DAILY WORD DEVOTIONAL - POWERFUL 52 WEEKLY THEMES, 365 DAYS SCRIPTURE SPEAKS FOR ITSELF

King James Version

LEE KOWAL ,MDIV

KINGDOM
LIFE
BOOKS™

Kingdom Life Books$_{TM}$

DAILY WORD DEVOTIONAL - Powerful 52 Weekly Themes, 365 Days Scripture Speaks For Itself: King James Version

Send inquiries to: Kingdom Life Books, PO Box 4, Lincoln City, Oregon 97367

www.KingdomLifeBooks.com

Print Edition © December 2019 ISBN: 978-1-949261-20-2

Christmas Hymns from www.Hymnary.org

For Jesus' Lambs and Sheep,
For their daily food, encouragement, joy, and guidance;
That His life-giving Word bring peace and restoration to their souls,
That their cup runs over with His countenance,
And His goodness and mercy follow them throughout their days.

CONTENTS

WEEK 1 - THE LORD'S PRAYER (MATTHEW 6:9–13)

Sunday: "*After this manner...pray ye: Our Father which art in heaven.*"
—Matthew 6:9

Jesus...lifted up his eyes to heaven, and said, "Father. —— My Father, and your Father..."

—John 17:1; 20:17

Ye are all the children of God by faith in Christ Jesus. —— Ye have not received the spirit of bondage again to fear; but ye have received the Spirit of adoption, whereby we cry, Abba, Father. The Spirit itself beareth witness with our spirit, that we are the children of God. —— Because ye are sons, God hath sent forth the Spirit of his Son into your hearts, crying, Abba, Father. Wherefore thou art no more a servant, but a son.

—Galatians 3:26; Romans 8:15–16; Galatians 4:6–7

"Verily, verily, I say unto you, Whatsoever ye shall ask the Father in my name, he will give it you. Hitherto have ye asked nothing in my name: ask, and ye shall receive, that your joy may be full."

—John 16:23–24

I will receive you, and will be a Father unto you, and ye shall be my sons and daughters, saith the Lord Almighty.

—2 Corinthians 6:17–18

. . .

Monday: "*Hallowed be thy name.*" —Matthew 6:9

Thou shalt worship no other god: for the Lord, whose name is Jealous, is a jealous God.

— Exodus 34:14

Who is like unto thee, O Lord, among the gods who is like thee, glorious in holiness, fearful in praises, doing wonders? —— Holy, holy, holy, Lord God Almighty.

— Exodus 15:11; Revelations 4:8

Worship the Lord in the beauty of holiness. —— I saw...the Lord sitting upon a throne, high and lifted up, and his train filled the temple. Above it stood the seraphims...And one cried unto another, and said, Holy, holy, holy, is the Lord of hosts: the whole earth is full of his glory. ...Then said I, Woe is me! for I am undone; —— I have heard of thee by the hearing of the ear: but now mine eye seeth thee. Wherefore I abhor myself.

—1 Chronicles 16:29; Isaiah 6:1–5; Job 42:5–6

The blood of Jesus Christ his Son cleanseth us from all sin. —— That we might be partakers of his holiness. —— Having therefore, brethren, boldness to enter into the holiest by the blood of Jesus...let us draw near with a true heart.

—1 John 1:7; Hebrews 12:10; 10:19–22

Tuesday: "*Thy kingdom come.*" —Matthew 6:10

In the days of these kings shall the God of heaven set up a kingdom, which shall never be destroyed: and the kingdom shall not be left to other people, but it shall break in pieces and consume all these kingdoms, and it shall stand for ever. —— A stone...cut out without hands. —— Not by might, nor by power, but by my spirit, saith the Lord of hosts. —— "The kingdom of God cometh not with observation: neither shall they say, Lo here! or, lo there! for, behold, the kingdom of God is within you."

—Daniel 2:44; 2:34; Zechariah 4:6; Luke 17:20–21

"Unto you it is given to know the mystery of the kingdom of God...So is the kingdom of God, as if a man should cast seed into the ground; And should sleep, and rise night and day, and the seed should spring and grow up, he knoweth not how. ...But when the fruit is brought forth, immediately he putteth in the sickle, because the harvest is come. —— Be ye...ready: for in such an hour as ye think not, the Son of man cometh."

—Mark 4:11,26–29; Matthew 24:44

The Spirit and the bride say, Come. And let him that heareth say, Come.

—Revelations 22:17

. . .

Wednesday: *"Thy will be done in earth, as it is in heaven."* —Matthew 6:10

Understanding what the will of the Lord is. —— "It is not the will of your Father which is in heaven, that one of these little ones should perish."

—Ephesians 5:17; Matthew 18:14

This is the will of God, even your sanctification, —— That he no longer should live the rest of his time in the flesh to the lusts of men, but to the will of God. —— Of his own will begat he us with the word of truth...wherefore lay apart all filthiness.

—1 Thessalonians 4:3; 1 Peter 4:2; James 1:18–21

Be ye holy; for I am holy. —— [Jesus said,] "Whosoever shall do the will of God, the same is my brother, and my sister, and mother. —— Whosoever heareth these sayings of mine, and doeth them, I will liken him unto a wise man, which built his house upon a rock: and the rain descended, and the floods came, and the winds blew, and beat upon that house; and it fell not: for it was founded upon a rock.". —— The world passeth away, and the lust thereof: but he that doeth the will of God abideth for ever.

—1 Peter 1:16; Mark 3:34–35; Matthew 7:24–25; 1 John 2:17

Thursday: *"Give us this day our daily bread."* —Matthew 6:11

I have been young, and now am old; yet have I not seen the righteous forsaken, nor his seed begging bread. —— Bread shall be given him; his waters shall be sure. —— The ravens brought him bread and flesh in the morning, and bread and flesh in the evening; and he drank of the brook.

—Psalm 37:25; Isaiah 33:16; 1 Kings 17:6

My God shall supply all your need according to his riches in glory by Christ Jesus. —— Be content with such things as ye have: for he hath said, I will never leave thee, nor forsake thee. —— He humbled thee, and suffered thee to hunger, and fed thee with manna...that he might make thee know that man doth not live by bread only, but by every word that proceedeth out of the mouth of the Lord doth man live. —— Jesus said unto them, "Verily, verily, I say unto you, Moses gave you not that bread from heaven; but my Father giveth you the true bread from heaven. For the bread of God is he which cometh down from heaven, and giveth life unto the world." Then said they unto him, Lord, evermore give us this bread.

—Philippians 4:19; Hebrews 13:5; Deuteronomy 8:3; John 6:32–34

. . .

Friday: *"Forgive us our debts, as we forgive our debtors."* —Matthew 6:12

Lord, how oft shall my brother sin against me, and I forgive him? till seven times? Jesus saith unto him," I say not unto thee, Until seven times: but, Until seventy times seven.". —— O thou wicked servant, I forgave thee all that debt, because thou desiredst me: shouldest not thou also have had compassion on thy fellow-servant, even as I had pity on thee? And his lord was wroth, and delivered him to the tormentors, till he should pay all that was due unto him. So likewise shall my heavenly Father do also unto you, if ye from your hearts forgive not every one his brother their trespasses.". —— Be ye kind one to another, tenderhearted, forgiving one another, even as God for Christ's sake hath forgiven you. —— You... hath he quickened...having forgiven you all trespasses; blotting out the handwriting of ordinances that was against us, which was contrary to us, and took it out of the way, nailing it to his cross. —— Even as Christ forgave you, so also do ye.

—Matthew 18:21–22; 18:32–35; Ephesians 4:32; Colossians 2:13–14; 3:13

Saturday: *"Lead us not into temptation, but deliver us from evil."* — Matthew 6:13

He that trusteth in his own heart is a fool: but whoso walketh wisely, he shall be delivered.

—Proverbs 28:26;

Let no man say when he is tempted, I am tempted of God: for God cannot be tempted with evil, neither tempteth he any man: But every man is tempted, when he is drawn away of his own lust, and enticed. —— Wherefore come out from among them, and be ye separate, saith the Lord, and touch not the unclean thing; and I will receive you.

—James 1:13–14; 2 Corinthians 6:17

Lot lifted up his eyes, and beheld all the plain of Jordan, that it was well watered every where...even as the garden of the Lord. ...Then Lot chose him all the plain of Jordan; ...But the men of Sodom were wicked and sinners before the Lord exceedingly. —— [The Lord] delivered just Lot, vexed with the filthy conversation of the wicked. ...The Lord knoweth how to deliver the godly out of temptations, —— Yea, he shall be holden up: for God is able to make him stand.

—Genesis 13:10–13; 2 Peter 2:7–9; Romans 14:4

. . .

BONUS: *"Thine is the kingdom, and the power, and the glory, for ever."* —Matthew 6:13

The Lord reigneth, he is clothed with majesty; the Lord is clothed with strength, wherewith he hath girded himself: the world also is stablished, that it cannot be moved. Thy throne is established of old: thou art from everlasting. —— The Lord of hosts, he is the King of glory. Selah.

—Psalm 93:1–2; 24:10

"I am Alpha and Omega, the beginning and the ending," saith the Lord, "which is, and which was, and which is to come, the Almighty." —— And he hath on his vesture and on his thigh a name written, King Of Kings, And Lord Of Lords.

—Revelations 1:8; 19:16

Jesus Christ, who is the faithful witness, and the first begotten of the dead, and the prince of the kings of the earth. Unto him that loved us, and washed us from our sins in his own blood, and hath made us kings and priests unto God and his Father; to him be glory and dominion for ever and ever. Amen.

—Revelations 1:5–6

Wherefore God also hath highly exalted him, and given him a name which is above every name: That at the name of Jesus every knee should bow, of things in heaven, and things in earth, and things under the earth; And that every tongue should confess that Jesus Christ is Lord, to the glory of God the Father.

—Philippians 2:9–11

Greater is he that is in you, than he that is in the world.

—1 John 4:4

WEEK 2 - JOY / REJOICING

S**unday**: *The joy of the Lord is your strength.* —Nehemiah 8:10

Sing, O heavens; and be joyful, O earth; and break forth with singing, O mountains: for the Lord hath comforted his people and will have mercy upon his afflicted. —— Behold, God is my salvation; I will trust, and not be afraid: for the Lord JEHOVAH is my strength and my song; he also is become my salvation.

—Isaiah 49:13; 12:2

The Lord is my strength and my shield; my heart trusted in Him, and I am helped: therefore my heart greatly rejoiceth; and with my song will I praise him. —— My soul shall be joyful in my God; for He hath clothed me with the garments of salvation, He hath covered me with the robe of righteousness, as a bridegroom decketh himself with ornaments, and as a bride adorneth herself with her jewels.

—Psalm 28:7; Isaiah 61:10

I have therefore whereof I may glory through Jesus Christ in those things which pertain to God. —— We...joy in God through our Lord Jesus Christ, by whom we have now received the atonement. —— I will joy in the God of my salvation.

—Romans 15:17; 5:11; Habakkuk 3:18

Monday: *I will greatly rejoice in the Lord, my soul shall be joyful in my God.* —Isaiah 61:10

Is any merry? let him sing psalms. —— Put on therefore, as the elect of God, holy and beloved, bowels of mercies, kindness, humbleness of mind, meekness, longsuffering; Forbearing one another, and forgiving one another. ...Let the word of Christ dwell in you richly in all wisdom; teaching and admonishing one another in psalms and hymns and spiritual songs, singing with grace in your hearts to the Lord. —— At midnight Paul and Silas prayed, and sang praises unto God: and the prisoners heard them.

—James 5:13; Colossians 3:12–16; Acts 16:25

I will bless the Lord at all times: his praise shall continually be in my mouth. My soul shall make her boast in the Lord: the humble shall hear thereof, and be glad. O magnify the Lord with me, and let us exalt his name together. —— The Lord will give grace and glory: no good thing will he withhold from them that walk uprightly. O Lord of hosts, blessed is the man that trusteth in thee. —— Bless the Lord, O my soul: and all that is within me, bless his holy name. —— Rejoice in the Lord alway: and again, I say, Rejoice.

—Psalm 34:1–3; 84:11–12; 103:1; Philippians 4:4

Tuesday: *Make a joyful noise unto the Lord, all ye lands. Serve the Lord with gladness: come before his presence with singing.*

—Psalm 100:1–2

Know ye that the Lord he is God: it is he that hath made us, and not we ourselves; we are his people, and the sheep of his pasture. Enter into his gates with thanksgiving, and into his courts with praise: be thankful unto him, and bless his name. For the Lord is good; his mercy is everlasting; and his truth endureth to all generations. —— The meek also shall increase their joy in the Lord, and the poor among men shall rejoice in the Holy One of Israel.

—Psalm 100:3–5; Isaiah 29:19

In the Lord have I righteousness and strength: even to Him shall men come; and all that are incensed against him shall be ashamed. In the Lord shall all the seed of Israel be justified, and shall glory. —— Be glad in the Lord, and rejoice, ye righteous: and shout for joy, all ye that are upright in heart.

—Isaiah 45:24–25; Psalm 32:11

Rejoice in the Lord alway: and again I say, Rejoice. —— Whom having not seen, ye love; in whom, though now ye see Him not, yet believing, ye rejoice with joy unspeakable and full of glory. —Philippians 4:4; 1 Peter 1:8

. . .

Wednesday: *Thou wilt shew me the path of life: in thy presence is fulness of joy.* —Psalm 16:11

"I am the true vine...Abide in Me and I in you. ...These things I have spoken unto you, that my joy may remain in you, and that that your joy may be full. —— But the fruit of the Spirit is love, joy, peace, longsuffering, gentleness, goodness, faith, Meekness, temperance: against such there is no law. And they that are Christ's have crucified the flesh with the affections and lusts. If we live in the Spirit, let us also walk in the Spirit.

—John 15:1–11; Galatians 5:22–25

Blessed is the people that know the joyful sound: they shall walk, O Lord, in the light of thy countenance. In thy name shall they rejoice all the day: and in thy righteousness shall they be exalted. For thou art the glory of their strength: and in thy favour our horn shall be exalted. ——

Glory ye in his holy name: let the heart of them rejoice that seek the Lord. —— This is the day which the Lord hath made; we will rejoice and be glad in it. —— Rejoice in the Lord, ye righteous; and give thanks at the remembrance of his holiness.

—Psalm 89:15–17; 105:3; 118:24; 97:12

Thursday: *He that is of a merry heart hath a continual feast.* —Proverbs 15:15

The joy of the Lord is your strength. —— The kingdom of God is not meat and drink; but righteousness, and peace, and joy in the Holy Ghost. —— Be filled with the Spirit; Speaking to yourselves in psalms and hymns and spiritual songs, singing and making melody in your heart to the Lord; Giving thanks always for all things unto God and the Father in the name of our Lord Jesus Christ. —— By him...let us offer the sacrifice of praise to God continually, that is, the fruit of our lips giving thanks to his name.

—Nehemiah 8:10; Romans 14:17; Ephesians 5:18–20; Hebrews 13:15

Although the fig tree shall not blossom, neither shall fruit be in the vines; the labour of the olive shall fail, and the fields shall yield no meat; the flock shall be cut off from the fold, and there shall be no herd in the stalls: yet I will rejoice in the Lord, I will joy in the God of my salvation. —— Sorrowful, yet alway rejoicing; —— We glory in tribulations also.

—Habakkuk 3:17–18; 2 Corinthians 6:10; Romans 5:3

. . .

Friday: *Rejoicing in hope.* —Romans 12:12

For the hope which is laid up for you in heaven, whereof ye heard before in the word of the truth of the gospel. —— No man should be moved by these afflictions: for yourselves know that we are appointed thereunto. —— Wherein ye greatly rejoice, though now for a season, if need be, ye are in heaviness through manifold temptations. —— But rejoice, inasmuch as ye are partakers of Christ's sufferings; that, when his glory shall be revealed, ye may be glad also with exceeding joy.

—Colossians 1:5; 1 Thessalonians 3:3; 1 Peter 1:6; 4:13

Rejoice with them that do rejoice, and weep with them that weep. —— The God of hope fill you with all joy and peace in believing, that ye may abound in hope, through the power of the Holy Ghost. —— Looking unto Jesus the author and finisher of our faith; who for the joy that was set before him endured the cross, despising the shame, and is set down at the right hand of the throne of God. —— Blessed be the God and Father of our Lord Jesus Christ, which according to his abundant mercy hath begotten us again unto a lively hope by the resurrection of Jesus Christ from the dead, —— By whom also we have access by faith into this grace wherein we stand, and rejoice in hope of the glory of God.

—Romans 12:15; 15:13; Hebrews 12:2; 1 Peter 1:3; Romans 5:2

Saturday: *Make a joyful noise unto the Lord, all the earth: make a loud noise, and rejoice, and sing praise.* —Psalm 98:4

Sing unto the Lord with the harp; with the harp, and the voice of a psalm. With trumpets and sound of cornet make a joyful noise before the Lord, the King.

—Psalm 98:5–6

O God, thou art my God; early will I seek thee: my soul thirsteth for thee, my flesh longeth for thee in a dry and thirsty land, where no water is...when I remember thee upon my bed, and meditate on thee in the night watches. Because thou hast been my help, therefore in the shadow of thy wings will I rejoice. My soul followeth hard after thee: thy right hand upholdeth me. —— In the multitude of my thoughts within me thy comforts delight my soul.

—Psalm 63:1–8; 94:19

How excellent is thy lovingkindness, O God! therefore the children of men put their trust under the shadow of thy wings. They shall be abundantly satisfied with the fatness of thy house; and thou shalt make them drink of the river of thy pleasures. For with thee is the fountain of life; in thy light shall we see light. —— Let my mouth be filled with thy praise and with thy honour all the day.

—Psalm 36:7-9; 71:8

WEEK 3 - WISDOM

Sunday: *Happy is the man that findeth wisdom,*
and the man that getteth understanding.

—Proverbs 3:13

Whoso findeth me findeth life, and shall obtain favour of the Lord.

—Proverbs 8:35

Thus saith the Lord, Let not the wise man glory in his wisdom, neither let the mighty man glory in his might...But let him that glorieth glory in this, that he understandeth and knoweth me, that I am the Lord.

—Jeremiah 9:23–24

The fear of the Lord is the beginning of wisdom. —— If ye fulfil the royal law according to the scripture, Thou shalt love thy neighbour as thyself, ye do well.

—Proverbs 9:10; James 2:8

What things were gain to me, those I counted loss for Christ. Yea doubtless, and I count all things but loss for the excellency of the knowledge of Christ Jesus my Lord: for whom I have suffered the loss of all things, and do count them but dung, that I may win Christ. —— In whom are hid all the treasures of wisdom and knowledge. —— Counsel is mine, and sound wisdom: I am understanding; I have strength.

—Philippians 3:7–8; Colossians 2:3; Proverbs 8:14

Christ Jesus...is made unto us wisdom, and righteousness, and sanctification, and redemption. —— He that winneth souls is wise.

—1 Corinthians 1:30; Proverbs 11:30

. . .

Monday: *There is a way which seemeth right unto a man, but the end thereof are the ways of death.* —Proverbs 14:12

He that trusteth in his own heart is a fool. —— For it is written, I will destroy the wisdom of the wise, and will bring to nothing the understanding of the prudent. —— Thy word is a lamp unto my feet, and a light unto my path.

—Proverbs 28:26; 1 Corinthians 1:19; Psalm 119:105

If there arise among you a prophet, or a dreamer of dreams...saying, Let us go after other gods, which thou hast not known, and let us serve them; Thou shalt not hearken unto the words of that prophet...for the Lord your God proveth you, to know whether ye love the Lord your God with all your heart and with all your soul. Ye shall walk after the Lord your God, and fear him, and keep his commandments, and obey his voice, and ye shall serve him, and cleave unto him.

—Deuteronomy 13:1–4

I will instruct thee and teach thee in the way which thou shalt go; I will guide thee with mine eye.

—Psalm 32:8

Tuesday: *I must work the works of him that sent me, while it is day.* —John 9:4

The soul of the sluggard desireth, and hath nothing: but the soul of the diligent shall be made fat. ...He that watereth shall be watered.

—Proverbs 13:4; 11:25

My meat is to do the will of him that sent me, and to finish his work. Say not ye, There are yet four months, and then cometh harvest? behold, I say unto you, Lift up your eyes, and look on the fields; for they are white already to harvest. And he that reapeth receiveth wages, and gathereth fruit unto life eternal: that both he that soweth and he that reapeth may rejoice together.

—John 4:34–36

Even so faith, if it hath not works, is dead, being alone. Yea, a man may say, Thou hast faith, and I have works: shew me thy faith without thy works, and I will shew thee my faith by my works. Thou believest that there is one God; thou doest well: the devils also believe, and tremble. But wilt thou know, O vain man, that faith without works is dead? —— Who is a wise man and endued with knowledge among you? let him shew out of a good conversation his works with meekness of wisdom. —— Preach the word; be instant in season, out of season. —— Occupy till I come.

—James 2:17–20; 3:13; 2 Timothy 4:2; Luke 19:13

. . .

Wednesday: *Boast not thyself of tomorrow; for thou knowest not what a day may bring forth.*

—Proverbs 27:1

Behold, now is the accepted time; behold, now is the day of salvation. —— Yet a little while is the light with you. Walk while ye have the light, lest darkness come upon you: for he that walketh in darkness knoweth not whither he goeth. While ye have light, believe in the light, that ye may be the children of light.

—2 Corinthians 6:2; John 12:35–36

Whatsoever thy hand findeth to do, do it with thy might; for there is no work, nor device, nor knowledge, nor wisdom, in the grave, whither thou goest.

—Ecclesiastes 9:10

Soul, thou hast much goods laid up for many years; take thine ease, eat, drink, and be merry"...Thou fool, this night thy soul shall be required of thee: then whose shall those things be, which thou hast provided? So is he that layeth up treasure for himself, and is not rich toward God. ——What is your life? It is even a vapour, that appeareth for a little time, and then vanisheth away. —— The world passeth away, and the lust thereof: but he that doeth the will of God abideth for ever.

—Luke 12:19–21; James 4:14; 1 John 2:17

Thursday: *Beloved, be not ignorant of this one thing, that one day is with the Lord as a thousand years, and a thousand years as one day. The Lord is not slack concerning his promise, as some men count slackness.*

—2 Peter 3:8–9

My thoughts are not your thoughts, neither are your ways my ways, saith the Lord. For as the heavens are higher than the earth, so are my ways higher than your ways, and my thoughts than your thoughts. For as the rain cometh down, and the snow from heaven, and returneth not thither, but watereth the earth...so shall my word be that goeth forth out of my mouth: it shall not return unto me void, but it shall accomplish that which I please, and it shall prosper in the thing whereto I sent it.

—Isaiah 55:8–11

God hath concluded them all in unbelief, that he might have mercy upon all. O the depth of the riches both of the wisdom and knowledge of God! how unsearchable are his judgments, and his ways past finding out! —— God hath chosen the foolish things of the world to confound the wise...That no flesh should glory in his presence.

—Romans 11:32–33; 1 Corinthians 1:27–29

. . .

Friday: *The Lord giveth wisdom: out of his mouth cometh knowledge and understanding.*

—Proverbs 2:6

Trust in the Lord with all thine heart; and lean not unto thine own understanding. —— If any of you lack wisdom, let him ask of God, that giveth to all men liberally, and upbraideth not; and it shall be given him. But let him ask in faith, nothing wavering. For he that wavereth is like a wave of the sea driven with the wind and tossed. —— But the wisdom that is from above is first pure, then peaceable, gentle, and easy to be intreated, full of mercy and good fruits, without partiality, and without hypocrisy. And the fruit of righteousness is sown in peace of them that make peace.

—Proverbs 3:5; James 1:5–6; 3:17–18

The entrance of thy words giveth light; it giveth understanding unto the simple. —— Thy word have I hid in mine heart, that I might not sin against thee.

—Psalm 119:130; 119:11

All bare him witness, and wondered at the gracious words which proceeded out of his mouth. —— Never man spake like this man. —— Of him are ye in Christ Jesus, who of God is made unto us wisdom, and righteousness, and sanctification, and redemption. —Luke 4:22; John 7:46; 1 Corinthians 1:30

Saturday: *Thy thoughts are very deep.* —Psalm 92:5

We...do not cease to pray for you, and to desire that ye might be filled with the knowledge of his will in all wisdom and spiritual understanding. —— That ye, being rooted and grounded in love, May be able to comprehend with all saints what is the breadth, and length, and depth, and height; And to know the love of Christ, which passeth knowledge, that ye might be filled with all the fulness of God.

—Colossians 1:9; Ephesians 3:17–19

O the depth of the riches both of the wisdom and knowledge of God! how unsearchable are his judgments, and his ways past finding out! —Romans 11:33

Many, O Lord my God, are thy wonderful works which thou hast done, and thy thoughts which are to us-ward: they cannot be reckoned up in order unto thee: if I would declare and speak of them, they are more than can be numbered. —— O give thanks unto the Lord; for he is good: because his mercy endureth for ever.

—Psalm 40:5; 118:1

Let the word of Christ dwell in you richly in all wisdom; teaching and admonishing one another in psalms and hymns and spiritual songs, singing with grace in your hearts to the Lord. —Colossians 3:16

Special Scripture Reading from 1 Corinthians 2:

1 And I, brethren, when I came to you, came not with excellency of speech or of wisdom, declaring unto you the testimony of God. 2 For I determined not to know any thing among you, save Jesus Christ, and him crucified. 3 And I was with you in weakness, and in fear, and in much trembling. 4 And my speech and my preaching was not with enticing words of man's wisdom, but in demonstration of the Spirit and of power: 5 That your faith should not stand in the wisdom of men, but in the power of God.

6 Howbeit we speak wisdom among them that are perfect: yet not the wisdom of this world, nor of the princes of this world, that come to nought: 7 But we speak the wisdom of God in a mystery, even the hidden wisdom, which God ordained before the world unto our glory: 8 Which none of the princes of this world knew: for had they known it, they would not have crucified the Lord of glory.

9 But as it is written, Eye hath not seen, nor ear heard, neither have entered into the heart of man, the things which God hath prepared for them that love him. 10 But God hath revealed them unto us by his Spirit: for the Spirit searcheth all things, yea, the deep things of God. 11 For what man knoweth the things of a man, save the spirit of man which is in him? even so the things of God knoweth no man, but the Spirit of God.

12 Now we have received, not the spirit of the world, but the spirit which is of God; that we might know the things that are freely given to us of God. 13 Which things also we speak, not in the words which man's wisdom teacheth, but which the Holy Ghost teacheth; comparing spiritual things with spiritual. 14 But the natural man receiveth not the things of the Spirit of God: for they are foolishness unto him: neither can he know them, because they are spiritually discerned.

15 But he that is spiritual judgeth all things, yet he himself is judged of no man. 16 For who hath known the mind of the Lord, that he may instruct him? but we have the mind of Christ.

WEEK 4 - THE LOVE & COMPASSION OF GOD – 1

S**unday**: *I will mention the lovingkindnesses of the Lord, and the praises of the Lord, according to all that the Lord hath bestowed on us.* —Isaiah 63:7

I am poor and needy; yet the Lord thinketh upon me. —— I know the thoughts that I think toward you, saith the Lord, thoughts of peace, and not of evil. —— How precious...are thy thoughts unto me, O God! how great is the sum of them! If I should count them, they are more in number than the sand: when I awake, I am still with thee. —— Many, O Lord my God, are thy wonderful works which thou hast done, and thy thoughts which are to us-ward.

—Psalm 40:17; Jeremiah 29:11; Psalm 139:17–18; 40:5

Thou hast in love to my soul delivered it from the pit of corruption. —— O Lord my God, I cried unto thee, and thou hast healed me. O Lord, thou hast brought up my soul from the grave: thou hast kept me alive, that I should not go down to the pit. —— The Son of God, who loved me, and gave himself for me —— Who hath also sealed us, and given the earnest of the Spirit in our hearts. —— Which is the earnest of our inheritance until the redemption of the purchased possession, unto the praise of his glory. —— The unsearchable riches of Christ —— Having nothing, and yet possessing all things. —— O give thanks unto the Lord; for he is good: because his mercy endureth for ever.

—Isaiah 38:17; Psalm 30:2–3; Galatians 2:20; 2 Corinthians 1:22; Ephesians 1:14; 3:8; 2 Corinthians 6:10; Psalm 118:1

. . .

Monday: *My delights were with the sons of men.* —Proverbs 8:31

As one whom his mother comforteth, so will I comfort you. —— They brought young children to him, that he should touch them...And he took them up in his arms, put his hands upon them, and blessed them. —— Jesus called his disciples unto him, and said, I have compassion on the multitude, because they continue with me now three days, and have nothing to eat; and I will not send them away fasting, lest they faint in the way. —— In his love and in his pity he redeemed them.

—Isaiah 66:13; Mark 10:13–16; Matthew 15:32; Isaiah 63:9

I will not leave you comfortless: I will come to you. —— Can a woman forget her sucking child, that she should not have compassion on the son of her womb? yea, they may forget, yet will I not forget thee. —— It is of the Lord's mercies that we are not consumed, because his compassions fail not. They are new every morning. —— They shall be abundantly satisfied with the fatness of thy house; and thou shalt make them drink of the river of thy pleasures. For with thee is the fountain of life. —— I am my beloved's, and his desire is toward me.

—John 14:18; Isaiah 49:15; Lamentations 3:22–23;
Psalm 36:8–9; Song 7:10

Tuesday: *God so loved the world, that he gave his only begotten Son, that whosoever believeth in him should not perish, but have everlasting life.* —John 3:16

God...hath reconciled us to himself by Jesus Christ, and hath given to us the ministry of reconciliation; To wit, that God was in Christ, reconciling the world unto himself, not imputing their trespasses unto them; and hath committed unto us the word of reconciliation. Now then we are ambassadors for Christ, as though God did beseech you by us: we pray you in Christ's stead, be ye reconciled to God. For he hath made him to be sin for us, who knew no sin; that we might be made the righteousness of God in him.

—2 Corinthians 5:18–21

God is love. In this was manifested the love of God toward us, because that God sent his only begotten Son into the world, that we might live through him. Herein is love, not that we loved God, but that he loved us, and sent his Son to be the propitiation for our sins. Beloved, if God so loved us, we ought also to love one another.

—1 John 4:8–11

. . .

Wednesday: *O taste and see that the Lord is good: blessed is the man that trusteth in him.* —Psalm 34:8

Thou shalt seek the Lord thy God, thou shalt find him, if thou seek him with all thy heart and with all thy soul. —— Ask, and it shall be given you; seek, and ye shall find; knock, and it shall be opened unto you: For every one that asketh receiveth; and he that seeketh findeth; and to him that knocketh it shall be opened."

—Deuteronomy 4:29; Matthew 7:7–8

Seek, 'taste,' and know God's love by praying Ephesians 3:14–21 personalized from you to Him:

For this reason, I bow my knees before You, oh Father, from whom every family in heaven and on earth derives its name, that You would grant me, according to the riches of Your glory, to be strengthened with power through Your Spirit in my inner-person; so that Christ may dwell in my heart through faith; and that I, being rooted and grounded in love, may be able to comprehend with all the saints what is the breadth and length and depth and height, and to know the love of Christ, which surpasses knowledge, that I may be filled up to all the fulness of God.

Now to You, who are able to do exceeding abundantly beyond all that I can ask or think, according to the power that works within me, to You be the glory in the church and in Christ Jesus to all generations forever and ever. Amen.

—Based on Ephesians 3:14–21

Thursday: *I have made, and I will bear.* —Isaiah 46:4

Thus saith the Lord that created thee, O Jacob, and he that formed thee, O Israel, Fear not: for I have redeemed thee, I have called thee by thy name; thou art mine. When thou passest through the waters, I will be with thee; and through the rivers, they shall not overflow thee. —— Even to your old age I am he; and even to hoar hairs will I carry you. —— He bare them, and carried them all the days of old. —— The very hairs of your head are all numbered. ...Are not two sparrows sold for a farthing? and one of them shall not fall on the ground without your Father. ...Fear ye not therefore, ye are of more value than many sparrows.

—Isaiah 43:1–2; 46:4; 63:9; Matthew 10:30, 29, 31

The Lord is very pitiful, and of tender mercy. —— Jesus Christ the same yesterday, and to day, and for ever. —— For I am persuaded, that neither...height, nor depth, nor any other creature, shall be able to separate us from the love of God, which is in Christ Jesus our Lord.

—James 5:11; Hebrews 13:8; Romans 8:38–39

. . .

Friday: *With lovingkindness have I drawn thee.* —Jeremiah 31:3

For the Lord delighteth in thee...and as the bridegroom rejoiceth over the bride, so shall thy God rejoice over thee. —— Thy love is better than wine. —— I sat down under his shadow with great delight, and his fruit was sweet to my taste. He brought me to the banqueting house, and his banner over me was love. —— Thou preparest a table before me in the presence of mine enemies: thou anointest my head with oil; my cup runneth over. Surely goodness and mercy shall follow me all the days of my life: and I will dwell in the house of the Lord for ever. —— I will greatly rejoice in the Lord, my soul shall be joyful in my God; for he hath clothed me with the garments of salvation, he hath covered me with the robe of righteousness, as a bridegroom decketh himself with ornaments, and as a bride adorneth herself with her jewels.

—Isaiah 62:4–5; Song 1:2; 2:3–4; Psalm 23:5–7; Isaiah 61:10

Let us be glad and rejoice, and give honour to him: for the marriage of the Lamb is come, and his wife hath made herself ready. And to her was granted that she should be arrayed in fine linen, clean and white: for the fine linen is the righteousness of saints. And he saith unto me, Write, Blessed are they which are called unto the marriage supper of the Lamb. And he saith unto me, These are the true sayings of God.

—Revelations 19:7–9

Saturday: *Draw me, we will run after thee.* —Song 1:4

I have loved thee with an everlasting love: therefore with lovingkindness have I drawn thee. —— I drew them with cords of a man, with bands of love. —— I, if I be lifted up from the earth, will draw all men unto me. —— Behold the Lamb of God. —— As Moses lifted up the serpent in the wilderness, even so must the Son of man be lifted up: That whosoever believeth in him should not perish, but have eternal life.

—Jeremiah 31:3; Hosea 11:4; John 12:32; 1:36; 3:14–15

My beloved spake, and said unto me, Rise up, my love, my fair one, and come away. For, lo, the winter is past, the rain is over and gone; The flowers appear on the earth; the time of the singing of birds is come, and the voice of the turtle is heard in our land; The fig tree putteth forth her green figs, and the vines with the tender grape give a good smell. Arise, my love, my fair one, and come away. ...My beloved is mine, and I am his.

—Song 2:10–16

WEEK 5 - FAITHFULNESS OF GOD

Sunday: *God is faithful.* —1 Corinthians 10:13

God is not a man that he should lie; neither the son of man, that he should repent: hath he said, and shall he not do it? or hath he spoken, and shall he not make it good? —— The Lord sware and will not repent.

—Numbers 23:19; Hebrews 7:21

God, willing more abundantly to shew unto the heirs of promise the immutability of his counsel, confirmed it by an oath: that by two immutable things, in which it was impossible for God to lie, we might have a strong consolation, who have fled for refuge to lay hold upon the hope set before us. —— Wherefore let them that suffer according to the will of God commit the keeping of their souls to him in well doing, as unto a faithful Creator. —— Wherefore in all things it behoved him to be made like unto his brethren, that he might be a merciful and faithful high priest in things pertaining to God, to make reconciliation for the sins of the people.

—Hebrews 6:17–18; 1 Peter 4:19; Hebrews 2:17

I know whom I have believed, and am persuaded that he is able to keep that which I have committed unto him against that day. —— Faithful is he that calleth you, who also will do it. —— All the promises of God in him are yea, and in him Amen, unto the glory of God by us. —— God is faithful, by whom ye were called unto the fellowship of his Son Jesus Christ our Lord.

—2 Timothy 1:12; 1 Thessalonians 5:24; 2 Corinthians 1:20; 1 Corinthians 1:9

. . .

Monday: *I will not fail thee, nor forsake thee.* —Joshua 1:5

There failed not ought of any good thing which the Lord had spoken unto the house of Israel; all came to pass. —— God is not a man, that he should lie; ...hath he said, and shall he not do it? or hath he spoken, and shall he not make it good?

—Joshua 21:45; Numbers 23:19

The Lord thy God, he is God, the faithful God, which keepeth covenant and mercy with them that love him. —— He will ever be mindful of his covenant. —— Can a woman forget her sucking child, that she should not have compassion on the son of her womb? yea, they may forget, yet will I not forget thee. Behold, I have graven thee upon the palms of my hands.

—Deuteronomy 7:9; Psalm 111:5; Isaiah 49:15–16

And from Jesus Christ, who is the faithful witness, and the first begotten of the dead, and the prince of the kings of the earth. Unto him that loved us, and washed us from our sins in his own blood, And hath made us kings and priests unto God and his Father; to him be glory and dominion for ever and ever. Amen. —— The Lord thy God in the midst of thee is mighty; he will save, he will rejoice over thee with joy; he will rest in his love, he will joy over thee with singing.

—Revelations 1:5–6; Zephaniah 3:17

Tuesday: *The Lord visited Sarah as he had said, and the Lord did unto Sarah as he had spoken.* —Genesis 21:1

Trust in him at all times; ye people, pour out your heart before him: God is a refuge for us. —— David encouraged himself in the Lord his God. —— God will surely visit you, and bring you out of this land unto the land which he sware to Abraham, to Isaac, and to Jacob. —— I have seen, I have seen the affliction of my people which is in Egypt, and I have heard their groaning, and am come down to deliver them. ...He brought them out, after that he had shewed wonders and signs in the land of Egypt, and in the Red sea, and in the wilderness forty years. —— There failed not ought of any good thing which the Lord had spoken unto the house of Israel; all came to pass.

—Psalm 62:8; 1 Samuel 30:6; Genesis 50:24; Acts .7:34–36; Joshua 21:45

Let us hold fast the profession of our faith without wavering; (for he is faithful that promised). —— Hath he said, and shall he not do it? or hath he spoken, and shall he not make it good? —— Heaven and earth shall pass away, but my words shall not pass away. —— The grass withereth, the flower fadeth: but the word of our God shall stand for ever.

—Hebrews 10:23; Numbers 23:19; Matthew 24:35; Isaiah 40:8

. . .

Wednesday: *The Lord thy God bare thee, as a man doth bear his son, in all the way that ye went.* —Deuteronomy 1:31

I bare you on eagles' wings, and brought you unto myself. — *In his love and in his pity he redeemed them; and he bare them, and carried them all the days of old.* — *As an eagle stirreth up her nest, fluttereth over her young, spreadeth abroad her wings, taketh them, beareth them on her wings: so the Lord alone did lead him.*

—Exodus 19:4; Isaiah 63:9; Deuteronomy 32:11–12

Even to your old age I am he; and even to hoar hairs will I carry you: I have made, and I will bear; even I will carry, and will deliver you. — *This God is our God for ever and ever: he will be our guide even unto death.*

—Isaiah 46:4; Psalm 48:14

Cast thy burden upon the Lord, and he shall sustain thee. — *Take no thought for your life, what ye shall eat, or what ye shall drink; nor yet for your body, what ye shall put on...For your heavenly Father knoweth that ye have need of all these things.* — *But the Lord is faithful, who shall stablish you, and keep you from evil.* — *It is of the Lord's mercies that we are not consumed, because his compassions fail not. They are new every morning: great is thy faithfulness. The Lord is my portion, saith my soul; therefore will I hope in him.*

—Psalm 55:22; Matthew 6:25–32; 2 Thessalonians 3:3; Lamentations 3:22–24

Thursday: *God is not a man, that he should lie; neither the son of man, that he should repent.* —Numbers 23:19

The Father of lights, with whom is no variableness, neither shadow of turning. — *Jesus Christ the same yesterday, and to day, and for ever.* — *His truth shall be thy shield and buckler.* — *God, willing more abundantly to shew unto the heirs of promise the immutability of his counsel, confirmed it by an oath: That by two immutable things, in which it was impossible for God to lie, we might have a strong consolation, who have fled for refuge to lay hold upon the hope set before us.*

—James 1:17; Hebrews 13:8; Psalm 91:4; Hebrews 6:17–18

The faithful God, which keepeth covenant and mercy with them that love him and keep his commandments to a thousand generations. — *All the paths of the Lord are mercy and truth unto such as keep his covenant and his testimonies.* — *Happy is he that hath the God of Jacob for his help, whose hope is in the Lord his God...which keepeth truth for ever.* —Deuteronomy 7:9; Psalm 25:10; 146:5–6

. . .

Friday: *Hitherto hath the Lord helped us.*
—1 Samuel 7:12

I was brought low, and he helped me. —— Blessed be the Lord, because he hath heard the voice of my supplications. The Lord is my strength and my shield; my heart trusted in him, and I am helped: therefore my heart greatly rejoiceth; and with my song will I praise him. —— It is a good thing to give thanks unto the Lord, and to sing praises unto thy name, O Most High: To shew forth thy lovingkindness in the morning, and thy faithfulness every night, Upon an instrument of ten strings, and upon the psaltery; upon the harp with a solemn sound.

—Psalm 116:6; 28:6–7; 92:92:1–3

It is better to trust in the Lord than to put confidence in man. It is better to trust in the Lord than to put confidence in princes. —— Happy is he that hath the God of Jacob for his help, whose hope is in the Lord his God. —— There failed not ought of any good thing which the Lord had spoken unto the house of Israel; all came to pass. —— When I sent you without purse, and scrip, and shoes, lacked ye any thing? And they said, Nothing. —— Because thou hast been my help, therefore in the shadow of thy wings will I rejoice.

—Psalm 118:8–9; 146:5; Joshua 21:45; Luke 22:35; Psalm 63:7

Saturday: *Lo, I am with you always, even unto the end of the world.*
—Matthew 28:20

If two of you shall agree on earth as touching any thing that they shall ask, it shall be done for them of my Father which is in heaven. For where two or three are gathered together in my name, there am I in the midst of them. —— If a man love me, he will keep my words: and my Father will love him, and we will come unto him, and make our abode with him. —— If we confess our sins, he is faithful and just to forgive us our sins, and to cleanse us from all unrighteousness.

—Matthew 18:19–20; John 14:23; 1 John 1:9

I will sing of the mercies of the Lord for ever: with my mouth will I make known thy faithfulness to all generations. —— O Lord: thy faithfulness also in the congregation of the saints. —— O Lord, thou art my God; I will exalt thee...thy counsels of old are faithfulness and truth. —— Unto him that is able to keep you from falling, and to present you faultless before the presence of his glory with exceeding joy, To the only wise God our Saviour, be glory and majesty, dominion and power, both now and ever. Amen.

—Psalm 89:1; Isaiah 25:1; Jude 1:24–25

WEEK 6 - PRAISE & GRATITUDE

S**unday**: *It is a good thing to give thanks unto the Lord,*
and to sing praises unto thy name, O Most High. —Psalm 92:1

Let the word of Christ dwell in you richly in all wisdom; teaching and admonishing one another in psalms and hymns and spiritual songs, singing with grace in your hearts to the Lord. And whatsoever ye do in word or deed, do all in the name of the Lord Jesus, giving thanks to God and the Father by him. —— Glorify God in your body, and in your spirit, which are God's.

—Colossians 3:16–17; 1 Corinthians 6:20

Ye are...a royal priesthood...that ye should shew forth the praises of him who hath called you out of darkness into his marvelous light. —— Ye...as lively stones, are built up a spiritual house, a holy priesthood, to offer up spiritual sacrifices, acceptable to God by Jesus Christ. —— By him...let us offer the sacrifice of praise to God continually, that is, the fruit of our lips giving thanks to his name. —— I beseech you...brethren, by the mercies of God, that ye present your bodies a living sacrifice, holy, acceptable unto God, which is your reasonable service. —— Giving thanks always for all things unto God and the Father in the name of our Lord Jesus Christ.

—1 Peter 2:9; 2:5; Hebrews 13:15; Romans 12:1; Ephesians 5:20

My soul shall make her boast in the Lord: the humble shall hear thereof, and be glad. O magnify the Lord with me, and let us exalt his name together.

—Psalm 34:2–3

. . .

Monday: *Whoso offereth praise glorifieth me.*
—Psalm 50:23

I will praise thee, O Lord my God, with all my heart: and I will glorify thy name for evermore. —— It is a good thing to give thanks unto the Lord, and to sing praises unto thy name, O most High: To shew forth thy lovingkindness in the morning, and thy faithfulness every night.

—Psalm 86:12; 92:1–2

Let every thing that hath breath praise the Lord. —— Rejoice in the Lord, O ye righteous: for praise is comely for the upright.

—Psalm 150:6; 33:1

And when he was come nigh...the whole multitude of the disciples began to rejoice and praise God with a loud voice for all the mighty works that they had seen; Saying, Blessed be the King that cometh in the name of the Lord: peace in heaven, and glory in the highest.

—Luke 19:37–38

I will freely sacrifice unto thee: I will praise thy name, O Lord; for it is good. —— I offer in his tabernacle sacrifices of joy; I will sing, yea, I will sing praises unto the Lord. —— Worthy is the Lamb that was slain to receive power, and riches, and wisdom, and strength, and honour, and glory, and blessing.

—Psalm 54:6; 27:6; Revelations 5:12

Tuesday: *I will sing with the spirit, and I will sing with the understanding also.*

—1 Corinthians 14:15

Be filled with the Spirit; Speaking to yourselves in psalms and hymns and spiritual songs, singing and making melody in your heart to the Lord. —— And the heavens shall praise thy wonders, O Lord: thy faithfulness also in the congregation of the saints. —— The Lord is my strength and my shield; my heart trusted in him, and I am helped: therefore my heart greatly rejoiceth; and with my song will I praise him.

—Ephesians 5:18–19; Psalm 89:5; 28:7

My mouth shall speak the praise of the Lord: and let all flesh bless his holy name for ever and ever. —— Praise ye the Lord: for it is good to sing praises unto our God; for it is pleasant; and praise is comely...Sing unto the Lord with thanksgiving; sing praise upon the harp unto our God. —— I heard a voice from heaven, as the voice of many waters, and as the voice of a great thunder: and I heard the voice of harpers harping with their harps.

—Psalm 145:21; Psalm 147:1–7; Revelations 14:2

. . .

Wednesday: *Praise waiteth for thee, O God, in Sion.*
—Psalm 65:1

O sing unto the Lord a new song; for he hath done marvellous things: his right hand, and his holy arm, hath gotten him the victory...Make a joyful noise unto the Lord, all the earth: make a loud noise, and rejoice, and sing praise. Sing unto the Lord with the harp; with the harp, and the voice of a psalm. With trumpets and sound of cornet make a joyful noise before the Lord, the King.

—Psalm 98:1,4–6

To us there is but one God, the Father, of whom are all things, and we in him; and one Lord Jesus Christ, by whom are all things, and we by him. —— All men should honour the Son, even as they honour the Father. He that honoureth not the Son honoureth not the Father which hath sent Him.

—1 Corinthians 8:6; John 5:23

I beheld, and, lo, a great multitude, which no man could number, of all nations, and kindreds, and people, and tongues, stood before the throne, and before the Lamb, clothed with white robes, and palms in their hands; and cried with a loud voice, saying, Salvation to our God which sitteth upon the throne, and unto the Lamb...Amen: Blessing, and glory, and wisdom, and thanksgiving, and honour, and power, and might, be unto our God for ever and ever. Amen.

—Revelations 7:9–12

Thursday: *All thy works shall praise thee, O Lord; and thy saints shall bless thee.* —Psalm 145:10

Bless the Lord, O my soul: and all that is within me, bless his holy name. Bless the Lord, O my soul, and forget not all his benefits. —— I will bless the Lord at all times: his praise shall continually be in my mouth. —— Every day will I bless thee; and I will praise thy name for ever and ever.

—Psalm 103:1–2; 34:1; 145:2

Because thy lovingkindness is better than life, my lips shall praise thee. Thus will I bless thee while I live: I will lift up my hands in thy name. My soul shall be satisfied as with marrow and fatness; and my mouth shall praise thee with joyful lips. —— My soul doth magnify the Lord, and my spirit hath rejoiced in God my Saviour. —— Thou art worthy, O Lord, to receive glory and honour and power: for thou hast created all things, and for thy pleasure they are and were created.

—Psalm 63:3–5; Luke 1:46–47; Revelations 4:11

. . .

Friday: *Make his praise glorious.* —Psalm 66:2

This people have I formed for myself; they shall shew forth my praise. —— I will cleanse them from all their iniquity, whereby they have sinned against me; and I will pardon all their iniquities, whereby they have sinned, and whereby they have transgressed against me. And it shall be to me a name of joy, a praise and an honour before all the nations of the earth. —— O Lord, thou art my God; I will exalt thee, I will praise thy name; for thou hast done wonderful things; thy counsels of old are faithfulness and truth. —— I will praise thee, O Lord, with my whole heart; I will shew forth all thy marvellous works. —— Make a joyful noise unto the Lord, all the earth: make a loud noise, and rejoice, and sing praise. —— Who is like unto thee, O Lord...glorious in holiness, fearful in praises, doing wonders?

—Isaiah 43:21; Jeremiah 33:8–9; Isaiah 25:1; Psalm 9:1; 98:4; Exodus 15:11

I will praise the name of God with a song, and will magnify him with thanksgiving. —— They sing the song of Moses the servant of God, and the song of the Lamb, saying, Great and marvellous are thy works, Lord God Almighty.

—Psalm 69:30; Revelations 15:3

Saturday: *Thanks be unto God for his unspeakable gift.* —2 Corinthians 9:15

Make a joyful noise unto the Lord, all ye lands. Serve the Lord with gladness: come before his presence with singing...Enter into his gates with thanksgiving, and into his courts with praise: be thankful unto him, and bless his name. —— For unto us a child is born, unto us a son is given: and the government shall be upon his shoulder: and his name shall be called Wonderful, Counsellor, The mighty God, The everlasting Father, The Prince of Peace. —— He...spared not his own Son, but delivered him up for us all. —— Having yet...one son, his wellbeloved, he sent him.

—Psalm 100:1–4; Isaiah 9:6; Romans 8:32; Mark 12:6

Oh that men would praise the Lord for his goodness, and for his wonderful works to the children of men! —— For the Lord is great, and greatly to be praised: he is to be feared above all gods. —— Bless the Lord, O my soul: and all that is within me, bless his holy name. —— The Lord is my strength and my shield; my heart trusted in him, and I am helped: therefore my heart greatly rejoiceth; and with my song will I praise him.

—Psalm 107:21; 96:4; 103:1; 28:7

WEEK 7 - FELLOWSHIP WITH GOD

Sunday: *Oh that I knew where I might find him!*
—Job 23:3

Ye shall seek me, and find me, when ye shall search for me with all your heart. —— Seek, and ye shall find; knock, and it shall be opened unto you. For every one that asketh receiveth; and he that seeketh findeth; and to him that knocketh it shall be opened.

—Jeremiah 29:13; Luke 11:9–10

Truly our fellowship is with the Father, and with his Son Jesus Christ. —— Now in Christ Jesus ye who sometime were far off are made nigh by the blood of Christ...For through him we both have access by one Spirit unto the Father.

—1 John 1:3; Ephesians 2:13–18

If we say that we have fellowship with him, and walk in darkness, we lie, and do not the truth. —— Who is among you that feareth the Lord, that obeyeth the voice of his servant, that walketh in darkness, and hath no light? let him trust in the name of the Lord, and stay upon his God.

—1 John 1:6; Isaiah 50:10

Lo, I am with you always. —— I will never leave thee, nor forsake thee. —— [The] Comforter...dwelleth with you, and shall be in you.

—Matthew 28:20; Hebrews 13:5; John 14:16–17

. . .

Monday: *Thou shalt put the mercy seat above upon the ark... and there I will meet with thee.*

—Exodus 25:21–22

The way into the holiest of all was not yet made manifest. —— Jesus, when he had cried again with a loud voice, yielded up the ghost. And, behold, the veil of the temple was rent in twain from the top to the bottom.

—Hebrews 9:8; Matthew 27:50–51

Having...brethren, boldness to enter into the holiest by the blood of Jesus, By a new and living way, which he hath consecrated for us, through the veil, that is to say, his flesh...Let us draw near with a true heart in full assurance of faith, having our hearts sprinkled from an evil conscience, and our bodies washed with pure water. —— Let us therefore come boldly unto the throne of grace, that we may obtain mercy, and find grace to help in time of need.

—Hebrews 10:19–22; 4:16

Christ Jesus: Whom God hath set forth to be a propitiation [mercy seat] through faith in his blood, to declare his righteousness for the remission of sins that are past, through the forbearance of God. —— Through Him we ... have access by one Spirit unto the Father. —— Behold, what manner of love the Father hath bestowed upon us, that we should be called the sons of God.

—Romans 3:24–25; Ephesians 2:18; 1 John 3:1

Tuesday: *The apostles gathered themselves together unto Jesus, and told him all things...they had done.*

—Mark 6:30

There is a friend that sticketh closer than a brother. —— The Lord spake unto Moses face to face, as a man speaketh unto his friend. —— Ye are my friends, if ye do whatsoever I command you. Henceforth I call you not servants; for the servant knoweth not what his lord doeth: but I have called you friends; for all things that I have heard of my Father I have made known unto you.

—Proverbs 18:24; Exodus 33:11; John 15:14–15

Ye have not received the spirit of bondage again to fear; but ye have received the Spirit of adoption, whereby we cry, Abba, Father. —— In every thing by prayer and supplication with thanksgiving let your requests be made known unto God. —— The prayer of the upright is his delight.

—Romans 8:15; Philippians 4:6; Proverbs 15:8

. . .

Wednesday: *Henceforth I call you not servants; for the servant knoweth not what his lord doeth: but I have called you friends.*

—John 15:15

The Lord said, Shall I hide from Abraham that thing which I do? —— It is given unto you to know the mysteries of the kingdom of heaven. —— God hath revealed them unto us by his Spirit: for the Spirit searcheth all things, yea, the deep things of God. —— Even the hidden wisdom, which God ordained before the world unto our glory.

—Genesis 18:17; Matthew 13:11; 1 Corinthians 2:10; 2:7

Blessed is the man whom thou choosest, and causest to approach unto thee, that he may dwell in thy courts: we shall be satisfied with the goodness of thy house, even of thy holy temple. —— The secret of the Lord is with them that fear him: and he will shew them his covenant. —— I have given unto them the words which thou gavest me; and they have received them, and have known surely that I came out from thee, and they have believed that thou didst send me.

—— This is my commandment, That ye love one another, as I have loved you. Greater love hath no man than this, that a man lay down his life for his friends. Ye are my friends, if ye do whatsoever I command you.

—Psalm 65:4; 25:14; John 17:8; 15:12–14

Thursday: *Abide in me, and I in you. As the branch cannot bear fruit of itself, except it abide in the vine.* —John 15:4

I pray for them: I pray not for the world, but for them which thou hast given me; for they are thine. And all mine are thine, and thine are mine; and I am glorified in them...And now come I to thee; and these things I speak in the world, that they might have my joy fulfilled in themselves...That they all may be one; as thou, Father, art in me, and I in thee, that they also may be one in us: that the world may believe that thou hast sent me. And the glory which thou gavest me I have given them; that they may be one, even as we are one: I in them, and thou in me, that they may be made perfect in one; and that the world may know that thou hast sent me, and hast loved them, as thou hast loved me.

—John 17:9–23

O righteous Father, the world hath not known thee: but I have known thee, and these have known that thou hast sent me. And I have declared unto them thy name, and will declare it: that the love wherewith thou hast loved me may be in them, and I in them.

—John 17:25–26

. . .

Friday: *God is faithful, by whom ye were called unto the fellowship of his Son Jesus Christ our Lord.*

—1 Corinthians 1:9

Let us hold fast the profession of our faith without wavering; (for he is faithful that promised). —— God hath said, I will dwell in them, and walk in them; and I will be their God, and they shall be my people. —— Truly our fellowship is with the Father, and with his Son Jesus Christ. —— Rejoice, inasmuch as ye are partakers of Christ's sufferings; that, when his glory shall be revealed, ye may be glad also with exceeding joy.

—Hebrews 10:23; 2 Corinthians 6:16; 1 John 1:3; 1 Peter 4:13

That ye, being rooted and grounded in love, may be able to comprehend with all saints what is the breadth, and length, and depth, and height; and to know the love of Christ, which passeth knowledge, that ye might be filled with all the fulness of God.

—Ephesians 3:17–19

Whosoever shall confess that Jesus is the Son of God, God dwelleth in him, and he in God. —— And he that keepeth his commandments dwelleth in him, and he in him.

—1 John 4:15; 3:24

Saturday: *(Master,) where dwellest thou? He saith unto them, Come and see.* —John 1:38–39

In my Father's house are many mansions: if it were not so, I would have told you. I go to prepare a place for you. And if I go and prepare a place for you, I will come again, and receive you unto myself; that where I am, there ye may be also. —— To him that overcometh will I grant to sit with me in my throne.

—John 14:2–3; Revelations 3:21

Thus saith the high and lofty One that inhabiteth eternity, whose name is Holy; I dwell in the high and holy place, with him also that is of a contrite and humble spirit, to revive the spirit of the humble, and to revive the heart of the contrite ones.

—Isaiah 57:15

Behold, I stand at the door, and knock: if any man hear my voice, and open the door, I will come in to him, and will sup with him, and he with me. —— Lo, I am with you always, even unto the end of the world. —— How excellent is thy lovingkindness, O God! therefore the children of men put their trust under the shadow of thy wings.

—Revelations 3:20; Matthew 28:20; Psalm 36:7

WEEK 8 - LIGHT IN DARKNESS

Sunday: *Let us put on the armour of light.* —Romans 13:12

Put...on the Lord Jesus Christ. —— That I may win Christ, and be found in him, not having mine own righteousness, which is of the law, but that which is through the faith of Christ, the righteousness which is of God by faith. —— The righteousness of God which is by faith of Jesus Christ unto all and upon all them that believe. —— I will go in the strength of the Lord God: I will make mention of thy righteousness, even of thine only. —— He hath covered me with the robe of righteousness.

—Romans 13:14; Philippians 3:8–9; Romans 3:22; Psalm 71:16; Isaiah 61:10

If we say that we have fellowship with him, and walk in darkness, we lie, and do not the truth: But if we walk in the light, as he is in the light, we have fellowship one with another, and the blood of Jesus Christ his Son cleanseth us from all sin. —— Again, a new commandment I write unto you...because the darkness is past, and the true light now shineth. He that saith he is in the light, and hateth his brother, is in darkness. ...He that loveth his brother abideth in the light, and there is none occasion of stumbling in him.

—1 John 1:6–7; 2:8–10

Ye were sometimes darkness, but now are ye light in the Lord: walk as children of light...Have no fellowship with the unfruitful works of darkness but rather reprove them...All things that are reproved are made manifest by the light: for whatsoever doth make manifest is light. ...See then that ye walk circumspectly. —Ephesians 5:8–15

. . .

Monday: *Awake thou that sleepest, and arise from the dead, and Christ shall give thee light.* —Ephesians 5:14

It is high time to awake out of sleep: for now is our salvation nearer than when we believed. —— Therefore let us not sleep, as do others; but let us watch and be sober. For they that sleep sleep in the night: and they that be drunken are drunken in the night. But let us, who are of the day, be sober, putting on the breastplate of faith and love; and for an helmet, the hope of salvation.

—Romans 13:11; 1 Thessalonians 5:6–8

Arise, shine; for thy light is come, and the glory of the Lord is risen upon thee. For, behold, the darkness shall cover the earth, and gross darkness the people: but the Lord shall arise upon thee, and his glory shall be seen upon thee.

—Isaiah 60:1–2

Wherefore gird up the loins of your mind, be sober, and hope to the end for the grace that is to be brought unto you at the revelation of Jesus Christ. —— Let your loins be girded about, and your lights burning; And ye yourselves like unto men that wait for their lord.

—1 Peter 1:13; Luke 12:35–36

Tuesday: *The things which are.* —Revelations 1:19

Now we see through a glass, darkly. —— Now we see not yet all things put under him. ——

We have...a more sure word of prophecy; whereunto ye do well that ye take heed, as unto a light that shineth in a dark place, until the day dawn, and the day star arise in your hearts. —— Thy word is a lamp unto my feet, and a light unto my path.

—1 Corinthians 13:12; Hebrews 2:8; 2 Peter 1:19; Psalm 119:105

Beloved, remember ye the words which were spoken before of the apostles of our Lord Jesus Christ; how that they told you there should be mockers in the last time, who should walk after their own ungodly lusts. —— The Spirit speaketh expressly, that in the latter times some shall depart from the faith, giving heed to seducing spirits, and doctrines of devils.

—Jude 1:17–18; 1 Timothy 4:1

Little children, it is the last time. —— The night is far spent, the day is at hand: let us therefore cast off the works of darkness, and let us put on the armour of light.

—1 John 2:18; Romans 13:12

. . .

Wednesday: *When shall I arise, and the night be gone?* —Job 7:4

Watchman, what of the night? The watchman said, The morning cometh. —Isaiah 21:11–12

Yet a little while, and he that shall come will come, and will not tarry. —— He shall be as the light of the morning, when the sun riseth, even a morning without clouds.

—Hebrews 10:37; 2 Samuel 23:4

I go to prepare a place for you. And if I go and prepare a place for you, I will come again, and receive you unto myself; that where I am, there ye may be also. —— Let not your heart be troubled, neither let it be afraid. Ye have heard how I said unto you, I go away, and come again unto you.

—John 14:2, 27–28

Let all thine enemies perish, O Lord: but let them that love him be as the sun when he goeth forth in his might. —— Ye are all the children of light, and the children of the day: we are not of the night, nor of darkness. —— There shall be no night there.

—Judges 5:31; 1 Thessalonians 5:5; Revelations 21:25

Thursday: *Unto the upright there ariseth light in the darkness.*

—Psalm 112:4

Who is among you that feareth the Lord, that obeyeth the voice of his servant, that walketh in darkness, and hath no light? let him trust in the name of the Lord, and stay upon his God. —— Though he fall, he shall not be utterly cast down: for the Lord upholdeth him with his hand. —— The commandment is a lamp, and the law is light.

—Isaiah 50:10; Psalm 37:24; Proverbs 6:23

Rejoice not against me, O mine enemy: when I fall, I shall arise; when I sit in darkness, the Lord shall be a light unto me. I will bear the indignation of the Lord, because I have sinned against him, until he plead my cause, and execute judgment for me: he will bring me forth to the light, and I shall behold his righteousness.

—Micah 7:8–9

The light of the body is the eye: if therefore thine eye be single, thy whole body shall be full of light. But if thine eye be evil, thy whole body shall be full of darkness. If therefore the light that is in thee be darkness, how great is that darkness!

—Matthew 6:22–23

. . .

Friday: *I am...the bright and morning star.* —Revelations 22:16

There shall come a star out of Jacob. —— And the city had no need of the sun, neither of the moon, to shine in it: for the glory of God did lighten it, and the Lamb is the light thereof. And the nations of them which are saved shall walk in the light of it: and the kings of the earth do bring their glory and honour into it. And the gates of it shall not be shut at all by day: for there shall be no night there. —— And they shall see his face; and his name shall be in their foreheads. And there shall be no night there; and they need no candle, neither light of the sun; for the Lord God giveth them light: and they shall reign for ever and ever.

—Numbers 24:17; Revelations 21:23–25; 22:4–5

Until the day break, and the shadows flee away, turn, my beloved, and be thou like a roe or a young hart upon the mountains of Bethel. —— I am the light of the world. —— I will give him the morning star.

—Song 2:17; John 8:12; Revelations 2:28

Take ye heed, watch and pray: for ye know not when the time is. For the Son of Man is as a man taking a far journey, who left his house, and gave authority to his servants, and to every man his work, and commanded the porter to watch. Watch ye therefore...Lest coming suddenly he find you sleeping. And what I say unto you I say unto all, Watch.

—Mark 13:33–37

Saturday: *When I sit in darkness, the Lord shall be a light unto me.* —Micah 7:8

When thou passest through the waters, I will be with thee; and through the rivers, they shall not overflow thee: when thou walkest through the fire, thou shalt not be burned; neither shall the flame kindle upon thee. For I am the Lord thy God, the Holy One of Israel, thy Saviour. —— I will bring the blind by a way that they knew not; I will lead them in paths that they have not known: I will make darkness light before them, and crooked things straight. These things will I do unto them, and not forsake them.

—Isaiah 43:2–3; 42:16

Yea, though I walk through the valley of the shadow of death, I will fear no evil: for thou art with me; thy rod and thy staff they comfort me. —— What time I am afraid, I will trust in thee. In God I will praise his word, in God I have put my trust; I will not fear what flesh can do unto me. —— The Lord is my light and my salvation; whom shall I fear? the Lord is the strength of my life; of whom shall I be afraid? —Psalm 23:4; 56:3–4; 27:1

WEEK 9 - JESUS 1

S**unday**: *I have trodden the winepress alone.* —Isaiah 63:3

Who is like unto thee, O Lord, among the gods? who is like thee, glorious in holiness, fearful in praises, doing wonders? —— Thou art fairer than the children of men: grace is poured into thy lips: therefore God hath blessed thee for ever. Gird thy sword upon thy thigh, O most mighty, with thy glory and thy majesty. And in thy majesty ride prosperously because of truth and meekness and righteousness; and thy right hand shall teach thee terrible things. Thine arrows are sharp in the heart of the king's enemies; whereby the people fall under thee. Thy throne, O God, is for ever and ever: the sceptre of thy kingdom is a right sceptre. Thou lovest righteousness, and hatest wickedness: therefore God, thy God, hath anointed thee with the oil of gladness above thy fellows. All thy garments smell of myrrh, and aloes, and cassia, out of the ivory palaces, whereby they have made thee glad.

—Exodus 15:11; Psalm 45:2–8

He saw that there was no man, and wondered that there was no intercessor: therefore his arm brought salvation unto him; and his righteousness, it sustained him. —— Who his own self bare our sins in his own body on the tree —— Being made a curse for us.

—Isaiah 59:16; 1 Peter 2:24; Galatians 3:13

O sing unto the Lord a new song; for he hath done marvellous things: his right hand, and his holy arm, hath gotten him the victory. —— We are more than conquerors through him that loved us.

—Psalm 98:1; Romans 8:37

. . .

Monday: *Giving thanks unto the Father, which hath made us meet to be partakers of the inheritance of the saints in light:*

Who hath delivered us from the power of darkness, and hath translated us into the kingdom of his dear Son: In whom we have redemption through his blood, even the forgiveness of sins:

Who is the image of the invisible God, the firstborn of every creature: For by him were all things created, that are in heaven, and that are in earth, visible and invisible, whether they be thrones, or dominions, or principalities, or powers: all things were created by him, and for him: And he is before all things, and by him all things consist.

—Colossians 1:12–17

And he is the head of the body, the church: who is the beginning, the firstborn from the dead; that in all things he might have the preeminence. For it pleased the Father that in him should all fulness dwell; And, having made peace through the blood of his cross, by him to reconcile all things unto himself; by him, I say, whether they be things in earth, or things in heaven.

—Colossians 1:18–20

Tuesday: *For in him dwelleth all the fulness of the Godhead bodily.*

—Colossians 2:9

And ye are complete in him, which is the head of all principality and power: In whom also ye are circumcised with the circumcision made without hands, in putting off the body of the sins of the flesh by the circumcision of Christ: Buried with him in baptism, wherein also ye are risen with him through the faith of the operation of God, who hath raised him from the dead.

And you, being dead in your sins and the uncircumcision of your flesh, hath he quickened together with him, having forgiven you all trespasses; Blotting out the handwriting of ordinances that was against us, which was contrary to us, and took it out of the way, nailing it to his cross; And having spoiled principalities and powers, he made a shew of them openly, triumphing over them in it.

—Colossians 2:10–15

But thanks be to God, which giveth us the victory through our Lord Jesus Christ.

—1 Corinthians 15:57

. . .

Wednesday: *Thou shalt put the two stones upon the shoulders of the ephod for stones of memorial unto the children of Israel: and Aaron shall bear their names before the Lord.*

—Exodus 28:12

This man [Jesus], because he continueth ever, hath an unchangeable priesthood. Wherefore he is able also to save them to the uttermost that come unto God by him, seeing he ever liveth to make intercession for them. —— Him that is able to keep you from falling, and to present you faultless before the presence of his glory.

—Hebrews 7:24–25; Jude 1:24

Seeing...that we have a great high priest, that is passed into the heavens, Jesus the Son of God, let us hold fast our profession. For we have not an high priest which cannot be touched with the feeling of our infirmities; but was in all points tempted like as we are, yet without sin. Let us therefore come boldly unto the throne of grace.

—Hebrews 4:14–16

The beloved of the Lord shall dwell in safety by him; and the Lord shall cover him all the day long, and he shall dwell between his shoulders.

—Deuteronomy 33:12

Thursday: *Who art thou Lord? And he said, I am Jesus.* —Acts 26:15

It is I; be not afraid. —— When thou passest through the waters, I will be with thee: and through the rivers, they shall not overflow thee: when thou walkest through the fire, thou shalt not be burned; neither shall the flame kindle upon thee. For I am the Lord thy God...thy Saviour.

—Matthew 14:27; Isaiah 43:2–3

Though I walk through the valley of the shadow of death, I will fear no evil: for thou art with me; thy rod and thy staff they comfort me. —— Emmanuel...God with us.

—Psalm 23:4; Matthew 1:23

Thou shalt call his name JESUS: for he shall save his people from their sins. —— If any man sin, we have an advocate with the Father, Jesus Christ the righteous. —— Who is he that condemneth? it is Christ that died, yea rather, that is risen again, who is even at the right hand of God, who also maketh intercession for us. Who shall separate us from the love of Christ? shall tribulation, or distress, or persecution, or famine, or nakedness, or peril, or sword?

—Matthew 1:21; 1 John 2:1; Romans 8:34–35

. . .

Friday: *As the Father hath life in himself; so hath he given to the Son to have life in himself.*

—John 5:26

Our Saviour Jesus Christ...hath abolished death, and hath brought life and immortality to light through the gospel. —— I am the resurrection, and the life. —— Because I live, ye shall live also. —— We are made partakers of Christ, —— Partakers of the Holy Ghost, —— Partakers of the divine nature. —— The first man Adam was made a living soul; the last Adam was made a quickening spirit... Behold, I shew you a mystery; We shall not all sleep, but we shall all be changed, In a moment, in the twinkling of an eye, at the last trump: for the trumpet shall sound, and the dead shall be raised incorruptible, and we shall be changed.

—2 Timothy 1:10; John 11:25; 14:19; Hebrews 3:14; 6:4; 2 Peter 1:4; 1 Corinthians 15:45–52

Holy, holy, holy, Lord God Almighty, which was, and is, and is to come...Who liveth for ever and ever. —— The blessed and only Potentate, the King of kings, and Lord of lords; Who only hath immortality. —— Unto the King eternal, immortal...be honour and glory for ever and ever. Amen.

—Revelations 4:8–9; 1 Timothy 6:15–16; 1:17

Saturday: *Suffer it to be so now: for thus it becometh us to fulfill all righteousness.*

—Matthew 3:15

I delight to do thy will, O my God: yea, thy law is within my heart.

—Psalm 40:8

Think not that I am come to destroy the law, or the prophets: I am not come to destroy, but to fulfil. For verily I say unto you, Till heaven and earth pass, one jot or one tittle shall in no wise pass from the law, till all be fulfilled. —— The Lord is well pleased for his righteousness' sake; he will magnify the law, and make it honourable. —— Except your righteousness shall exceed the righteousness of the scribes and Pharisees, ye shall in no case enter into the kingdom of heaven.

—Matthew 5:17–18; Isaiah 42:21; Matthew 5:20

What the law could not do, in that it was weak through the flesh, God sending his own Son in the likeness of sinful flesh, and for sin, condemned sin in the flesh: that the righteousness of the law might be fulfilled in us, who walk not after the flesh, but after the Spirit. —— Christ is the end of the law for righteousness to every one that believeth.

—Romans 8:3–4; 10:4

WEEK 10 - JESUS OUR EXAMPLE

Sunday: *I must work the works of him that sent me, while it is day: the night cometh, when no man can work.* —John 9:4

Ye know that your labour is not in vain in the Lord. —— As ye have...received Christ Jesus the Lord, so walk ye in him: Rooted and built up in him, and stablished in the faith, as ye have been taught, abounding therein with thanksgiving. —— He that shall endure unto the end, the same shall be saved. —— That on the good ground are they, which in an honest and good heart, having heard the word, keep it, and bring forth fruit with patience.

—1 Corinthians 15:58; Colossians 2:6–7; Matthew 24:13; Luke 8:15

By faith ye stand.

—2 Corinthians 1:24

Be ye stedfast, unmoveable, always abounding in the work of the Lord.

—1 Corinthians 15:58

He that soweth to his flesh shall of the flesh reap corruption; but he that soweth to the Spirit shall of the Spirit reap life everlasting. —— It is the spirit that quickeneth; the flesh profiteth nothing: the words that I speak unto you, they are spirit, and they are life. —— And let us not be weary in well doing: for in due season we shall reap, if we faint not. As we have therefore opportunity, let us do good unto all men, especially unto them who are of the household of faith.

—Galatians 6:8; John 6:63; Galatians 6:9–10

. . .

Monday: *Ever follow that which is good.* —1 Thessalonians 5:15.

For even hereunto were ye called: because Christ also suffered for us, leaving us an example, that ye should follow his steps: Who did no sin, neither was guile found in his mouth: Who, when he was reviled, reviled not again...but committed himself to him that judgeth righteously. —— Consider him that endured such contradiction of sinners against himself, lest ye be wearied and faint in your minds.

—1 Peter 2:21–23; Hebrews 12:3

Let us lay aside every weight, and the sin which doth so easily beset us, and let us run with patience the race that is set before us, Looking unto Jesus the author and finisher of our faith; who for the joy that was set before him endured the cross, despising the shame, and is set down at the right hand of the throne of God.

—Hebrews 12:1–2

Finally, brethren, whatsoever things are true, whatsoever things are honest, whatsoever things are just, whatsoever things are pure, whatsoever things are lovely, whatsoever things are of good report; if there be any virtue, and if there be any praise, think on these things.

—Philippians 4:8

Tuesday: *Though he [Jesus] were a Son, yet learned he obedience by the things which he suffered.* —Hebrews 5:8

We glory in tribulations...knowing that tribulation worketh patience; And patience, experience; and experience, hope: And hope maketh not ashamed; because the love of God is shed abroad in our hearts by the Holy Ghost which is given unto us. —— No chastening for the present seemeth to be joyous, but grievous: nevertheless afterward it yieldeth the peaceable fruit of righteousness unto them which are exercised thereby. —— The fruit of the Spirit.

—Romans 5:3–5; Hebrews 12:11; Galatians 5:22

As the sufferings of Christ abound in us, so our consolation also aboundeth by Christ. —— Like as a father pitieth his children, so the Lord pitieth them that fear him.

—2 Corinthians 1:5; Psalm 103:13

Though our outward man perish, yet the inward man is renewed day by day. For our light affliction, which is but for a moment, worketh for us a far more exceeding and eternal weight of glory; while we look not at the things which are seen, but at the things which are not seen.

—2 Corinthians 4:16–18

. . .

Wednesday: *Reckon ye...yourselves to be dead indeed unto sin, but alive unto God through Jesus Christ our Lord.*

—Romans 6:11

Know ye not, that so many of us as were baptized into Jesus Christ were baptized into his death? Therefore we are buried with him by baptism into death: that like as Christ was raised up from the dead by the glory of the Father, even so we also should walk in newness of life...Knowing this, that our old man is crucified with him, that the body of sin might be destroyed, that henceforth we should not serve sin. For he that is dead is freed from sin. Now if we be dead with Christ, we believe that we shall also live with him: Knowing that Christ being raised from the dead dieth no more; death hath no more dominion over him. For in that he died, he died unto sin once: but in that he liveth, he liveth unto God. —— I am crucified with Christ; nevertheless I live; yet not I, but Christ liveth in me: and the life which I now live in the flesh I live by the faith of the Son of God, who loved me, and gave himself for me.

—Romans 6:3–10; Galatians 2:20

If ye then be risen with Christ, seek those things which are above, where Christ sitteth on the right hand of God...For ye are dead, and your life is hid with Christ in God.

—Colossians 3:1–3

Thursday: *The disciple is not above his master.* —Matthew 10:24

Ye call me Master and Lord: and ye say well; for so I am. —— It is enough for the disciple that he be as his master, and the servant as his lord. —— If they have persecuted me, they will also persecute you; if they have kept my saying, they will keep yours also. —— I have given them thy word; and the world hath hated them, because they are not of the world, even as I am not of the world.

—John 13:13; Matthew 10:25; John 15:20; 17:14

Let us run with patience the race that is set before us, Looking unto Jesus the author and finisher of our faith; who for the joy that was set before him endured the cross, despising the shame, and is set down at the right hand of the throne of God. For consider him that endured such contradiction of sinners against himself, lest ye be wearied and faint in your minds. —— Forasmuch...as Christ hath suffered for us in the flesh, arm yourselves likewise with the same mind. —— But rejoice, inasmuch as ye are partakers of Christ's sufferings; that, when his glory shall be revealed, ye may be glad also with exceeding joy.

—Hebrews 12:1–3; 1 Peter 4:1, 13

. . .

Friday: *In all points tempted like as we are, yet without sin.*
—Hebrews 4:15

When the woman saw that the tree was good for food [the lust of the flesh], and that it was pleasant to the eyes [the lust of the eyes], and a tree to be desired to make one wise [the pride of life], she took of the fruit thereof, and did eat, and gave also unto her husband with her; and he did eat. —— When the tempter came to him [Jesus], he said, If thou be the Son of God, command that these stones be made bread [the lust of the flesh]. But he answered, ...Man shall not live by bread alone, but by every word that proceedeth out of the mouth of God. Then the devil...sheweth him all the kingdoms of the world, and the glory of them [the lust of the eyes, and the pride of life]...Then saith Jesus unto him, Get thee hence, Satan.

—Genesis 3:6; Matthew 4:3–10

Blessed is the man that endureth temptation: for when he is tried, he shall receive the crown of life, which the Lord hath promised to them that love him. Let no man say when he is tempted, I am tempted of God: for God cannot be tempted with evil, neither tempteth he any man: But every man is tempted, when he is drawn away of his own lust, and enticed.

—James 1:12–14

Saturday: *Jesus wept.* —John 11:35

A man of sorrows, and acquainted with grief. —— We have not an high priest which cannot be touched with the feeling of our infirmities. —— It became him, for whom are all things, and by whom are all things, in bringing many sons unto glory, to make the captain of their salvation perfect through sufferings. —— Though he were a Son, yet learned he obedience by the things which he suffered.

—Isaiah 53:3; Hebrews 4:15; 2:10; 5:8

I was not rebellious, neither turned away back. I gave my back to the smiters, and my cheeks to them that plucked off the hair: I hid not my face from shame and spitting.

—Isaiah 50:5–6

Behold how he loved! —— He took not on him the nature of angels; but he took on him the seed of Abraham. Wherefore in all things it behooved him to be made like unto his brethren, that he might be a merciful and faithful high priest in things pertaining to God, to make reconciliation for the sins of the people.

—John 11:36; Hebrews 2:16–17

WEEK 11 - CHRIST'S CHURCH

S**unday**: *Thy Maker is thine husband; the Lord of hosts is his name.*
—Isaiah 54:5

This is a great mystery: but I speak concerning Christ and the church. —— Thou shalt also be a crown of glory in the hand of the Lord, and a royal diadem in the hand of thy God. Thou shalt no more be termed Forsaken...but thou shalt be called Hephzibah...for the Lord delighteth in thee...And as the bridegroom rejoiceth over the bride, so shall thy God rejoice over thee. —— He hath sent me... to comfort all that mourn; to appoint unto them that mourn in Zion, to give unto them beauty for ashes, the oil of joy for mourning, the garment of praise for the spirit of heaviness.

—Ephesians 5:32; Isaiah 62:3–5; 61:1–3

I will greatly rejoice in the Lord, my soul shall be joyful in my God; for he hath clothed me with the garments of salvation...as a bridegroom decketh himself with ornaments, and as a bride adorneth herself with her jewels. —— I will betroth thee unto me for ever; yea, I will betroth thee unto me in righteousness, and in judgment, and in lovingkindness, and in mercies.

— Isaiah 61:10; Hosea 2:19

Let us be glad and rejoice, and give honour to him: for the marriage of the Lamb is come, and his wife hath made herself ready. And to her was granted that she should be arrayed in fine linen, clean and white: for the fine linen is the righteousness of saints. And he saith unto me, Write, Blessed are they which are called unto the marriage supper of the Lamb. —— Who shall separate us from the love of Christ? —Revelations 19:7–9; Romans 8:35

. . .

M**onday**: *Fellowship in the gospel.* —Philippians 1:5

As the body is one, and hath many members, and all the members of that one body, being many, are one body: so also is Christ. For by one Spirit are we all baptized into one body, whether we be Jews or Gentiles, whether we be bond or free; and have been all made to drink into one Spirit.

—1 Corinthians 12:12–13

God is faithful, by whom ye were called unto the fellowship of his Son Jesus Christ our Lord. —— That which we have seen and heard declare we unto you, that ye also may have fellowship with us: and truly our fellowship is with the Father, and with his Son Jesus Christ.

—1 Corinthians 1:9; 1 John 1:3

If we walk in the light, as he is in the light, we have fellowship one with another, and the blood of Jesus Christ his Son cleanseth us from all sin. —— These words spake Jesus, ...Neither pray I for these alone, but for them also which shall believe on me through their word; That they all may be one; as thou, Father, art in me, and I in thee, that they also may be one in us.

—1 John 1:7; John 17:1, 20–21

T**uesday**: *When ye come together in the church, I hear that there be divisions among you.* —1 Corinthians 11:18

And if a house be divided against itself, that house cannot stand. —— For, brethren, ye have been called unto liberty; only use not liberty for an occasion to the flesh, but by love serve one another. For all the law is fulfilled in one word, even in this; Thou shalt love thy neighbour as thyself. But if ye bite and devour one another, take heed that ye be not consumed one of another.

—Mark 3:25; Galatians 5:13–15

This I say then, Walk in the Spirit, and ye shall not fulfil the lust of the flesh. For the flesh lusteth against the Spirit, and the Spirit against the flesh: and these are contrary the one to the other: so that ye cannot do the things that ye would...But the fruit of the Spirit is love, joy, peace, longsuffering, gentleness, goodness, faith, Meekness, temperance: against such there is no law. And they that are Christ's have crucified the flesh with the affections and lusts. If we live in the Spirit, let us also walk in the Spirit. Let us not be desirous of vain glory, provoking one another, envying one another.

—Galatians 5:16–17, 22–26

As we have therefore opportunity, let us do good unto all men, especially unto them who are of the household of faith. —Galatians 6:10

. . .

Wednesday: *They shall be mine, saith the Lord of hosts, in that day when I make up my jewels.* —Malachi 3:17

I have manifested thy name unto the men which thou gavest me out of the world: thine they were, and thou gavest them me; and they have kept thy word. —— I pray for them: I pray not for the world, but for them which thou hast given me; for they are thine. And all mine are thine, and thine are mine; and I am glorified in them. —— Father, I will that they also, whom thou hast given me, be with me where I am; that they may behold my glory, which thou hast given me: for thou lovedst me before the foundation of the world. —John 17:6, 9-10, 24

I will come again, and receive you unto myself. —— He shall come to be glorified in his saints, and to be admired in all them that believe...in that day. —— We which are alive and remain shall be caught up together with them in the clouds, to meet the Lord in the air: and so shall we ever be with the Lord. —— Thou shalt also be a crown of glory in the hand of the Lord, and a royal diadem in the hand of thy God.

—John 14:3; 2 Thessalonians 1:10; 1 Thessalonians 4:17; Isaiah 62:3

Thursday: *As the body is one, and hath many members... so also is Christ.* —1 Corinthians 12:12

He is the head of the body, the church: —— The head over all things to the church, Which is his body, the fulness of him that filleth all in all. —— We are members of his body, of his flesh, and of his bones.

—Colossians 1:18; Ephesians 1:22–23; 5:30

A body hast thou prepared me. —— Thine eyes did see my substance, yet being unperfect; and in thy book all my members were written, which in continuance were fashioned, when as yet there was none of them.

—Hebrews 10:5; Psalm 139:16

Thine they were, and thou gavest them me. —— He hath chosen us in him before the foundation of the world. —— Whom he did foreknow, he also did predestinate to be conformed to the image of his Son. —— Christ...loved the church, and gave himself for it; That he might sanctify and cleanse it with the washing of water by the word.

—John 17:6; Ephesians 1:4; Romans 8:29; Ephesians 5:25–26

Grow up into him in all things, which is the head, even Christ: From whom the whole body fitly joined together, and compacted by that which every joint supplieth...maketh increase of the body unto the edifying of itself in love.

—Ephesians 4:15–16

. . .

Friday: *Thou shalt call thy walls Salvation, and thy gates Praise.*
—Isaiah 60:18

The wall of the city had twelve foundations, and in them the names of the twelve apostles of the Lamb.

—Revelations 21:14

Ye are no more strangers and foreigners, but fellowcitizens with the saints, and of the household of God, And are built upon the foundation of the apostles and prophets, Jesus Christ himself being the chief corner stone; In whom all the building fitly framed together groweth unto an holy temple in the Lord: in whom ye also are builded together for an habitation of God through the Spirit. —— If so be ye have tasted that the Lord is gracious. To whom coming, as unto a living stone, disallowed indeed of men, but chosen of God, and precious, Ye also, as lively stones, are built up a spiritual house, an holy priesthood, to offer up spiritual sacrifices, acceptable to God by Jesus Christ.

—Ephesians 2:19–22; 1 Peter 2:3–5

Praise waiteth for thee, O God, in Sion.

—Psalm 65:1

Saturday: *The Lord's portion is his people.*
—Deuteronomy 32:9

Ye are Christ's; and Christ is God's. —— I am my beloved's, and his desire is toward me. —— I am his. —— The Son of God...loved me, and gave himself for me.

—1 Corinthians 3:23; Song 7:10; 2:16; Galatians 2:20

Ye are not your own...ye are bought with a price: therefore glorify God in your body, and in your spirit, which are God's. —— The Lord hath taken you, and brought you forth out of the iron furnace, even out of Egypt, to be unto him a people of inheritance, as ye are this day.

—1 Corinthians 6:19–20; Deuteronomy 4:20

Ye are God's husbandry, ye are God's building. —— Christ as a son over his own house; whose house are we, if we hold fast the confidence and the rejoicing of the hope firm unto the end. —— A spiritual house, an holy priesthood.

—1 Corinthians 3:9; Hebrews 3:6; 1 Peter 2:5

They shall be mine, saith the Lord of hosts, in that day when I make up my jewels. —— All mine are thine, and thine are mine; and I am glorified in them. —— The glory of his inheritance in the saints.

—Malachi 3:17; John 17:10; Ephesians 1:18

WEEK 12 - ETERNITY VS. TIME

Sunday: *Brethren, the time is short.*
—1 Corinthians 7:29

Man that is born of a woman is of few days, and full of trouble. He cometh forth like a flower, and is cut down: he fleeth also as a shadow, and continueth not. —— The world passeth away, and the lust thereof: but he that doeth the will of God abideth for ever. —— As in Adam all die, even so in Christ shall all be made alive. —— Death is swallowed up in victory. —— Whether we live, we live unto the Lord; and whether we die, we die unto the Lord: whether we live therefore, or die, we are the Lord's. —— To live is Christ, and to die is gain.

—Job 14:1–2; 1 John 2:17; 1 Corinthians 15:22, 54;
Romans 14:8; Philippians 1:21

Cast not away...your confidence, which hath great recompence of reward. For ye have need of patience, that, after ye have done the will of God, ye might receive the promise. For yet a little while, and he that shall come will come, and will not tarry.

—Hebrews 10:35–37

The night is far spent, the day is at hand: let us therefore cast off the works of darkness, and let us put on the armour of light. —— The end of all things is at hand: be ye therefore sober, and watch unto prayer.

—Romans 13:12; 1 Peter 4:7

. . .

Monday: *What is your life? It is even a vapour, that appeareth for a little time, and then vanisheth away.*

—James 4:14

My days are swifter than a post: they flee away, they see no good. They are passed away as the swift ships: as the eagle that hasteth to the prey. —— Thou carriest them away as with a flood; they are as a sleep...in the morning they are like grass which groweth up. In the morning it flourisheth, and groweth up: in the evening it is cut down, and withereth...So teach us to number our days, that we may apply our hearts unto wisdom. —— Man that is born of a woman is of few days, and full of trouble. He cometh forth like a flower, and is cut down.

—Job 9:25–26; Psalm 90:5–12; Job 14:1–2

The world passeth away, and the lust thereof: but he that doeth the will of God abideth for ever. —— And this is the promise that he hath promised us, even eternal life. —— And this is life eternal, that they might know thee the only true God, and Jesus Christ, whom thou hast sent —— Which God, that cannot lie, promised before the world began. —— To them who by patient continuance in well doing seek for glory and honour and immortality, eternal life.

—1 John 2:17; 2:25; John 17:3; Titus 1:2; Romans 2:7

Tuesday: *Vanity of vanities; all is vanity.*

—Ecclesiastes 1:2

We spend our years as a tale that is told. The days of our years are threescore years and ten; and if by reason of strength they be fourscore years, yet is their strength labour and sorrow; for it is soon cut off, and we fly away.

—Psalm 90:9–10

If in this life only we have hope in Christ, we are of all men most miserable. —— Here have we no continuing city, but we seek one to come. —— I am the Lord, I change not. —— Our conversation [citizenship] *is in heaven; from whence also we look for the Saviour, the Lord Jesus Christ: Who shall change our vile body, that it may be fashioned like unto his glorious body, according to the working whereby he is able even to subdue all things unto himself. —— The creature was made subject to vanity, not willingly, but by reason of him who hath subjected the same in hope. —— Holy, holy, holy, Lord God Almighty, which was, and is, and is to come.*

—1 Corinthians 15:19; Hebrews 13:14; Malachi 3:6; Philippians 3:20–21; Romans 8:20; Revelations 4:8

. . .

Wednesday: *Everlasting consolation.* —2 Thessalonians 2:16

I will remember my covenant with thee in the days of thy youth, and I will establish unto thee an everlasting covenant. —— By one offering he hath perfected for ever them that are sanctified. —— He is able to save them to the uttermost that come unto God by him, seeing he ever liveth to make intercession for them. —— I know whom I have believed, and am persuaded that he is able to keep that which I have committed unto him against that day.

—Ezekiel 16:60; Hebrews 10:14; 7:25; 2 Timothy 1:12

The gifts and calling of God are without repentance. —— Who shall separate us from the love of Christ? —— The Lamb which is in the midst of the throne shall feed them, and shall lead them unto living fountains of waters: and God shall wipe away all tears from their eyes. —— So shall we ever be with the Lord. Wherefore comfort one another with these words.

—Romans 11:29; 8:35; Revelations 7:17; 1 Thessalonians 4:17–18

This is not your rest. —— These all died in faith, not having received the promises, but having seen them afar off, and were persuaded of them, and embraced them, and confessed that they were strangers and pilgrims on the earth. —— Thy statutes have been my songs in the house of my pilgrimage.

—Micah 2:10; Hebrews 11:13; Psalm 119:54

Thursday: *I will make the place of my feet glorious.* —Isaiah 60:13

Thus saith the Lord, The heaven is my throne, and the earth is my footstool. —— Will God in very deed dwell with men on the earth? behold, heaven and the heaven of heavens cannot contain thee; how much less this house which I have built!

—Isaiah 66:1; 2 Chronicles 6:18

Thus saith the Lord of hosts, Yet once, it is a little while, and I will shake the heavens, and the earth, and the sea, and the dry land; And I will shake all nations, and the desire of all nations shall come: and I will fill this house with glory, saith the Lord of hosts. ...The glory of this latter house shall be greater than of the former, saith the Lord of hosts.

—Haggai 2:6–9

I saw a new heaven and a new earth: for the first heaven and the first earth were passed away; and there was no more sea...And I heard a great voice out of heaven saying, Behold, the tabernacle of God is with men, and he will dwell with them, and they shall be his people, and God himself shall be with them, and be their God.

—Revelations 21:1–3

. . .

Friday: *We look not at the things which are seen, but at the things which are not seen: for the things which are seen are temporal; but the things which are not seen are eternal.*

—2 Corinthians 4:18

Here have we no continuing city. —— Ye have in heaven a better and an enduring substance. —— Fear not, little flock; for it is your Father's good pleasure to give you the kingdom. ——

Now for a season, if need be, ye are in heaviness through manifold temptations. —— There the wicked cease from troubling; and there the weary be at rest.

—Hebrews 13:14; 10:34; Luke 12:32; 1 Peter 1:6; Job 3:17

We that are in this tabernacle do groan, being burdened. —— God shall wipe away all tears from their eyes; and there shall be no more death, neither sorrow, nor crying, neither shall there be any more pain: for the former things are passed away.

—2 Corinthians 5:4; Revelations 21:4

The sufferings of this present time are not worthy to be compared with the glory which shall be revealed in us. —— Our light affliction, which is but for a moment, worketh for us a far more exceeding and eternal weight of glory.

—Romans 8:18; 2 Corinthians 4:17

Saturday: *There was a rainbow round about the throne, in sight like unto an emerald.*

—Revelations 4:3

This is the token of the covenant which I make between me and you and every living creature that is with you, for perpetual generations: I do set my bow in the cloud...and I will look upon it, that I may remember the everlasting covenant between God and every living creature of all flesh that is upon the earth. —— An everlasting covenant, ordered in all things, and sure. —— That by two immutable things, in which it was impossible for God to lie, we might have a strong consolation, who have fled for refuge to lay hold upon the hope set before us.

—Genesis 9:12–16; 2 Samuel 23:5; Hebrews 6:18

We declare unto you glad tidings, how that the promise which was made unto the fathers, God hath fulfilled the same unto their children, in that he hath raised up Jesus again. —— Jesus Christ the same yesterday, and to day, and for ever.

—Acts 13:32; Hebrews 13:8

WEEK 13 - JESUS OUR REDEEMER

S**unday**: *It is I; be not afraid.* —John 6:20

Fear not; I am the first and the last: I am he that liveth, and was dead; and, behold, I am alive for evermore, Amen; and have the keys of hell and of death. —— I, even I, am he that blotteth out thy transgressions for mine own sake, and will not remember thy sins.

—Revelations 1:17–18; Isaiah 43:25

There is therefore now no condemnation to them which are in Christ Jesus.

—Romans 8:1

Ye know the grace of our Lord Jesus Christ, that, though he was rich, yet for your sakes he became poor, that ye through his poverty might be rich. —— Being justified by faith, we have peace with God through our Lord Jesus Christ. —— Christ hath redeemed us from the curse of the law, being made a curse for us.

—2 Corinthians 8:9; Romans 5:1; Galatians 3:13

There is no God else beside me; a just God and a Saviour; there is none beside me. Look unto me, and be ye saved, all the ends of the earth: for I am God, and there is none else. —— There is none other name under heaven given among men, whereby we must be saved.

—Isaiah 45:21–22; Acts 4:12

God sent his only begotten Son into the world, that we might live through him. Herein is love, not that we loved God, but that he loved us, and sent his Son to be the propitiation for our sins. —— That he might be just, and the justifier of him which believeth in Jesus.

—1 John 4:9–10; Romans 3:26

. . .

M**onday**: *Great is thy mercy toward me: and thou hast delivered my soul from the lowest hell.*

—Psalm 86:13

Fear him which is able to destroy both soul and body in hell.

—Matthew 10:28

Fear not: for I have redeemed thee, I have called thee by thy name; thou art mine...I, even I, am the Lord; and beside me there is no saviour...I, even I, am he that blotteth out thy transgressions for mine own sake, and will not remember thy sins. —— They that trust in their wealth, and boast themselves in the multitude of their riches; None of them can by any means redeem his brother, nor give to God a ransom for him: (for the redemption of their soul is precious). —— I have found a ransom. —— God, who is rich in mercy, for his great love wherewith he loved us, Even when we were dead in sins, hath quickened us together with Christ.

—Isaiah 43:1, 11, 25; Psalm 49:6–8; Job 33:24; Ephesians 2:4–5

Neither is there salvation in any other: for there is none other name under heaven given among men, whereby we must be saved.

—Acts 4:12

T**uesday**: *The grace of our Lord was exceeding abundant with faith and love which is in Christ Jesus.*

—1 Timothy 1:14

He hath sent me to bind up the brokenhearted, to proclaim liberty to the captives, and the opening of the prison to them that are bound...To appoint unto them that mourn in Zion, to give unto them beauty for ashes, the oil of joy for mourning, the garment of praise for the spirit of heaviness...that he might be glorified...Everlasting joy shall be unto them. —— In all their affliction he was afflicted, and the angel of his presence saved them: in his love and in his pity he redeemed them; and he bare them, and carried them all the days of old. —— But where sin abounded, grace did much more abound.

—Isaiah 61:1, 3, 7; 63:9; Romans 5:20

That in the ages to come he might shew the exceeding riches of his grace in his kindness toward us through Christ Jesus. For by grace are ye saved through faith; and that not of yourselves: it is the gift of God: Not of works, lest any man should boast. —— According to his mercy he saved us, by the washing of regeneration, and renewing of the Holy Ghost; Which he shed on us abundantly through Jesus Christ our Saviour.

—Ephesians 2:7–9; Titus 3:5–6

. . .

Wednesday: *O my Father, if it be possible, let this cup pass from me: nevertheless not as I will, but as thou wilt.*

—Matthew 26:39

Now is my soul troubled; and what shall I say? Father, save me from this hour: but for this cause came I unto this hour.

—John 12:27

I came down from heaven, not to do mine own will, but the will of him that sent me. —— He...became obedient unto death, even the death of the cross. —— In the days of his flesh, when he had offered up prayers and supplications with strong crying and tears unto him that was able to save him from death.

—John 6:38; Philippians 2:8; Hebrews 5:7

Thinkest thou that I cannot now pray to my Father, and he shall presently give me more than twelve legions of angels? —— Thus it is written, and thus it behooved Christ to suffer, and to rise from the dead the third day: And that repentance and remission of sins should be preached in his name among all nations, beginning at Jerusalem.

—Matthew 26:53; Luke 24:46–47

Thursday: *Fear not: for I have redeemed thee.*

—Isaiah 43:1

Fear not; for thou shalt not be ashamed: neither be thou confounded; for thou shalt not be put to shame: for thou shalt forget the shame of thy youth, and shalt not remember the reproach of thy widowhood any more. For thy Maker is thine husband; the Lord of hosts is his name; and thy Redeemer the Holy One of Israel. —— I have blotted out, as a thick cloud, thy transgressions, and, as a cloud, thy sins: return unto me; for I have redeemed thee. —— With the precious blood of Christ, as of a lamb without blemish and without spot.

—Isaiah 54:4–5; 44:22; 1 Peter 1:19

Their Redeemer is strong; the Lord of hosts is his name: he shall throughly plead their cause. —— My Father, which gave them me, is greater than all; and no man is able to pluck them out of my Father's hand.

—Jeremiah 50:34; John 10:29

Grace be to you and peace from God the Father, and from our Lord Jesus Christ, Who gave himself for our sins, that he might deliver us from this present evil world, according to the will of God and our Father: To whom be glory for ever and ever. Amen.

—Galatians 1:3–5

. . .

Friday: *Mercy and truth are met together;*
righteousness and peace have kissed each other.

—Psalm 85:10

A just God and a Saviour.

—Isaiah 45:21

The Lord is well pleased for his righteousness' sake; he will magnify the law, and make it honourable.

—Isaiah 42:21

God was in Christ, reconciling the world unto himself, not imputing their trespasses unto them. —— Whom God hath set forth to be a propitiation through faith in his blood, to declare his righteousness for the remission of sins that are past, through the forbearance of God; to declare, I say, at this time his righteousness: that he might be just, and the justifier of him which believeth in Jesus. —— He was wounded for our transgressions, he was bruised for our iniquities: the chastisement of our peace was upon him; and with his stripes we are healed. —— Who shall lay any thing to the charge of God's elect? It is God that justifieth. —— To him that worketh not, but believeth on him that justifieth the ungodly, his faith is counted for righteousness.

—2 Corinthians 5:19; Romans 3:25–26; Isaiah 53:5; Romans 8:33; 4:5

Saturday: *I know that my redeemer liveth.* —Job 19:25

If, when we were enemies, we were reconciled to God by the death of his Son, much more, being reconciled, we shall be saved by his life. —— This man, because he continueth ever, hath an unchangeable priesthood. Wherefore he is able also to save them to the uttermost that come unto God by him, seeing he ever liveth to make intercession for them.

—Romans 5:10; Hebrews 7:24–25

Because I live, ye shall live also. —— But now is Christ risen from the dead, and become the firstfruits of them that slept.

—John 14:19; 1 Corinthians 15:20

The Redeemer shall come to Zion, and unto them that turn from transgression in Jacob, saith the Lord. —— We have redemption through his blood, the forgiveness of sins, according to the riches of his grace. —— Ye were not redeemed with corruptible things, as silver and gold, from your vain conversation received by tradition from your fathers; But with the precious blood of Christ, as of a lamb without blemish and without spot.

—Isaiah 59:20; Ephesians 1:7; 1 Peter 1:18–19

WEEK 14 - HOLY WEEK 1 - PASSOVER / GETHSEMANE

Christ our passover is sacrificed for us:
therefore let us keep the feast.
—1 Corinthians 5:7–8

It is a night to be much observed unto the Lord
for bringing them out from the land of Egypt.
—Exodus 12:42

Sunday: Feast of Unleavened Bread - The Passover

Now the feast of unleavened bread drew nigh, which is called the Passover. —— After two days was the feast of the passover, and of unleavened bread: and the chief priests and the scribes sought how they might take him by craft, and put him to death. But they said, Not on the feast day, lest there be an uproar of the people.

—Luke 22:1; Mark 14:1–2

Jesus' Betrayal Planned

And Judas Iscariot, one of the twelve, went unto the chief priests, to betray him unto them. And when they heard it, they were glad, and promised to give him money. And he sought how he might conveniently betray him. —Mark 14:10–11

. . .

Monday: The Last Supper

Then came the day of unleavened bread, when the passover must be killed. And he sent Peter and John , saying, Go and prepare us the passover, that we may eat.

—Luke 22:7–8

And the disciples did as Jesus had appointed them; and they made ready the passover. Now when the even was come, he sat down with the twelve. And as they did eat, he said, Verily I say unto you, that one of you shall betray me. And they were exceeding sorrowful, and began every one of them to say unto him, Lord, is it I? And he answered and said, He that dippeth his hand with me in the dish, the same shall betray me. The Son of man goeth as it is written of him: but woe unto that man by whom the Son of man is betrayed! it had been good for that man if he had not been born.

Then Judas, which betrayed him, answered and said, Master, is it I?

He said unto him, Thou hast said.

—Matthew 26:19–25

Tuesday: The Lord's Supper Instituted

And he said unto them, With desire I have desired to eat this passover with you before I suffer: For I say unto you, I will not any more eat thereof, until it be fulfilled in the kingdom of God...And as they were eating, Jesus took bread, and blessed it, and brake it, and gave it to the disciples, and said, Take, eat; this is my body. And he took the cup, and gave thanks, and gave it to them, saying, Drink ye all of it; For this is my blood of the new testament, which is shed for many for the remission of sins. But I say unto you, I will not drink henceforth of this fruit of the vine, until that day when I drink it new with you in my Father's kingdom.

—Luke 22:15–16; Matthew 26:26–29

The Way To Gethsemane

And when they had sung an hymn, they went out into the mount of Olives.

Then saith Jesus unto them, All ye shall be offended because of me this night: for it is written, I will smite the shepherd, and the sheep of the flock shall be scattered abroad. But after I am risen again, I will go before you into Galilee.

—Matthew 26:30–32

. . .

Wednesday: Gethsemane

And they came to a place which was named Gethsemane: and he saith to his disciples, Sit ye here, while I shall pray. And he taketh with him Peter and James and John, and began to be sore amazed, and to be very heavy; And saith unto them, My soul is exceeding sorrowful unto death: tarry ye here, and watch. And he went forward a little, and fell on the ground, and prayed that, if it were possible, the hour might pass from him.

And he said, Abba, Father, all things are possible unto thee; take away this cup from me: nevertheless not what I will, but what thou wilt. And he cometh, and findeth them sleeping, and saith unto Peter, Simon, sleepest thou? couldest not thou watch one hour?

Watch ye and pray, lest ye enter into temptation. The spirit truly is ready, but the flesh is weak. And again he went away, and prayed, and spake the same words.

And when he returned, he found them asleep again, (for their eyes were heavy,) neither wist they what to answer him. And he cometh the third time, and saith unto them, Sleep on now, and take your rest: it is enough, the hour is come; behold, the Son of man is betrayed into the hands of sinners.

Rise up, let us go; lo, he that betrayeth me is at hand.

—Mark 14:32–42

Thursday: Jesus Betrayed

And while he yet spake, lo, Judas, one of the twelve, came, and with him a great multitude with swords and staves, from the chief priests and elders of the people.

Now he that betrayed him gave them a sign, saying, Whomsoever I shall kiss, that same is he: hold him fast. And forthwith he came to Jesus, and said, Hail, master; and kissed him.

And Jesus said unto him, Friend, wherefore art thou come?

—Matthew 26:47–50a

Jesus therefore, knowing all things that should come upon him, went forth, and said unto them, Whom seek ye?

They answered him, Jesus of Nazareth.

Jesus saith unto them, I am he. And Judas also, which betrayed him, stood with them.

As soon then as he had said unto them, I am he, they went backward, and fell to the ground.

—John 18:4–6

Jesus Taken Captive

Then came they, and laid hands on Jesus and took him.

And, behold, one of them which were with Jesus stretched out his hand, and drew his sword, and struck a servant of the high priest's, and smote off his ear. Then said Jesus unto him, Put up again thy sword into his place: for all they that take the sword shall perish with the sword. Thinkest thou that I cannot now pray to my Father, and he shall presently give me more than twelve legions of angels? But how then shall the scriptures be fulfilled, that thus it must be?

—Matthew 26:50b–54

And Jesus answered and said, Suffer ye thus far. And he touched his ear, and healed him.

—Luke 22:51

In that same hour said Jesus to the multitudes, Are ye come out as against a thief with swords and staves for to take me? I sat daily with you teaching in the temple, and ye laid no hold on me. But all this was done, that the scriptures of the prophets might be fulfilled.

Then all the disciples forsook him, and fled.

And they that had laid hold on Jesus led him away to Caiaphas the high priest, where the scribes and the elders were assembled.

—Matthew 26:55–57

F**riday**: Jesus Before the Jewish Religious Leaders

Now the chief priests, and elders, and all the council, sought false witness against Jesus, to put him to death; But found none: yea, though many false witnesses came, yet found they none. At the last came two false witnesses, And said, This fellow said, I am able to destroy the temple of God, and to build it in three days. And the high priest arose, and said unto him, Answerest thou nothing? what is it which these witness against thee?

But Jesus held his peace, And the high priest answered and said unto him, I adjure thee by the living God, that thou tell us whether thou be the Christ, the Son of God.

Jesus saith unto him, Thou hast said: nevertheless I say unto you, Hereafter shall ye see the Son of man sitting on the right hand of power, and coming in the clouds of heaven.

—Matthew 26:59–64

Jewish Religious Leaders Sentence Jesus to Death, But First Required Pilot's Approval

Then the high priest rent his clothes, saying, He hath spoken blasphemy; what

further need have we of witnesses? behold, now ye have heard his blasphemy. What think ye?

They answered and said, He is guilty of death. Then did they spit in his face, and buffeted him; and others smote him with the palms of their hands, Saying, Prophesy unto us, thou Christ, Who is he that smote thee?

—Matthew 26:65–68

When the morning was come, all the chief priests and elders of the people took counsel against Jesus to put him to death: And when they had bound him, they led him away, and delivered him to Pontius Pilate the governor.

—Matthew 27:1–2

Saturday: Jesus Delivered to Pilot for Judgment

And they began to accuse him, saying, We found this fellow perverting the nation, and forbidding to give tribute to Caesar, saying that he himself is Christ a King.

—Luke 23:2

And Jesus stood before the governor: and the governor asked him, saying, Art thou the King of the Jews? And Jesus said unto him, Thou sayest. And when he was accused of the chief priests and elders, he answered nothing.

Then said Pilate unto him, Hearest thou not how many things they witness against thee? And he answered him to never a word; insomuch that the governor marvelled greatly.

—Matthew 27:11–14

Then said Pilate to the chief priests and to the people, I find no fault in this man. And they were the more fierce, saying, He stirreth up the people, teaching throughout all Jewry, beginning from Galilee to this place. When Pilate heard of Galilee, he asked whether the man were a Galilaean. And as soon as he knew that he belonged unto Herod's jurisdiction, he sent him to Herod, who himself also was at Jerusalem at that time.

—Luke 23:4–7

Jesus Delivered to Herod

And when Herod saw Jesus, he was exceeding glad: for he was desirous to see him of a long season, because he had heard many things of him; and he hoped to have seen some miracle done by him.

Then he questioned with him in many words; but he answered him nothing. And the chief priests and scribes stood and vehemently accused him. And Herod with his men of war set him at nought, and mocked him, and arrayed him in a gorgeous robe, and sent him again to Pilate.

—Luke 23:8–11

WEEK 15 - HOLY WEEK 2 - CRUCIFIXION / RESURRECTION

Sunday: Jesus Sent Back To Pilot Who Attempts To Release Jesus

And Pilate, when he had called together the chief priests and the rulers and the people,

Said unto them, Ye have brought this man unto me, as one that perverteth the people: and, behold, I, having examined him before you, have found no fault in this man touching those things whereof ye accuse him:

No, nor yet Herod: for I sent you to him; and, lo, nothing worthy of death is done unto him. I will therefore chastise him, and release him.

—Luke 23:13–16

Then said Pilate unto them, Take ye him, and judge him according to your law.

The Jews therefore said unto him, It is not lawful for us to put any man to death: That the saying of Jesus might be fulfilled, which he spake, signifying what death he should die.

Then Pilate entered into the judgment hall again, and called Jesus, and said unto him, Art thou the King of the Jews?

Jesus answered him, Sayest thou this thing of thyself, or did others tell it thee of me?

Pilate answered, Am I a Jew? Thine own nation and the chief priests have delivered thee unto me: what hast thou done?

Jesus answered, My kingdom is not of this world: if my kingdom were of this world, then would my servants fight, that I should not be delivered to the Jews: but now is my kingdom not from hence.

Pilate therefore said unto him, Art thou a king then?

Jesus answered, Thou sayest that I am a king. To this end was I born, and for this cause came I into the world, that I should bear witness unto the truth. Every one that is of the truth heareth my voice.

Pilate saith unto him, What is truth? And when he had said this, he went out again unto the Jews, and saith unto them, I find in him no fault at all.

But ye have a custom, that I should release unto you one at the passover: will ye therefore that I release unto you the King of the Jews?

Then cried they all again, saying, Not this man, but Barabbas. Now Barabbas was a robber.

—Luke 23:13–16; John 18:31–40

Monday: Pilot Tries To Release Jesus' A Second Time

Now at that feast he released unto them one prisoner, whomsoever they desired. And there was one named Barabbas, which lay bound with them that had made insurrection with him, who had committed murder in the insurrection.

—Mark 15:6–7

The governor answered and said unto them, Whether of the twain will ye that I release unto you?

They said, Barabbas.

Pilate saith unto them, What shall I do then with Jesus which is called Christ?

They all say unto him, Let him be crucified.

And the governor said, Why, what evil hath he done?

But they cried out the more, saying, Let him be crucified.

—Matthew 27:21–23

When the chief priests therefore and officers saw him, they cried out, saying, Crucify him, crucify him.

Pilate saith unto them, Take ye him, and crucify him: for I find no fault in him.

The Jews answered him, We have a law, and by our law he ought to die, because he made himself the Son of God.

When Pilate therefore heard that saying, he was the more afraid; And went again into the judgment hall, and saith unto Jesus, Whence art thou? But Jesus gave him no answer. Then saith Pilate unto him, Speakest thou not unto me? knowest thou not that I have power to crucify thee, and have power to release thee?

Jesus answered, Thou couldest have no power at all against me, except it were given thee from above: therefore he that delivered me unto thee hath the greater sin.

And from thenceforth Pilate sought to release him: but the Jews cried out, saying, If thou let this man go, thou art not Caesar's friend: whosoever maketh himself a king speaketh against Caesar.

—John 19:6–12

Tuesday: Jesus Sentenced To Death By The Jews

When Pilate saw that he could prevail nothing, but that rather a tumult was made, he took water, and washed his hands before the multitude, saying, I am innocent of the blood of this just person: see ye to it.

Then answered all the people, and said, His blood be on us, and on our children.

Then released he Barabbas unto them: and when he had scourged Jesus, he delivered him to be crucified.

—Matthew 27:24–26

The Mocking of Christ

Then the soldiers of the governor took Jesus into the common hall, and gathered unto him the whole band of soldiers. And they stripped him, and put on him a scarlet robe. And when they had platted a crown of thorns, they put it upon his head, and a reed in his right hand: and they bowed the knee before him, and mocked him, saying, Hail, King of the Jews! And they spit upon him, and took the reed, and smote him on the head. And after that they had mocked him, they took the robe off from him, and put his own raiment on him, and led him away to crucify him.

—Matthew 27:27–31

Wednesday: The Via Dolorosa

And Pilate gave sentence that it should be as they required. And he released unto them him that for sedition and murder was cast into prison, whom they had desired; but he delivered Jesus to their will. And as they led him away, they laid hold upon one Simon, a Cyrenian, coming out of the country, and on him they laid the cross, that he might bear it after Jesus. And there followed him a great company of people, and of women, which also bewailed and lamented him.

But Jesus turning unto them said, Daughters of Jerusalem, weep not for me, but weep for yourselves, and for your children. For, behold, the days are coming, in the which they shall say, Blessed are the barren, and the wombs that never bare, and the paps which never gave suck.

Then shall they begin to say to the mountains, Fall on us; and to the hills, Cover us. For if they do these things in a green tree, what shall be done in the dry?

And there were also two other, malefactors, led with him to be put to death. And when they were come to the place, which is called Calvary, there they crucified him, and the malefactors, one on the right hand, and the other on the left.

—Luke 23:24–42

Thursday: Jesus' Crucifixion - The Third Hour

And they gave him to drink wine mingled with myrrh: but he received it not...And it was the third hour, and they crucified him.

—Mark 15:23–25

Then said Jesus, Father, forgive them; for they know not what they do. And they parted his raiment, and cast lots.

And the people stood beholding. And the rulers also with them derided him, saying, He saved others; let him save himself, if he be Christ, the chosen of God.

—Luke 23:34–35

And with him they crucify two thieves; the one on his right hand, and the other on his left. And the scripture was fulfilled, which saith, And he was numbered with the transgressors. And they that passed by railed on him, wagging their heads, and saying, Ah, thou that destroyest the temple, and buildest it in three days, Save thyself, and come down from the cross.

Likewise also the chief priests mocking said among themselves with the scribes, He saved others; himself he cannot save. Let Christ the King of Israel descend now from the cross, that we may see and believe. And they that were crucified with him reviled him.

—Mark 15:27–32

And a superscription also was written over him in letters of Greek, and Latin, and Hebrew, ***THIS IS THE KING OF THE JEWS.***

And one of the malefactors which were hanged railed on him, saying, If thou be Christ, save thyself and us. But the other answering rebuked him, saying, Dost not thou fear God, seeing thou art in the same condemnation? And we indeed justly; for we receive the due reward of our deeds: but this man hath done nothing amiss. And he said unto Jesus, Lord, remember me when thou comest into thy kingdom.

And Jesus said unto him, Verily I say unto thee, Today shalt thou be with me in paradise.

—Luke 23:38–43

Jesus' Crucifixion - The Sixth to Ninth Hour

Now from the sixth hour there was darkness over all the land unto the ninth hour. And about the ninth hour Jesus cried with a loud voice, saying, Eli, Eli, lama sabachthani? that is to say, My God, my God, why hast thou forsaken me?

—Matthew 27:45–46

Now there stood by the cross of Jesus his mother, and his mother's sister, Mary the wife of Cleophas, and Mary Magdalene. When Jesus therefore saw his mother, and the disciple standing by, whom he loved, he saith unto his mother, Woman, behold thy son! Then saith he to the disciple, Behold thy mother! And from that hour that disciple took her unto his own home.

After this, Jesus knowing that all things were now accomplished, that the scripture might be fulfilled, saith, I thirst. Now there was set a vessel full of vinegar: and they filled a spunge with vinegar, and put it upon hyssop, and put it to his mouth.

When Jesus therefore had received the vinegar, he said, It is finished.

—John 19:25–30a

Jesus' Death

And when Jesus had cried with a loud voice, he said, Father, into thy hands I commend my spirit: and having said thus, he gave up the ghost.

—Luke 23:46

Friday: Jesus' Burial

And, behold, the veil of the temple was rent in twain from the top to the bottom; and the earth did quake, and the rocks rent; And the graves were opened; and many bodies of the saints which slept arose, And came out of the graves after his resurrection, and went into the holy city, and appeared unto many.

Now when the centurion, and they that were with him, watching Jesus, saw the earthquake, and those things that were done, they feared greatly, saying, Truly this was the Son of God.

—Matthew 27:51–54

And, behold, there was a man named Joseph, a counsellor; and he was a good man, and a just: (The same had not consented to the counsel and deed of them;) he was of Arimathaea, a city of the Jews: who also himself waited for the kingdom of God. This man went unto Pilate, and begged the body of Jesus. And he took it down, and wrapped it in linen, and laid it in a sepulchre that was hewn in stone, wherein never man before was laid. And that day was the preparation, and the sabbath drew on. And the women also, which came with him from Galilee, followed after, and beheld the sepulchre, and how his body was laid. And they returned, and prepared spices and ointments; and rested the sabbath day according to the commandment.

—Luke 23:50–56

Saturday: Resurrection Sunday

And when the sabbath was past, Mary Magdalene, and Mary the mother of James, and Salome, had bought sweet spices, that they might come and anoint him. And very early in the morning the first day of the week, they came unto the sepulchre at the rising of the sun. And they said among themselves, Who shall roll us away the stone from the door of the sepulchre?

—Mark 16:1–3

And, behold, there was a great earthquake: for the angel of the Lord descended from heaven, and came and rolled back the stone from the door, and sat upon it. His countenance was like lightning, and his raiment white as snow.

—Matthew 28:2–3

And they found the stone rolled away from the sepulchre. And they entered in, and found not the body of the Lord Jesus. And it came to pass, as they were much perplexed thereabout, behold, two men stood by them in shining garments: And as they were afraid, and bowed down their faces to the earth, they said unto them, Why seek ye the living among the dead? He is not here, but is risen: remember how he spake unto you when he was yet in Galilee, Saying, The Son of man must be delivered into the hands of sinful men, and be crucified, and the third day rise again.

—Luke 24:2–7

Jesus, Risen from the Dead

And he saith unto them, Be not affrighted: Ye seek Jesus of Nazareth, which was crucified: he is risen; he is not here: behold the place where they laid him. But go your way, tell his disciples and Peter that he goeth before you into Galilee: there shall ye see him, as he said unto you.

And they went out quickly, and fled from the sepulchre; for they trembled and were amazed: neither said they any thing to any man; for they were afraid.

—Mark 16:6–8

But Mary stood without at the sepulchre weeping: and as she wept, she stooped down, and looked into the sepulchre,

And seeth two angels in white sitting, the one at the head, and the other at the feet, where the body of Jesus had lain.

And they say unto her, Woman, why weepest thou?

She saith unto them, Because they have taken away my Lord, and I know not where they have laid him. And when she had thus said, she turned herself back, and saw Jesus standing, and knew not that it was Jesus.

Jesus saith unto her, Woman, why weepest thou? whom seekest thou?

She, supposing him to be the gardener, saith unto him, Sir, if thou have borne him hence, tell me where thou hast laid him, and I will take him away.

Jesus saith unto her, Mary.

She turned herself, and saith unto him, Rabboni; which is to say, Master.

Jesus saith unto her, Touch me not; for I am not yet ascended to my Father: but go to my brethren, and say unto them, I ascend unto my Father, and your Father; and to my God, and your God.

—John 20:11–17

And as they went to tell his disciples, behold, Jesus met them, saying, All hail. And they came and held him by the feet, and worshipped him. Then said Jesus unto them, Be not afraid: go tell my brethren that they go into Galilee, and there shall they see me.

—Matthew 28:9–10

WEEK 16 - JESUS' "I AM" DECLARATIONS

Sunday: *I am the true vine, and my Father is the husbandman. Every branch in me that beareth not fruit he taketh away: and every branch that beareth fruit, he purgeth it, that it may bring forth more fruit. Now ye are clean through the word which I have spoken unto you. Abide in me, and I in you. As the branch cannot bear fruit of itself, except it abide in the vine; no more can ye, except ye abide in me.*

I am the vine, ye are the branches: He that abideth in me, and I in him, the same bringeth forth much fruit: for without me ye can do nothing. If a man abide not in me, he is cast forth as a branch, and is withered; and men gather them, and cast them into the fire, and they are burned. If ye abide in me, and my words abide in you, ye shall ask what ye will, and it shall be done unto you.

Herein is my Father glorified, that ye bear much fruit; so shall ye be my disciples. As the Father hath loved me, so have I loved you: continue ye in my love. If ye keep my commandments, ye shall abide in my love; even as I have kept my Father's commandments, and abide in his love. These things have I spoken unto you, that my joy might remain in you, and that your joy might be full. This is my commandment, That ye love one another, as I have loved you. Greater love hath no man than this, that a man lay down his life for his friends.

—John 15:1–13

. . .

Monday: *I am come a light into the world.* —John 12:46

Then spake Jesus again unto them, saying, I am the light of the world: he that followeth me shall not walk in darkness, but shall have the light of life. —— I must work the works of him that sent me, while it is day: the night cometh, when no man can work. As long as I am in the world, I am the light of the world.

—John 8:12; 9:4–5

In the beginning was the Word, and the Word was with God, and the Word was God. The same was in the beginning with God. All things were made by him; and without him was not any thing made that was made. In him was life; and the life was the light of men. And the light shineth in darkness; and the darkness comprehended it not...That was the true Light, which lighteth every man that cometh into the world.

He was in the world, and the world was made by him, and the world knew him not. He came unto his own, and his own received him not. But as many as received him, to them gave he power to become the sons of God, even to them that believe on his name: Which were born, not of blood, nor of the will of the flesh, nor of the will of man, but of God. And the Word was made flesh, and dwelt among us, (and we beheld his glory, the glory as of the only begotten of the Father,) full of grace and truth.

—John 1:1–5; 9–14

Tuesday: *I am the door of the sheep...I am the good shepherd.*

—John 10:7–14

All that ever came before me are thieves and robbers: but the sheep did not hear them. I am the door: by me if any man enter in, he shall be saved, and shall go in and out, and find pasture. The thief cometh not, but for to steal, and to kill, and to destroy: I am come that they might have life, and that they might have it more abundantly. I am the good shepherd: the good shepherd giveth his life for the sheep. But he that is an hireling, and not the shepherd, whose own the sheep are not, seeth the wolf coming, and leaveth the sheep...and careth not for the sheep.

I am the good shepherd, and know my sheep, and am known of mine. As the Father knoweth me, even so know I the Father: and I lay down my life for the sheep. And other sheep I have, which are not of this fold: them also I must bring, and they shall hear my voice; and there shall be one fold, and one shepherd. Therefore doth my Father love me, because I lay down my life, that I might take it again.

—John 10:8–17

. . .

Wednesday: *Jesus said unto them, Verily, verily, I say unto you, Before Abraham was, I am.*

—John 8:58

I am from above: ye are of this world; I am not of this world. —— Again the high priest asked him, and said unto him, Art thou the Christ, the Son of the Blessed? And Jesus said, I am: and ye shall see the Son of man sitting on the right hand of power, and coming in the clouds of heaven.

—John 8:23; Mark 14:61–62

Pilate therefore said unto him, Art thou a king then? Jesus answered, Thou sayest that I am a king. To this end was I born, and for this cause came I into the world, that I should bear witness unto the truth. Every one that is of the truth heareth my voice.

—John 18:37

Believest thou not that I am in the Father, and the Father in me? the words that I speak unto you I speak not of myself: but the Father that dwelleth in me, he doeth the works.

—John 14:10

Thursday: *I am the way, the truth, and the life: no man cometh unto the Father, but by me.*

—John 14:6

It is the spirit that quickeneth; the flesh profiteth nothing: the words that I speak unto you, they are spirit, and they are life. —— I am the resurrection, and the life: he that believeth in me, though he were dead, yet shall he live.

—John 6:63; 11:25

Come unto me, all ye that labour and are heavy laden, and I will give you rest. Take my yoke upon you, and learn of me; for I am meek and lowly in heart: and ye shall find rest unto your souls. For my yoke is easy, and my burden is light. —— For whether is greater, he that sitteth at meat, or he that serveth? is not he that sitteth at meat? but I am among you as he that serveth.

—Matthew 11:28–30; Luke 22:27

I have given them thy word; and the world hath hated them, because they are not of the world, even as I am not of the world...And all mine are thine, and thine are mine; and I am glorified in them.

—John 17:14, 10

. . .

Friday: *I am that bread of life.*

—John 6:48

Our fathers did eat manna in the desert; as it is written, He gave them bread from heaven to eat. Then Jesus said unto them, Verily, verily, I say unto you, Moses gave you not that bread from heaven; but my Father giveth you the true bread from heaven. For the bread of God is he which cometh down from heaven, and giveth life unto the world.

—John 6:31–33

And Jesus said unto them, I am the bread of life: he that cometh to me shall never hunger; and he that believeth on me shall never thirst. ...And this is the will of him that sent me, that every one which seeth the Son, and believeth on him, may have everlasting life: and I will raise him up at the last day. ...No man can come to me, except the Father which hath sent me draw him: and I will raise him up at the last day. It is written in the prophets, And they shall be all taught of God. Every man therefore that hath heard, and hath learned of the Father, cometh unto me. ...Your fathers did eat manna in the wilderness, and are dead. This is the bread which cometh down from heaven, that a man may eat thereof, and not die.

—John 6:35, 40, 44–45, 49–50

Saturday: *I am the living bread which came down from heaven: if any man eat of this bread, he shall live for ever: and the bread that I will give is my flesh, which I will give for the life of the world...Then Jesus said unto them, Verily, verily, I say unto you, Except ye eat the flesh of the Son of man, and drink his blood, ye have no life in you. Whoso eateth my flesh, and drinketh my blood, hath eternal life; and I will raise him up at the last day. For my flesh is meat indeed, and my blood is drink indeed. He that eateth my flesh, and drinketh my blood, dwelleth in me, and I in him. As the living Father hath sent me, and I live by the Father: so he that eateth me, even he shall live by me. This is that bread which came down from heaven: not as your fathers did eat manna, and are dead: he that eateth of this bread shall live for ever.*

—John 6:51–58

Ho, every one that thirsteth, come ye to the waters, and he that hath no money; come ye, buy, and eat; yea, come, buy wine and milk without money and without price. Wherefore do ye spend money for that which is not bread? and your labour for that which satisfieth not? hearken diligently unto me, and eat ye that which is good, and let your soul delight itself in fatness. Incline your ear, and come unto me: hear, and your soul shall live.

—Isaiah 55:1–3

WEEK 17 - NEW LIFE IN CHRIST

Sunday: *A new and living way.*
—Hebrews 10:20

Cain went out from the presence of the Lord. —— Your iniquities have separated between you and your God, and your sins have hid his face from you. —— Holiness without which no man shall see the Lord.

—Genesis 4:16; Isaiah 59:2; Hebrews 12:14

I am the way, the truth, and the life: no man cometh unto the Father, but by me. —— Our Saviour Jesus Christ...hath abolished death, and hath brought life and immortality to light through the gospel.

—John 14:6; 2 Timothy 1:10

The way into the holiest of all was not yet made manifest, while as the first tabernacle was yet standing. —— He is our peace, who hath made both one, and hath broken down the middle wall of partition between us. —— The veil of the temple was rent in twain from the top to the bottom.

—Hebrews 9:8; Ephesians 2:14; Matthew 27:51

Strait is the gate, and narrow is the way, which leadeth unto life, and few there be that find it. —— Thou wilt shew me the path of life: in thy presence is fulness of joy; at thy right hand there are pleasures for evermore.

—Matthew 7:14; Psalm 16:11

. . .

Monday: *And hath raised us up together, and made us sit together in heavenly places in Christ Jesus.*

—Ephesians 2:6

Fear not...I am he that liveth. —— Father, I will that they also, whom thou hast given me, be with me where I am.

—Revelations 1:17–18; John 17:24

We are members of his body, of his flesh, and of his bones. —— He is the head of the body, the church: who is the beginning, the firstborn from the dead. —— Ye are complete in him, which is the head.

—Ephesians 5:30; Colossians 1:18; 2:10

Forasmuch...as the children are partakers of flesh and blood, he also himself likewise took part of the same; that through death he might destroy him that had the power of death, that is, the devil; And deliver them who through fear of death were all their lifetime subject to bondage.

—Hebrews 2:14–15

This corruptible must put on incorruption, and this mortal must put on immortality. So when this corruptible shall have put on incorruption, and this mortal shall have put on immortality, then shall be brought to pass the saying that is written, Death is swallowed up in victory.

—1 Corinthians 15:53–54

Tuesday: *Behold, I make all things new.* —Revelations 21:5

Except a man be born of water and of the Spirit, he cannot enter into the kingdom of God. That which is born of the flesh is flesh; and that which is born of the Spirit is spirit. —— If any man be in Christ, he is a new creature: old things are passed away; behold, all things are become new. —— A new heart also will I give you, and a new spirit will I put within you: and I will take away the stony heart out of your flesh, and I will give you an heart of flesh. —— Purge out therefore the old leaven, that ye may be a new lump. —— The new man, which after God is created in righteousness and true holiness.

—John 3:5–6; 2 Corinthians 5:17; Ezekiel 36:26; 1 Corinthians 5:7; Ephesians 4:24

Thou shalt be called by a new name, which the mouth of the Lord shall name. —— Behold, I create new heavens and a new earth: and the former shall not be remembered, nor come into mind. —— Seeing...that all these things shall be dissolved, what manner of persons ought ye to be in all holy conversation and godliness?

—Isaiah 62:2; 65:17; 2 Peter 3:11

. . .

Wednesday: *He hath made him to be sin for us... that we might be made the righteousness of God in him.*

—2 Corinthians 5:21

The Lord hath laid on him the iniquity of us all. —— Who his own self bare our sins in his own body on the tree, that we, being dead to sins, should live unto righteousness: by whose stripes ye were healed. —— As by one man's disobedience many were made sinners, so by the obedience of one shall many be made righteous.

—Isaiah 53:6; 1 Peter 2:24; Romans 5:19

After that the kindness and love of God our Saviour toward man appeared, Not by works of righteousness which we have done, but according to his mercy he saved us, by the washing of regeneration, and renewing of the Holy Ghost; which he shed on us abundantly through Jesus Christ our Saviour; That being justified by his grace, we should be made heirs according to the hope of eternal life. —— There is therefore now no condemnation to them which are in Christ Jesus, who walk not after the flesh, but after the Spirit. —— ***THE LORD OUR RIGHTEOUSNESS.***

—Titus 3:4–7; Romans 8:1; Jeremiah 23:6

Thursday: *A servant of Jesus Christ.* —Romans 1:1

Ye call me Master and Lord: and ye say well; for so I am. —— If any man serve me, let him follow me; and where I am, there shall also my servant be: if any man serve me, him will my Father honour. —— Take my yoke upon you, and learn of me; for I am meek and lowly in heart: and ye shall find rest unto your souls. For my yoke is easy, and my burden is light.

—John 13:13; 12:26; Matthew 11:29–30

What things were gain to me, those I counted loss for Christ. —— Being made free from sin, and become servants to God, ye have your fruit unto holiness, and the end everlasting life.

—Philippians 3:7; Romans 6:22

Henceforth I call you not servants; for the servant knoweth not what his lord doeth: but I have called you friends; for all things that I have heard of my Father I have made known unto you. —— Thou art no more a servant, but a son. —— Stand fast therefore in the liberty wherewith Christ hath made us free, and be not entangled again with the yoke of bondage...For, brethren, ye have been called unto liberty; only use not liberty for an occasion to the flesh.

—John 15:15; Galatians 4:7; 5:1; 5:13

. . .

Friday: *I will be as the dew unto Israel.* —Hosea 14:5

The meekness and gentleness of Christ. —— A bruised reed shall he not break, and the smoking flax shall he not quench. —— The Spirit of the Lord is upon me, because he hath anointed me to preach the gospel to the poor; he hath sent me to heal the brokenhearted, to preach deliverance to the captives, and recovering of sight to the blind, to set at liberty them that are bruised, To preach the acceptable year of the Lord. ...And he began to say unto them, This day is this scripture fulfilled in your ears.

—2 Corinthians 10:1; Isaiah 42:3; Luke 4:18–21

They shall be abundantly satisfied with the fatness of thy house; and thou shalt make them drink of the river of thy pleasures. For with thee is the fountain of life: in thy light shall we see light. —— The desert shall rejoice, and blossom as the rose. It shall blossom abundantly, and rejoice even with joy and singing. ... They shall see the glory of the Lord, and the excellency of our God...Then the eyes of the blind shall be opened, and the ears of the deaf shall be unstopped. Then shall the lame man leap as an hart, and the tongue of the dumb sing: for in the wilderness shall waters break out, and streams in the desert.

—Psalm 36:8–9; Isaiah 35:1–6

He shall feed his flock like a shepherd: he shall gather the lambs with his arm, and carry them in his bosom, and shall gently lead those that are with young.

—Isaiah 40:11

Saturday: *Ye shall know the truth, and the truth shall make you free.*

—John 8:32

Where the Spirit of the Lord is, there is liberty. —— The law of the Spirit of life in Christ Jesus hath made me free from the law of sin and death. —— If the Son...shall make you free, ye shall be free indeed. —— Brethren, we are not children of the bondwoman, but of the free. —— Knowing that a man is not justified by the works of the law, but by the faith of Jesus Christ, even we have believed in Jesus Christ, that we might be justified by the faith of Christ, and not by the works of the law: for by the works of the law shall no flesh be justified. —— Whoso looketh into the perfect law of liberty, and continueth therein, he being not a forgetful hearer, but a doer of the work, this man shall be blessed in his deed. —— Stand fast therefore in the liberty wherewith Christ hath made us free, and be not entangled again with the yoke of bondage.

—2 Corinthians 3:17; Romans 8:2; John 8:36; Galatians 4:31; 2:16; James 1:25; Galatians 5:1

WEEK 18 - FAITH

Sunday: *He [Abraham] believed in the Lord;*
and he counted it to him for righteousness. —Genesis 15:6

What doth it profit, my brethren, though a man say he hath faith, and have not works? can faith save him?..Faith, if it hath not works, is dead, being alone. —— By faith Abraham, when he was tried, offered up Isaac: and he that had received the promises offered up his only begotten son, ...Accounting that God was able to raise him up, even from the dead.

—James 2:14–17; Hebrews 11:17–19

Was not Abraham our father justified by works, when he had offered Isaac his son upon the altar? ...Ye see then how that by works a man is justified, and not by faith only. —— He staggered not at the promise of God through unbelief; but was strong in faith, giving glory to God; And being fully persuaded that, what he had promised, he was able also to perform. And therefore it was imputed to him for righteousness. Now it was not written for his sake alone, that it was imputed to him; But for us also, to whom it shall be imputed, if we believe on him that raised up Jesus our Lord from the dead. —— Whoso looketh into the perfect law of liberty, and continueth therein, he being not a forgetful hearer, but a doer of the work, this man shall be blessed in his deed. —— By their fruits ye shall know them. Not every one that saith unto me, Lord, Lord, shall enter into the kingdom of heaven; but he that doeth the will of my Father which is in heaven. —— If ye know these things, happy are ye if ye do them.

—James 2:21–24; Romans 4:20–24; James 1:25; Matthew 7:20–21; John 13:17

. . .

Monday: *The fruit of the Spirit is . . . faith.* —Galatians 5:22

The righteousness of God which is by faith of Jesus Christ unto all and upon all them that believe. —— By grace are ye saved through faith; and that not of yourselves: it is the gift of God. —— Without faith it is impossible to please him. —— He that believeth on him is not condemned: but he that believeth not is condemned already, because he hath not believed in the name of the only begotten Son of God. —— Lord, I believe; help thou mine unbelief.

—Romans 3:22; Ephesians 2:8; Hebrews 11:6; John 3:18; Mark 9:24

Whoso keepeth his word, in him verily is the love of God perfected: hereby know we that we are in him. —— Faith...worketh by love. —— Faith without works is dead. —— I am crucified with Christ: nevertheless I live; yet not I, but Christ liveth in me: and the life which I now live in the flesh I live by the faith of the Son of God, who loved me, and gave himself for me. —— Whom having not seen, ye love; in whom, though now ye see him not, yet believing, ye rejoice with joy unspeakable and full of glory; Receiving the end of your faith, even the salvation of your souls.

—1 John 2:5; Galatians 5:6; James 2:20; Galatians 2:20; 1 Peter 1:8–9

Tuesday: *Faith is the substance of things hoped for, the evidence of things not seen.*

—Hebrews 11:1

If in this life only we have hope in Christ, we are of all men most miserable. —— Eye hath not seen, nor ear heard, neither have entered into the heart of man, the things which God hath prepared for them that love him. But God hath revealed them unto us by his Spirit. —— After that ye believed, ye were sealed with that holy Spirit of promise, Which is the earnest of our inheritance until the redemption of the purchased possession.

—1 Corinthians 15:19; 2:9–10; Ephesians 1:13–14

Jesus saith unto him, Thomas, because thou hast seen me, thou hast believed: blessed are they that have not seen, and yet have believed. —— Whom having not seen, ye love; in whom, though now ye see him not, yet believing, ye rejoice with joy unspeakable and full of glory: Receiving the end of your faith, even the salvation of your souls.

—John 20:29; 1 Peter 1:8–9

We walk by faith, not by sight. —— Cast not away therefore your confidence, which hath great recompence of reward.

—2 Corinthians 5:7; Hebrews 10:35

. . .

Wednesday: *Faith as a grain of mustard seed.*
—Matthew 17:20

And in the fourth watch of the night Jesus went unto them, walking on the sea. And when the disciples saw him walking on the sea, they were troubled, saying, It is a spirit; and they cried out for fear. But straightway Jesus spake unto them, saying, Be of good cheer; it is I; be not afraid.

And Peter answered him and said, Lord, if it be thou, bid me come unto thee on the water. And he said, Come. And when Peter was come down out of the ship, he walked on the water, to go to Jesus.

But when he saw the wind boisterous, he was afraid; and beginning to sink, he cried, saying, Lord, save me. And immediately Jesus stretched forth his hand, and caught him, and said unto him, O thou of little faith, wherefore didst thou doubt?

—Matthew 14:25–31

"Lord, increase our faith."

—Luke 17:5

Thursday: *Have faith in God.* —Mark 11:22

The just shall live by his faith. —— Let us hold fast the profession of our faith without wavering; (for he is faithful that promised). —— Our God is in the heavens: he hath done whatsoever he hath pleased. —— With God nothing shall be impossible. ...And blessed is she that believed: for there shall be a performance of those things which were told her from the Lord.

—Habakkuk 2:4; Hebrews 10:23; Psalm 115:3; Luke 1:37–45

With God all things are possible. —— Is my hand shortened at all, that it cannot redeem? or have I no power to deliver? —— My thoughts are not your thoughts, neither are your ways my ways, saith the Lord. For as the heavens are higher than the earth, so are my ways higher than your ways, and my thoughts than your thoughts. —— Prove me now herewith, saith the Lord of hosts, if I will not open you the windows of heaven, and pour you out a blessing, that there shall not be room enough to receive it. —— Behold, the Lord's hand is not shortened, that it cannot save; neither his ear heavy, that it cannot hear. —— Lord, it is nothing with thee to help, whether with many, or with them that have no power. —— We should not trust in ourselves, but in God which raiseth the dead.

—Matthew 19:26; Isaiah 50:2; 55:8–9; Malachi 3:10; Isaiah 59:1; 2 Chronicles 14:11; 2 Corinthians 1:9

. . .

Friday: *With God all things are possible.*
—Matthew 19:26

We are bound to thank God always for you, brethren, as it is meet, because that your faith groweth exceedingly. —— Let us, who are of the day, be sober, putting on the breastplate of faith and love; and for an helmet, the hope of salvation. —— If ye will not drive out the inhabitants of the land from before you...those which ye let remain of them shall be pricks in your eyes, and thorns in your sides, and shall vex you in the land wherein ye dwell. —— The flesh lusteth against the Spirit, and the Spirit against the flesh; and these are contrary the one to the other.

—2 Thessalonians 1:3; 1 Thessalonians 5:8; Numbers 33:55; Galatians 5:17

But without faith it is impossible to please him: for he that cometh to God must believe that he is, and that he is a rewarder of them that diligently seek him. —— Have faith in God. ...Whosoever shall say unto this mountain, Be thou removed, and be thou cast into the sea; and shall not doubt in his heart, but shall believe that those things which he saith shall come to pass; he shall have whatsoever he saith. —— Is any thing too hard for the Lord?

—Hebrews 11:6; Mark 11:22–23; Genesis 18:14

Saturday: *Fight the good fight of faith.*
—1 Timothy 6:12

(The weapons of our warfare are not carnal, but mighty through God to the pulling down of strong holds;) casting down imaginations...and bringing into captivity every thought to the obedience of Christ. —— Brethren, we are debtors, not to the flesh, to live after the flesh. For if ye live after the flesh, ye shall die: but if ye through the Spirit do mortify the deeds of the body, ye shall live.

—2 Corinthians 10:4–5; Romans 8:12–13

David and Goliath

Now the Philistines gathered together their armies to battle, and were gathered together at Shochoh, which belongeth to Judah. —— And there went out a champion out of the camp of the Philistines, named Goliath, of Gath, whose height was six cubits and a span. And he had an helmet of brass upon his head, and he was armed with a coat of mail; and the weight of the coat was five thousand shekels of brass. And he had greaves of brass upon his legs, and a target of brass between his shoulders. And the staff of his spear was like a weaver's beam; and his spear's head weighed six hundred shekels of iron: and one bearing a shield went before him. And he stood and cried unto the armies of Israel, and said unto them, Why are ye come out to set your battle in array? am not I a Philistine, and ye servants to Saul? choose you a man for you, and let him come down to me. If he be able to fight with me, and to kill me, then will we be your servants: but if I prevail against him, and kill him, then shall ye be our servants, and serve us.

And the Philistine said, I defy the armies of Israel this day; give me a man, that we may fight together. —— And all the men of Israel, when they saw the man, fled from him, and were sore afraid. And the men of Israel said, Have ye seen this man that is come up? surely to defy Israel is he come up. ... And David spake to the men that stood by him, saying, What shall be done to the man that killeth this Philistine, and taketh away the reproach from Israel? for who is this uncircumcised Philistine, that he should defy the armies of the living God? ——

And he took his staff in his hand, and chose him five smooth stones out of the brook, and put them in a shepherd's bag which he had, even in a scrip; and his sling was in his hand: and he drew near to the Philistine.

And the Philistine came on and drew near unto David; and the man that bare the shield went before him. And when the Philistine looked about, and saw David, he disdained him: for he was but a youth, and ruddy, and of a fair countenance. —— And the Philistine said to David, Come to me, and I will give thy flesh unto the fowls of the air, and to the beasts of the field.

Then said David to the Philistine, Thou comest to me with a sword, and with a spear, and with a shield: but I come to thee in the name of the Lord of hosts, the God of the armies of Israel, whom thou hast defied. This day will the Lord deliver thee into mine hand; and I will smite thee, and take thine head from thee; and I will give the carcases of the host of the Philistines this day unto the fowls of the air, and to the wild beasts of the earth; that all the earth may know that there is a God in Israel. And all this assembly shall know that the Lord saveth not with sword and spear: for the battle is the Lord's, and he will give you into our hands.

And it came to pass, when the Philistine arose, and came, and drew nigh to meet David, that David hastened, and ran toward the army to meet the Philistine. And David put his hand in his bag, and took thence a stone, and slang it, and smote the Philistine in his forehead, that the stone sunk into his forehead; and he fell upon his face to the earth. So David prevailed over the Philistine with a sling and with a stone, and smote the Philistine, and slew him; but there was no sword in the hand of David.

—1 Samuel 17:1, 4–10, 24–26, 40–42, 44–50

We are more than conquerors through him that loved us. —— For whatsoever is born of God overcometh the world: and this is the victory that overcometh the world, even our faith.

—Romans 8:37; 1 John 5:4

WEEK 19 - PATH OF LIFE

S**unday**: *Thou wilt shew me the path of life.*
—Psalm 16:11

Thus saith the Lord; Behold, I set before you the way of life, and the way of death. —— I will teach you the good and the right way. —— I am the way, the truth, and the life: no man cometh unto the Father, but by me. —— Follow me.

—Jeremiah 21:8; 1 Samuel 12:23; John 14:6; Matthew 4:19

There is a way which seemeth right unto a man, but the end thereof are the ways of death. —— Wide is the gate, and broad is the way, that leadeth to destruction, and many there be which go in thereat: Because strait is the gate, and narrow is the way, which leadeth unto life, and few there be that find it.

—Proverbs 14:12; Matthew 7:13–14

An highway shall be there, and a way, and it shall be called The way of holiness; the unclean shall not pass over it; but it shall be for those: the wayfaring men, though fools, shall not err therein. —— Then shall we know, if we follow on to know the Lord.

—Isaiah 35:8; Hosea 6:3; Hebrews 10:20

A new and living way, which he hath consecrated for us.

—Hebrews 10:20

Monday: *The path of the just is as the shining light, that shineth more and more unto the perfect day.*

—Proverbs 4:18

Not as though I had already attained, either were already perfect: but I follow after, if that I may apprehend that for which also I am apprehended of Christ Jesus. —— Then shall we know, if we follow on to know the Lord.

—Philippians 3:12; Hosea 6:3

Then shall the righteous shine forth as the sun in the kingdom of their Father. —— We all, with open face beholding as in a glass the glory of the Lord, are changed into the same image from glory to glory, even as by the Spirit of the Lord. —— When that which is perfect is come, then that which is in part shall be done away. ...For now we see through a glass, darkly; but then face to face: now I know in part; but then shall I know even as also I am known. —— Beloved, now are we the sons of God; and it doth not yet appear what we shall be: but we know that, when he shall appear, we shall be like him; for we shall see him as he is. And every man that hath this hope in him purifieth himself, even as he is pure.

—Matthew 13:43; 2 Corinthians 3:18; 1 Corinthians 13:10–12; 1 John 3:2–3

Tuesday: *I will give them one heart, and one way, that they may fear me forever, for the good of them, and of their children after them.*

—Jeremiah 32:39

A new heart...will I give you, and a new spirit will I put within you. —— Good and upright is the Lord: therefore will he teach sinners in the way. The meek will he guide in judgment: and the meek will he teach his way. All the paths of the Lord are mercy and truth unto such as keep his covenant and his testimonies.

—Ezekiel 36:26; Psalm 25:8–10

That they all may be one; as thou, Father, art in me, and I in thee, that they also may be one in us: that the world may believe that thou hast sent me.

—John 17:21

I...beseech you that ye walk worthy of the vocation wherewith ye are called, With all lowliness and meekness...Endeavouring to keep the unity of the Spirit in the bond of peace. There is one body, and one Spirit, even as ye are called in one hope of your calling; One Lord, one faith, one baptism, One God and Father of all, who is above all, and through all, and in you all.

—Ephesians 4:1–6

. . .

Wednesday: *My feet were almost gone;*
my steps had well nigh slipped. —Psalm 73:2

When I said, My foot slippeth; thy mercy, O Lord, held me up. —— The Lord said, Simon, Simon, behold, Satan hath desired to have you, that he may sift you as wheat: But I have prayed for thee, that thy faith fail not. —— A just man falleth seven times, and riseth up again. —— Though he fall, he shall not be utterly cast down: for the Lord upholdeth him with his hand.

—Psalm 94:18; Luke 22:31–32; Proverbs 24:16; Psalm 37:24

Rejoice not against me, O my enemy: when I fall, I shall arise; when I sit in darkness, the Lord shall be a light unto me. —— He shall deliver thee in six troubles: yea, in seven there shall no evil touch thee.

—Micah 7:8; Job 5:19

If any man sin, we have an advocate with the Father, Jesus Christ the righteous. —— He leadeth me in the paths of righteousness for his name's sake. Yea, though I walk through the valley of the shadow of death, I will fear no evil: for thou art with me; thy rod and thy staff they comfort me.

—1 John 2:1; Psalm 23:3–4

Thursday: *Shew me thy ways, O Lord; teach me thy paths.*
—Psalm 25:4

Moses said unto the Lord... I pray thee, if I have found grace in thy sight, shew me now thy way, that I may know thee. ...And he said, My presence shall go with thee, and I will give thee rest. —— He made known his ways unto Moses, his acts unto the children of Israel.

—Exodus 33:12–14; Psalm 103:7

The meek will he guide in judgment: and the meek will he teach his way. ... What man is he that feareth the Lord? him shall he teach in the way that he shall choose. —— Trust in the Lord with all thine heart; and lean not unto thine own understanding. In all thy ways acknowledge him, and he shall direct thy paths.

—Psalm 25:9–12; Proverbs 3:5–6

Thou wilt shew me the path of life: in thy presence is fulness of joy; at thy right hand there are pleasures for evermore. —— I will instruct thee and teach thee in the way which thou shalt go: I will guide thee with mine eye. —— The path of the just is as the shining light, that shineth more and more unto the perfect day.

—Psalm 16:11; 32:8; Proverbs 4:18

. . .

Friday: *I have set before you life and death, blessing and cursing: therefore choose life.* —Deuteronomy 30:19

For I have no pleasure in the death of him that dieth, saith the Lord God: wherefore turn yourselves, and live ye. —— Know ye not, that to whom ye yield yourselves servants to obey, his servants ye are to whom ye obey; whether of sin unto death, or of obedience unto righteousness?

—Ezekiel 18:32; Romans 6:16

As ye have therefore received Christ Jesus the Lord, so walk ye in him: Rooted and built up in him, and stablished in the faith, as ye have been taught, abounding therein with thanksgiving. Beware lest any man spoil you through philosophy and vain deceit, after the tradition of men, after the rudiments of the world, and not after Christ. For in him dwelleth all the fulness of the Godhead bodily. And ye are complete in him, which is the head of all principality and power. —— If ye then be risen with Christ, seek those things which are above, where Christ sitteth on the right hand of God. Set your affection on things above, not on things on the earth. For ye are dead, and your life is hid with Christ in God. When Christ, who is our life, shall appear, then shall ye also appear with him in glory. —— If any man serve me, let him follow me; and where I am, there shall also my servant be: if any man serve me, him will my Father honour.

—Colossians 2:6–10; 3:1–4; John 12:26

Saturday: *He will keep the feet of his saints.* —1 Samuel 2:9

If we say that we have fellowship with him, and walk in darkness, we lie, and do not the truth: But if we walk in the light, as he is in the light, we have fellowship one with another, and the blood of Jesus Christ his Son cleanseth us from all sin. —— He that is washed needeth not save to wash his feet, but is clean every whit.

—1 John 1:6–7; John 13:10

I have taught thee in the way of wisdom; I have led thee in right paths. When thou goest, thy steps shall not be straitened; and when thou runnest, thou shalt not stumble. —— Enter not into the path of the wicked, and go not in the way of evil men. Avoid it, pass not by it, turn from it, and pass away. —— Let thine eyes look right on, and let thine eyelids look straight before thee. Ponder the path of thy feet, and let all thy ways be established. Turn not to the right hand nor to the left: remove thy foot from evil.

—Proverbs 4:11–12, 14–15, 25–27

The Lord shall deliver me from every evil work, and will preserve me unto his heavenly kingdom: to whom be glory for ever and ever. Amen. —2 Timothy 4:18

WEEK 20 - LOVE ONE ANOTHER

Sunday: *Hereby perceive we the love of God,*
because he laid down his life for us. —1 John 3:16

The love of Christ, which passeth knowledge. —— Greater love hath no man than this, that a man lay down his life for his friends. —— Ye know the grace of our Lord Jesus Christ, that, though he was rich, yet for your sakes he became poor, that ye through his poverty might be rich. —— Beloved, if God so loved us, we ought also to love one another. —— Be ye kind one to another, tenderhearted, forgiving one another, even as God for Christ's sake hath forgiven you. —— Forbearing one another, and forgiving one another, if any man have a quarrel against any: even as Christ forgave you, so also do ye. —— For even the Son of man came not to be ministered unto, but to minister, and to give his life a ransom for many. —— Christ...suffered for us, leaving us an example, that ye should follow his steps.

—Ephesians 3:19; John 15:13; 2 Corinthians 8:9; 1 John 4:11; Ephesians 4:32; Colossians 3:13; Mark 10:45; 1 Peter 2:21

Ye also ought to wash one another's feet. For I have given you an example, that ye should do as I have done to you. —— We ought to lay down our lives for the brethren.

—John 13:14–15; 1 John 3:16

. . .

Monday: *By love serve one another.*
—Galatians 5:13

Brethren, if a man be overtaken in a fault, ye which are spiritual, restore such an one in the spirit of meekness; considering thyself, lest thou also be tempted. Bear ye one another's burdens, and so fulfil the law of Christ.

—Galatians 6:1–2

Brethren, if any of you do err from the truth, and one convert him; Let him know, that he which converteth the sinner from the error of his way shall save a soul from death, and shall hide a multitude of sins. —— Seeing ye have purified your souls in obeying the truth through the Spirit unto unfeigned love of the brethren, see that ye love one another with a pure heart fervently. —— Owe no man any thing, but to love one another: for he that loveth another hath fulfilled the law. —— Be kindly affectioned one to another with brotherly love; in honour preferring one another. —— Yea, all of you be subject one to another, and be clothed with humility: for God resisteth the proud, and giveth grace to the humble.

—James 5:19–20; 1 Peter 1:22; Romans 13:8; 12:10; 1 Peter 5:5

We...that are strong ought to bear the infirmities of the weak, and not to please ourselves.

—Romans 15:1

Tuesday: *Thy lovingkindness is before mine eyes.*
—Psalm 26:3

The Lord is gracious, and full of compassion; slow to anger, and of great mercy. —— Your Father which is in heaven...maketh his sun to rise on the evil and on the good, and sendeth rain on the just and on the unjust.

—Psalm 145:8; Matthew 5:45

Be ye...followers of God, as dear children; And walk in love, as Christ also hath loved us, and hath given himself for us an offering and a sacrifice to God for a sweetsmelling savour. —— Seeing ye have purified your souls in obeying the truth through the Spirit unto unfeigned love of the brethren, see that ye love one another with a pure heart fervently. —— The love of Christ constraineth us.

—Ephesians 5:1–2; 1 Peter 1:22; 2 Corinthians 5:14

Love ye your enemies, and do good, and lend, hoping for nothing again; and your reward shall be great, and ye shall be the children of the Highest: for he is kind unto the unthankful and to the evil. Be ye therefore merciful, as your Father also is merciful.

—Luke 6:35–36

. . .

Wednesday: *The unity of the Spirit.*
—Ephesians 4:3

There is one body, and one Spirit. —— Through him we both have access by one Spirit unto the Father. Now therefore ye are no more strangers and foreigners, but fellowcitizens with the saints and of the household of God; And are built upon the foundation of the apostles and prophets, Jesus Christ himself being the chief cornerstone; In whom all the building fitly framed together groweth unto an holy temple in the Lord: In whom ye also are builded together for an habitation of God through the Spirit.

—Ephesians 4:4; 2:18–22

Behold, how good and how pleasant it is for brethren to dwell together in unity! It is like the precious ointment upon the head, that ran down upon the beard, even Aaron's beard: that went down to the skirts of his garments.

—Psalm 133:1–2

Seeing ye have purified your souls in obeying the truth through the Spirit unto unfeigned love of the brethren, see that ye love one another with a pure heart fervently.

—1 Peter 1:22

Thursday: *Beloved, let us love one another: for love is of God; and every one that loveth is born of God, and knoweth God.*

—1 John 4:7

The love of God is shed abroad in our hearts by the Holy Ghost which is given unto us. —— Ye have not received the spirit of bondage again to fear; but ye have received the Spirit of adoption, whereby we cry, Abba, Father. The Spirit itself beareth witness with our spirit, that we are the children of God. —— My little children, let us not love in word, neither in tongue; but in deed and in truth.

—Romans 5:5; 8:15–16; 1 John 3:18

In this was manifested the love of God toward us, because that God sent his only begotten Son into the world, that we might live through him. —— In whom we have redemption through his blood, the forgiveness of sins, according to the riches of his grace. —— That in the ages to come he might shew the exceeding riches of his grace in his kindness toward us through Christ Jesus.

—1 John 4:9; Ephesians 1:7; 2:7

Beloved, if God so loved us, we ought also to love one another.

—1 John 4:11

. . .

Friday: *Let not the sun go down upon your wrath.*
—Ephesians 4:26

If thy brother shall trespass against thee, go and tell him his fault between thee and him alone: if he shall hear thee, thou hast gained thy brother. ...Lord, how oft shall my brother sin against me, and I forgive him? till seven times? Jesus saith unto him, I say not unto thee, Until seven times: but, Until seventy times seven. —— When ye stand praying, forgive, if ye have ought against any: that your Father also which is in heaven may forgive you your trespasses.

—Matthew 18:15–22; Mark 11:25

Put on, therefore, as the elect of God, holy and beloved, bowels of mercies, kindness, humbleness of mind, meekness, longsuffering; Forbearing one another, and forgiving one another, if any man have a quarrel against any: even as Christ forgave you, so also do ye. —— Be ye kind one to another, tenderhearted, forgiving one another, even as God for Christ's sake hath forgiven you.

—Colossians 3:12–13; Ephesians 4:32

The apostles said unto the Lord, Increase our faith.

—Luke 17:5

Saturday: *Walk in love.*
—Ephesians 5:2

A new commandment I give unto you, That ye love one another; as I have loved you, that ye also love one another. —— Above all things have fervent charity among yourselves: for charity shall cover the multitude of sins. —— Love covereth all sins.

—John 13:34; 1 Peter 4:8; Proverbs 10:12

When ye stand praying, forgive, if ye have ought against any: that your Father also which is in heaven may forgive you your trespasses. —— Love ye your enemies, and do good, and lend, hoping for nothing again. —— Rejoice not when thine enemy falleth, and let not thine heart be glad when he stumbleth. —— Not rendering evil for evil, or railing for railing: but contrariwise blessing; knowing that ye are thereunto called, that ye should inherit a blessing. —— If it be possible, as much as lieth in you, live peaceably with all men. —— Be ye kind one to another, tenderhearted, forgiving one another, even as God for Christ's sake hath forgiven you.

—Mark 11:25; Luke 6:35; Proverbs 24:17; 1 Peter 3:9; Romans 12:18; Ephesians 4:32

WEEK 21 - HUMILITY 1

Sunday: *Serving the Lord with all humility of mind.*

—Acts 20:19

Whosoever will be great among you, let him be your minister; And whosoever will be chief among you, let him be your servant: Even as the Son of man came not to be ministered unto, but to minister, and to give his life a ransom for many.

—Matthew 20:26–28

If a man think himself to be something, when he is nothing, he deceiveth himself. —— I say, through the grace given unto me, to every man...not to think of himself more highly than he ought to think; but to think soberly, according as God hath dealt to every man the measure of faith. —— When ye shall have done all those things which are commanded you, say, We are unprofitable servants: we have done that which was our duty to do.

—Galatians 6:3; Romans 12:3; Luke 17:10

Our rejoicing is this...that in simplicity and godly sincerity, not with fleshly wisdom, but by the grace of God, we have had our conversation in the world. —— We have this treasure in earthen vessels, that the excellency of the power may be of God, and not of us.

—2 Corinthians 1:12; 4:7

Monday: *The Lord thy God accept thee.*
—2 Samuel 24:23

Wherewith shall I come before the Lord, and bow myself before the high God? shall I come before him with burnt offerings, with calves of a year old? Will the Lord be pleased with thousands of rams, or with ten thousands of rivers of oil? shall I give my firstborn for my transgression, the fruit of my body for the sin of my soul? He hath shewed thee, O man, what is good; and what doth the Lord require of thee, but to do justly, and to love mercy, and to walk humbly with thy God?

—Micah 6:6–8

For all have sinned, and come short of the glory of God; Being justified freely by his grace through the redemption that is in Christ Jesus: Whom God hath set forth to be a propitiation through faith in his blood, to declare...at this time his righteousness: that he might be just, and the justifier of him which believeth in Jesus.

—Romans 3:23–26

The sacrifices of God are a broken spirit: a broken and a contrite heart, O God, thou wilt not despise. —— Ye are complete in him, —— accepted in the beloved.

—Psalm 51:17; Colossians 2:10; Ephesians 1:6

Tuesday: *Better it is to be of an humble spirit with the lowly, than to divide the spoil with the proud.* —Proverbs 16:19

Thus saith the high and lofty One that inhabiteth eternity, whose name is Holy; I dwell in the high and holy place, with him also that is of a contrite and humble spirit, to revive the spirit of the humble, and to revive the heart of the contrite ones. —— Blessed are the poor in spirit: for theirs is the kingdom of heaven.

—Isaiah 57:15; Matthew 5:3

These six things doth the Lord hate: yea, seven are an abomination unto him: a proud look. —— Every one that is proud in heart is an abomination to the Lord. —— Search me, O God, and know my heart: try me, and know my thoughts: And see if there be any wicked way in me, and lead me in the way everlasting.

—Proverbs 6:16–17; 16:5; Psalm 139:23–24

Grace be unto you, and peace, from God our Father, and from the Lord Jesus Christ. I thank my God upon every remembrance of you.—Blessed are the meek: for they shall inherit the earth.

—Philippians 1:2–3; Matthew 5:5

. . .

W**ednesday**: *Who maketh thee to differ from another? And what hast thou that thou didst not receive?* —1 Corinthians 4:7

By the grace of God I am what I am. —— Of his own will begat he us with the word of truth. —— It is not of him that willeth, nor of him that runneth, but of God that sheweth mercy. —— Where is boasting then? It is excluded. —— Christ Jesus...is made unto us wisdom, and righteousness, and sanctification, and redemption...He that glorieth, let him glory in the Lord.

—1 Corinthians 15:10; James 1:18; Romans 9:16; 3:27; 1 Corinthians 1:30–31

You hath he quickened, who were dead in trespasses and sins; Wherein in time past ye walked according to the course of this world, according to the prince of the power of the air, the spirit that now worketh in the children of disobedience: Among whom also we all had our conversation in times past in the lusts of our flesh, fulfilling the desires of the flesh and of the mind; and were by nature the children of wrath, even as others. —— Ye are washed...ye are sanctified...ye are justified in the name of the Lord Jesus, and by the Spirit of our God.

—Ephesians 2:1–3; 1 Corinthians 6:11

T**hursday**: *One star differeth from another star in glory.* —1 Corinthians 15:41

By the way they had disputed among themselves, who should be the greatest. And he sat down, and called the twelve, and saith unto them, If any man desire to be first, the same shall be last of all. —— But he that is greatest among you shall be your servant. And whosoever shall exalt himself shall be abased; and he that shall humble himself shall be exalted.

—Mark 9:34–35; Matthew 23:11–12

Be clothed with humility: for God resisteth the proud, and giveth grace to the humble. Humble yourselves therefore under the mighty hand of God, that he may exalt you in due time. ——

Let this mind be in you, which was also in Christ Jesus: Who...made himself of no reputation, and took upon him the form of a servant, and was made in the likeness of men...Wherefore God also hath highly exalted him, and given him a name which is above every name: that at the name of Jesus every knee should bow.

—1 Peter 5:5–6; Philippians 2:5–10

They that be wise shall shine as the brightness of the firmament; and they that turn many to righteousness as the stars for ever and ever. —Daniel 12:3

. . .

F**riday**: *Humble yourselves...under the mighty hand of God, that he may exalt you in due time.* —1 Peter 5:6

Every one that is proud in heart is an abomination to the Lord: though hand join in hand, he shall not be unpunished.

—Proverbs 16:5

O Lord, thou art our father; we are the clay, and thou our potter; and we all are the work of thy hand. Be not wroth very sore, O Lord, neither remember iniquity for ever: behold, see, we beseech thee, we are all thy people. —— Thou hast chastised me, and I was chastised, as a bullock unaccustomed to the yoke: turn thou me, and I shall be turned; for thou art the Lord my God. Surely after that I was turned, I repented; and after that I was instructed, I smote upon my thigh: I was ashamed, yea, even confounded, because I did bear the reproach of my youth.

—Isaiah 64:8–9; Jeremiah 31:18–19

Thus saith the high and lofty One that inhabiteth eternity, whose name is Holy; I dwell in the high and holy place, with him also that is of a contrite and humble spirit, to revive the spirit of the humble, and to revive the heart of the contrite ones.

—Isaiah 57:15

S**aturday**: *It is good for a man that he bear the yoke in his youth.*

—Lamentations 3:27

Train up a child in the way he should go: and when he is old, he will not depart from it. ——

We have had fathers of our flesh which corrected us, and we gave them reverence: shall we not much rather be in subjection unto the Father of spirits, and live? For they verily for a few days chastened us after their own pleasure; but he for our profit, that we might be partakers of his holiness.

—Proverbs 22:6; Hebrews 12:9–10

Before I was afflicted I went astray: but now have I kept thy word. ...It is good for me that I have been afflicted; that I might learn thy statutes. —— I know the thoughts that I think toward you, saith the Lord, thoughts of peace, and not of evil, to give you an expected end.

—Psalm 119:67–71; Jeremiah 29:11

Humble yourselves therefore under the mighty hand of God, that he may exalt you in due time.

—1 Peter 5:6

WEEK 22 - PRAYER

Sunday: *We made our prayer unto our God, and set a watch against them.* —Nehemiah 4:9

Watch and pray, that ye enter not into temptation. —— Continue in prayer, and watch in the same with thanksgiving. —— Casting all your care upon him; for he careth for you. Be sober, be vigilant; because your adversary the devil, as a roaring lion, walketh about, seeking whom he may devour: Whom resist stedfast in the faith. —— Why call ye me, Lord, Lord, and do not the things which I say? —— Be ye doers of the word, and not hearers only, deceiving your own selves. —— Be careful for nothing; but in every thing by prayer and supplication with thanksgiving let your requests be made known unto God. And the peace of God, which passeth all understanding, shall keep your hearts and minds through Christ Jesus.

—Matthew 26:41; Colossians 4:2; 1 Peter 5:7–9; Luke 6:46; James 1:22; Phil. 4:6–7

Men ought always to pray, and not to faint. ...Which of you shall have a friend, and shall go unto him at midnight, and say unto him, Friend, lend me three loaves; For a friend of mine in his journey is come to me, and I have nothing to set before him? And he from within shall answer and say, Trouble me not: the door is now shut, and my children are with me in bed; I cannot rise and give thee. I say unto you, Though he will not rise and give him, because he is his friend, yet because of his importunity he will rise and give him as many as he needeth.

—Luke 18:1; 11:5–8

. . .

Monday: *Let my prayer be set forth before thee as incense; and the lifting up of my hands as the evening sacrifice.*

—Psalm 141:2

Thou shalt make an altar to burn incense upon...And thou shalt put it before the veil that is by the ark of the testimony, before the mercy seat that is over the testimony, where I will meet with thee. And Aaron shall burn thereon sweet incense every morning...And when Aaron lighteth the lamps at even, he shall burn incense upon it, a perpetual incense before the Lord throughout your generations.

—Exodus 30:1–8

[Jesus] is able to save them to the uttermost that come unto God by him, seeing he ever liveth to make intercession for them. —— The smoke of the incense, which came with the prayers of the saints, ascended up before God out of the angel's hand. —— Ye also, as lively stones, are built up a spiritual house, an holy priesthood, to offer up spiritual sacrifices, acceptable to God by Jesus Christ. —— Pray without ceasing.

—Hebrews 7:25; Revelations 8:4; 1 Peter 2:5; 1 Thessalonians 5:17

Tuesday: *Thus saith the Lord God; I will yet for this be enquired of.*

—Ezekiel 36:37

Ye have not, because ye ask not. —— Ask, and it shall be given you; seek, and ye shall find; knock, and it shall be opened unto you: For every one that asketh receiveth; and he that seeketh findeth; and to him that knocketh it shall be opened. —— This is the confidence that we have in him, that, if we ask anything according to his will, He heareth us: And if we know that he hear us, whatsoever we ask, we know that we have the petitions that we desired of him. —— If any of you lack wisdom, let him ask of God, that giveth to all men liberally, and upbraideth not; and it shall be given him. —— Open thy mouth wide, and I will fill it. —— Men ought always to pray, and not to faint.

—James 4:2; Matthew 7:7–8; 1 John 5:14–15; James 1:5; Psalm 81:10; Luke 18:1

The eyes of the Lord are upon the righteous, and his ears are open unto their cry. ...The Lord heareth, and delivereth them out of all their troubles. —— Ye shall ask in my name: and I say not unto you, that I will pray the Father for you: For the Father himself loveth you, because ye have loved me. —— Ask, and ye shall receive, that your joy may be full.

—Psalm 34:15–17; John 16:26–27; 16:24

. . .

Wednesday: *Pray every where, lifting up holy hands, without wrath and doubting.*

—1 Timothy 2:8

The true worshippers shall worship the Father in spirit and in truth: for the Father seeketh such to worship him. God is a Spirit: and they that worship him must worship him in spirit and in truth. —— Then shalt thou call, and the Lord shall answer; thou shalt cry, and he shall say, Here I am. —— When ye stand praying, forgive, if ye have ought against any.

—John 4:23–24; Isaiah 58:9; Mark 11:25

Without faith it is impossible to please him: for he that cometh to God must believe that he is, and that he is a rewarder of them that diligently seek him. —— Let him ask in faith, nothing wavering. For he that wavereth is like a wave of the sea driven with the wind and tossed. For let not that man think that he shall receive any thing of the Lord.

—Hebrews 11:6; James 1:6–7

If I regard iniquity in my heart, the Lord will not hear me. —— My little children, these things write I unto you, that ye sin not. And if any man sin, we have an advocate with the Father, Jesus Christ the righteous: And he is the propitiation for our sins.

—Psalm 66:18; 1 John 2:1–2

Thursday: *Brethren, pray for us.* —1 Thessalonians 5:25

Is any sick among you? let him call for the elders of the church; and let them pray over him...And the prayer of faith shall save the sick, and the Lord shall raise him up. ...Pray one for another, that ye may be healed. The effectual fervent prayer of a righteous man availeth much. Elias was a man subject to like passions as we are, and he prayed earnestly that it might not rain: and it rained not on the earth by the space of three years and six months. And he prayed again, and the heaven gave rain, and the earth brought forth her fruit.

—James 5:14–18

Praying always with all prayer and supplication in the Spirit, and watching thereunto with all perseverance and supplication for all saints.

—Ephesians 6:18

Without ceasing I make mention of you always in my prayers. —— Always labouring fervently for you in prayers, that ye may stand perfect and complete in all the will of God.

—Romans 1:9; Colossians 4:12

. . .

Friday: *Thou hearest me always.* —John 11:42

Jesus lifted up his eyes, and said, Father, I thank thee that thou hast heard me. —— Father, glorify thy name. Then came there a voice from heaven, saying, I have both glorified it, and will glorify it again. —— Lo, I come... to do thy will, O God. —— Not My will, but thine, be done.

—John 11:41; 12:28; Hebrews 10:7; Luke 22:42

[Jesus] went out into a mountain to pray, and continued all night in prayer to God. —— As he is, so are we in this world. —— This is the confidence that we have in him, that, if we ask anything according to his will, he heareth us.

—Luke 6:12; 1 John 4:17; 5:14

Whatsoever we ask, we receive of him, because we keep his commandments, and do those things that are pleasing in his sight.

—1 John 3:22

Without faith it is impossible to please him: for he that cometh to God must believe that he is, and that he is a rewarder of them that diligently seek him.

—Hebrews 11:6

He ever liveth to make intercession for them. —— We have an advocate with the Father, Jesus Christ the righteous.

—Hebrews 7:25; 1 John 2:1

Saturday: *Praying in the Holy Ghost.* —Jude 20:1

God is a Spirit: and they that worship him must worship him in spirit and in truth. —— We...have access by one Spirit unto the Father.

—John 4:24; Ephesians 2:18

O my Father, if it be possible, let this cup pass from me: nevertheless not as I will, but as thou wilt.

—Matthew 26:39

The Spirit...helpeth our infirmities: for we know not what we should pray for as we ought: but the Spirit itself maketh intercession for us with groanings which cannot be uttered. And he that searcheth the hearts knoweth what is the mind of the Spirit, because he maketh intercession for the saints according to the will of God. —— When he, the Spirit of truth, is come, he will guide you into all truth: for he shall not speak of himself; but whatsoever he shall hear, that shall he speak: and he will shew you things to come.

—Romans 8:26–27; John 16:13

Praying always with all prayer and supplication in the Spirit, and watching thereunto with all perseverance and supplication.

—Ephesians 6:18

WEEK 23 - LIFE IN THE SPIRIT 1

Sunday: *It is the spirit that quickeneth.*

—John 6:63

The first man Adam was made a living soul; the last Adam was made a quickening spirit. —— That which is born of the flesh is flesh; and that which is born of the Spirit is spirit.

—1 Corinthians 15:45; John 3:6

Not by works of righteousness which we have done, but according to his mercy he saved us, by the washing of regeneration, and renewing of the Holy Ghost.

—Titus 3:5

If any man have not the Spirit of Christ, he is none of his. And if Christ be in you, the body is dead because of sin; but the Spirit is life because of righteousness. But if the Spirit of him that raised up Jesus from the dead dwell in you, he that raised up Christ from the dead shall also quicken your mortal bodies by his Spirit that dwelleth in you.

—Romans 8:9–11

I live; yet not I, but Christ liveth in me: and the life which I now live in the flesh I live by the faith of the Son of God. —— Reckon ye...yourselves to be dead indeed unto sin, but alive unto God through Jesus Christ our Lord.

—Galatians 2:20; Romans 6:11

. . .

Monday: *Sin shall not have dominion over you: for ye are not under the law, but under grace.* —Romans 6:14

What then? shall we sin, because we are not under the law, but under grace? God forbid.

—Romans 6:15

My brethren, ye...are become dead to the law by the body of Christ; that ye should be married to another, even to him who is raised from the dead, that we should bring forth fruit unto God. —— Being not without law to God, but under the law to Christ. —— The sting of death is sin; and the strength of sin is the law. But thanks be to God, which giveth us the victory through our Lord Jesus Christ.

—Romans 7:4; 1 Corinthians 9:21; 15:56–57

The law of the Spirit of life in Christ Jesus hath made me free from the law of sin and death. —— Whosoever committeth sin is the servant of sin. ...If the Son... shall make you free, ye shall be free indeed.

—Romans 8:2; John 8:34–36

Stand fast therefore in the liberty wherewith Christ hath made us free, and be not entangled again with the yoke of bondage.

—Galatians 5:1

Tuesday: *Ask me of things to come concerning my sons, and concerning the work of my hands command ye me.*

—Isaiah 45:11

A new heart...will I give you, and a new spirit will I put within you: and I will take away the stony heart out of your flesh, and I will give you an heart of flesh. And I will put my Spirit within you, and cause you to walk in my statutes. ...Thus saith the Lord God; I will yet for this be enquired of by the house of Israel, to do it for them.

—Ezekiel 36:26–37

If two of you shall agree on earth as touching anything that they shall ask, it shall be done for them of my Father which is in heaven. For where two or three are gathered together in my name, there am I in the midst of them.

— Matthew 18:19–20

Have faith in God. ...Verily I say unto you, That whosoever shall say unto this mountain, Be thou removed, and be thou cast into the sea; and shall not doubt in his heart, but shall believe that those things which he saith shall come to pass; he shall have whatsoever he saith.

—Mark 11:22–23

. . .

Wednesday: *The spirit indeed is willing, but the flesh is weak.*
—Matthew 26:41

In the way of thy judgments, O Lord, have we waited for thee; the desire of our soul is to thy name, and to the remembrance of thee. With my soul have I desired thee in the night; yea, with my spirit within me will I seek thee early.

—Isaiah 26:8–9

I know that in me (that is, in my flesh,) dwelleth no good thing: for to will is present with me; but how to perform that which is good I find not...For I delight in the law of God after the inward man: But I see another law in my members, warring against the law of my mind, and bringing me into captivity to the law of sin which is in my members. —— The flesh lusteth against the Spirit, and the Spirit against the flesh: and these are contrary the one to the other: so that ye cannot do the things that ye would.

—Romans 7:18–23; Galatians 5:17

I can do all things through Christ which strengtheneth me. —— Our sufficiency is of God. —— My grace is sufficient for thee.

—Philippians 4:13; 2 Corinthians 3:5; 12:9

Thursday: *None of us liveth to himself, and no man dieth to himself.*
—Romans 14:7

Whether we live, we live unto the Lord; and whether we die, we die unto the Lord: whether we live therefore, or die, we are the Lord's. —— Let no man seek his own, but every man another's wealth. —— Ye are bought with a price: therefore glorify God in your body, and in your spirit, which are God's.

—Romans 14:8; 1 Corinthians 10:24; 6:20

Christ shall be magnified in my body, whether it be by life, or by death. For to me to live is Christ, and to die is gain. But if I live in the flesh, this is the fruit of my labour: yet what I shall choose I wot not. For I am in a strait betwixt two, having a desire to depart, and to be with Christ; which is far better.

—Philippians 1:20–23

I through the law am dead to the law, that I might live unto God. I am crucified with Christ: nevertheless I live; yet not I, but Christ liveth in me: and the life which I now live in the flesh I live by the faith of the Son of God, who loved me, and gave himself for me.

—Galatians 2:19–20

. . .

Friday: *The God of peace...make you perfect in every good work to do his will.* —Hebrews 13:20–21

Be perfect, be of good comfort, be of one mind, live in peace; and the God of love and peace shall be with you.

—2 Corinthians 13:11

By grace are ye saved through faith; and that not of yourselves: it is the gift of God: Not of works, lest any man should boast. —— Every good gift and every perfect gift is from above, and cometh down from the Father of lights, with whom is no variableness, neither shadow of turning.

—Ephesians 2:8–9; James 1:17

Work out your own salvation with fear and trembling. For it is God which worketh in you both to will and to do of his good pleasure. —— Be ye transformed by the renewing of your mind, that ye may prove what is that good, and acceptable, and perfect, will of God. —— Being filled with the fruits of righteousness, which are by Jesus Christ, unto the glory and praise of God.

—Philippians 2:12–13; Romans 12:2; Philippians 1:11

Not that we are sufficient of ourselves to think any thing as of ourselves; but our sufficiency is of God.

—2 Corinthians 3:5

Saturday: *The Spirit...helpeth our infirmities.* —Romans 8:26

The Comforter, which is the Holy Ghost. —— What? know ye not that your body is the temple of the Holy Ghost which is in you, which ye have of God? —— It is God which worketh in you.

—John 14:26; 1 Corinthians 6:19; Philippians 2:13

We know not what we should pray for as we ought: but the Spirit itself maketh intercession for us with groanings which cannot be uttered. And he that searcheth the hearts knoweth what is the mind of the Spirit, because he maketh intercession for the saints according to the will of God.

—Romans 8:26–27

He knoweth our frame; he remembereth that we are dust. —— A bruised reed shall he not break, and the smoking flax shall he not quench.

—Psalm 103:14; Isaiah 42:3

The spirit indeed is willing, but the flesh is weak.

—Matthew 26:41

The Lord is my shepherd; I shall not want. He maketh me to lie down in green pastures: he leadeth me beside the still waters.

—Psalm 23:1–2

WEEK 24 - SPIRITUAL WARFARE

Sunday: *For this purpose the Son of God was manifested, that he might destroy the works of the devil.*

—1 John 3:8

We wrestle not against flesh and blood, but against principalities, against powers, against the rulers of the darkness of this world, against spiritual wickedness in high places. —— Forasmuch...as the children are partakers of flesh and blood, he also himself likewise took part of the same; that through death he might destroy him that had the power of death, that is, the devil. —— And having spoiled principalities and powers, he made a shew of them openly, triumphing over them. ——

I heard a loud voice saying in heaven, Now is come salvation, and strength, and the kingdom of our God, and the power of his Christ: for the accuser of our brethren is cast down, which accused them before our God day and night. And they overcame him by the blood of the Lamb, and by the word of their testimony; and they loved not their lives unto the death.

—Ephesians 6:12; Hebrews 2:14; Colossians 2:15; Revelations 12:10–11

Thanks be to God, which giveth us the victory through our Lord Jesus Christ.

—1 Corinthians 15:57

Monday: *Be watchful, and strengthen the things which remain, that are ready to die.*

—Revelations 3:2

The end of all things is at hand: be ye therefore sober, and watch unto prayer. —— Be sober, be vigilant; because your adversary the devil, as a roaring lion, walketh about, seeking whom he may devour: Whom resist stedfast in the faith, knowing that the same afflictions are accomplished in your brethren that are in the world. —— Take heed to thyself, and keep thy soul diligently, lest thou forget the things which thine eyes have seen, and lest they depart from thy heart all the days of thy life. —— The just shall live by faith: but if any man draw back, my soul shall have no pleasure in him. But we are not of them who draw back unto perdition; but of them that believe to the saving of the soul. —— What I say unto you I say unto all, Watch.

—1 Peter 4:7; 5:8–9; Deuteronomy 4:9; Hebrews 10:38–39; Mark 13:37

Fear thou not; for I am with thee: be not dismayed; for I am thy God: I will strengthen thee; yea, I will help thee; yea, I will uphold thee with the right hand of my righteousness. ...I the Lord thy God will hold thy right hand.

—Isaiah 41:10–13

Tuesday: *Shall the throne of iniquity have fellowship with thee?*

—Psalm 94:20

Truly our fellowship is with the Father, and with his Son Jesus Christ. —— Beloved, now are we the sons of God, and it doth not yet appear what we shall be: but we know that, when he shall appear, we shall be like him; for we shall see him as he is. And every man that hath this hope in him purifieth himself, even as he is pure.

—1 John 1:3; 3:2–3

The prince of this world cometh, and hath nothing in me. —— An high priest...holy, harmless, undefiled.

—John 14:30; Hebrews 7:26

We wrestle not against flesh and blood, but against principalities, against powers, against the rulers of the darkness of this world, against spiritual wickedness in high places. —— The prince of the power of the air, the spirit that now worketh in the children of disobedience. —— Whosoever is born of God sinneth not; but he that is begotten of God keepeth himself, and that wicked one toucheth him not. And we know that we are of God, and the whole world lieth in wickedness. —Ephesians 6:12; Ephesians 2:2; 1 John 5:18–19

. . .

W**ednesday**: *The accuser of our brethren is cast down, which accused them before our God day and night.* —Revelations 12:10

They overcame him by the blood of the Lamb, and by the word of their testimony. —— Who shall lay any thing to the charge of God's elect? It is God that justifieth. Who is he that condemneth? It is Christ that died, yea rather, that is risen again, who is even at the right hand of God, who also maketh intercession for us.

—Revelations 12:11; Romans 8:33–34

Having spoiled principalities and powers, he made a shew of them openly. —— That through death he might destroy him that had the power of death, that is, the devil; And deliver them who through fear of death were all their lifetime subject to bondage. —— In all these things we are more than conquerors through him that loved us. —— Put on the whole armour of God, that ye may be able to stand against the wiles of the devil...And take the...sword of the Spirit, which is the word of God. —— Thanks be to God, which giveth us the victory through our Lord Jesus Christ.

—Colossians 2:15; Hebrews 2:14–15; Romans 8:37; Ephesians 6:11,17; 1 Corinthians 15:57

T**hursday**: *Resist the devil, and he will flee from you.* —James 4:7

When the enemy shall come in like a flood, the Spirit of the Lord shall lift up a standard against him. —— Get thee hence, Satan: for it is written, Thou shalt worship the Lord thy God, and him only shalt thou serve. Then the devil leaveth him. —— For the word of God is quick, and powerful, and sharper than any twoedged sword.

—Isaiah 59:19; Matthew 4:10–11; Hebrews 4:12

Be strong in the Lord, and in the power of his might. —— For he put on righteousness as a breastplate, and an helmet of salvation upon his head. —— Put on the whole armour of God, that ye may be able to stand against the wiles of the devil. —— For we walk by faith, not by sight. —— And have no fellowship with the unfruitful works of darkness, but rather reprove them. ...See then that ye walk circumspectly, not as fools, but as wise, Redeeming the time, because the days are evil. —— Lest Satan should get an advantage of us: for we are not ignorant of his devices. —— This is the victory that overcometh the world, even our faith. —— Who shall lay anything to the charge of God's elect? It is God that justifieth.

—Ephesians 6:10; Isaiah 59:17; Ephesians 6:11; 2 Corinthians 5:7; Ephesians 5:11–16; 2 Corinthians 2:11; 1 John 5:4; Romans 8:33

. . .

F**riday**: *The triumphing of the wicked is short.* —Job 20:5

In quietness and in confidence shall be your strength. —— He shall cover thee with his feathers, and under his wings shalt thou trust: his truth shall be thy shield and buckler.

— Isaiah 30:15; Psalm 91:4

O our God, wilt thou not judge them? for we have no might against this great company that cometh against us; neither know we what to do: but our eyes are upon thee. ...Thus saith the Lord unto you, Be not afraid nor dismayed by reason of this great multitude; for the battle is not yours, but God's. ...Ye shall not need to fight in this battle: set yourselves, stand ye still, and see the salvation of the Lord with you...for the Lord will be with you. ...As they went out...to say, Praise the Lord; for his mercy endureth for ever. ...the Lord set ambushments...and they were smitten.

—2 Chronicles 20:12–22

And the Lord God said unto the serpent...I will put enmity between thee and the woman, and between thy seed and her seed; it shall bruise thy head. —— The wicked plotteth against the just, and gnasheth upon him with his teeth. The Lord shall laugh at him: for he seeth that his day is coming. —— The God of peace shall bruise Satan under your feet shortly. —— The devil...was cast into the lake of fire and brimstone...and shall be tormented day and night for ever and ever.

—Genesis 3:14–15; Psalm 37:12–13; Romans 16:20; Revelations 20:10

S**aturday**: *Finally, my brethren, be strong in the Lord, and in the power of his might.* —Ephesians 6:10

Put on the whole armour of God, that ye may be able to stand against the wiles of the devil. For we wrestle not against flesh and blood, but against principalities, against powers, against the rulers of the darkness of this world, against spiritual wickedness in high places.

Wherefore take unto you the whole armour of God, that ye may be able to withstand in the evil day, and having done all, to stand. Stand therefore, having your loins girt about with truth, and having on the breastplate of righteousness; And your feet shod with the preparation of the gospel of peace; Above all, taking the shield of faith, wherewith ye shall be able to quench all the fiery darts of the wicked. And take the helmet of salvation, and the sword of the Spirit, which is the word of God: Praying always with all prayer and supplication in the Spirit, and watching thereunto with all perseverance and supplication for all saints.

—Ephesians 6:11–18

WEEK 25 - GOODNESS OF GOD

Sunday: *Bless the Lord, O my soul, and forget not all his benefits...Who redeemeth thy life from destruction; who crowneth thee with lovingkindness and tender mercies; Who satisfieth thy mouth with good things; so that thy youth is renewed like the eagle's.*

—Psalm 103:2–5

Adam...begat a son in his own likeness. —— Behold, I was shapen in iniquity; and in sin did my mother conceive me. —— Dead in trespasses and sins...by nature the children of wrath, even as others. —— By one man sin entered into the world, —— by one man's disobedience many were made sinners. —— If through the offence of one many be dead, much more the grace of God, and the gift by grace, which is by one man, Jesus Christ, hath abounded unto many.

—Genesis 5:3; Psalm 51:5; Ephesians 2:1–3; Romans 5:12, 19, 15

But after that the kindness and love of God our Saviour toward man appeared, Not by works of righteousness which we have done, but according to his mercy he saved us, by the washing of regeneration, and renewing of the Holy Ghost; Which he shed on us abundantly through Jesus Christ our Saviour; That being justified by his grace, we should be made heirs according to the hope of eternal life. —— Therefore being justified by faith, we have peace with God through our Lord Jesus Christ. —— Thanks be to God, which giveth us the victory through our Lord Jesus Christ.

—Titus 3:4–7; Romans 5:1; 1 Corinthians 15:57

. . .

Monday: *We shall be satisfied with the goodness of thy house.* —Psalm 65:4

One thing have I desired of the Lord, that will I seek after; that I may dwell in the house of the Lord all the days of my life, to behold the beauty of the Lord, and to enquire in his temple.

—Psalm 27:4

Blessed are they which do hunger and thirst after righteousness: for they shall be filled. —— He hath filled the hungry with good things; and the rich he hath sent empty away.

—Matthew 5:6; Luke 1:53

He satisfieth the longing soul, and filleth the hungry soul with goodness. —— I am the bread of life: he that cometh to me shall never hunger; and he that believeth on me shall never thirst.

—Psalm 107:9; John 6:35

How excellent is thy lovingkindness, O God! therefore the children of men put their trust under the shadow of thy wings. They shall be abundantly satisfied with the fatness of thy house; and thou shalt make them drink of the river of thy pleasures. For with thee is the fountain of life: in thy light shall we see light.

—Psalm 36:7–9

Tuesday: *Oh that men would praise the Lord for his goodness, and for his wonderful works to the children of men!*

—Psalm 107:8

O taste and see that the Lord is good: blessed is the man that trusteth in him. —— How great is thy goodness, which thou hast laid up for them that fear thee!

—Psalm 34:8; 31:19

This people have I formed for myself; they shall shew forth my praise. —— Having predestinated us unto the adoption of children by Jesus Christ to himself, according to the good pleasure of his will, to the praise of the glory of his grace, wherein he hath made us accepted in the beloved...That we should be to the praise of his glory, who first trusted in Christ.

—Isaiah 43:21; Ephesians 1:5–12

How great is his goodness, and how great is his beauty! —— The Lord is good to all: and his tender mercies are over all his works. All thy works shall praise thee, O Lord; and thy saints shall bless thee. They shall speak of the glory of thy kingdom, and talk of thy power; To make known to the sons of men his mighty acts, and the glorious majesty of his kingdom.

—Zechariah 9:17; Psalm 145:9–12

. . .

Wednesday: *The Lord is good, a strong hold in the day of trouble; and he knoweth them that trust in him.*

—Nahum 1:7

Praise the Lord of hosts: for the Lord is good; for his mercy endureth for ever. —— God is our refuge and strength, a very present help in trouble.

—Jeremiah 33:11; Psalm 46:1

I will say of the Lord, He is my refuge and my fortress: my God; in him will I trust. ——

Who is like unto thee, O people saved by the Lord, the shield of thy help, and who is the sword of thy excellency! —— As for God, his way is perfect; the word of the Lord is tried: he is a buckler to all them that trust in him. For who is God, save the Lord? and who is a rock, save our God?

—Psalm 91:2; Deuteronomy 33:29; 2 Samuel 22:31–32

If any man love God, the same is known of him. —— The foundation of God standeth sure, having this seal, The Lord knoweth them that are his. And, let every one that nameth the name of Christ depart from iniquity. —— The Lord knoweth the way of the righteous: but the way of the ungodly shall perish. —— Thou hast found grace in my sight, and I know thee by name.

—1 Corinthians 8:3; 2 Timothy 2:19; Psalm 1:6; Exodus 33:17

Thursday: *Think upon me, my God, for good.*

—Nehemiah 5:19

Thus saith the Lord; I remember thee, the kindness of thy youth, the love of thine espousals, when thou wentest after me in the wilderness. —— I will remember my covenant with thee in the days of thy youth, and I will establish unto thee an everlasting covenant. —— I will visit you, and perform my good word toward you...For I know the thoughts that I think toward you, saith the Lord, thoughts of peace, and not of evil, to give you an expected end.

—Jeremiah 2:2; Ezekiel 16:60; Jeremiah 29:10–11

As the heavens are higher than the earth, so are my ways higher than your ways, and my thoughts than your thoughts. —— I would seek unto God, and unto God would I commit my cause: Which doeth great things and unsearchable; marvelous things without number. —— Many, O Lord my God, are thy wonderful works which thou hast done, and thy thoughts which are to us-ward: they cannot be reckoned up in order unto thee: if I would declare and speak of them, they are more than can be numbered.

—Isaiah 55:9; Job 5:8–9; Psalm 40:5

. . .

Friday: *The living God...giveth us richly all things to enjoy.* —1 Timothy 6:17

Beware that thou forget not the Lord thy God, in not keeping his commandments, and his judgments, and his statutes, which I command thee this day: Lest when thou hast eaten and art full, and hast built goodly houses, and dwelt therein...Then thine heart be lifted up, and thou forget the Lord thy God... For it is he that giveth thee power to get wealth.

—Deuteronomy 8:11–18

Except the Lord build the house, they labour in vain that build it: except the Lord keep the city, the watchman waketh but in vain. It is vain for you to rise up early, to sit up late, to eat the bread of sorrows: for so he giveth his beloved sleep.

—Psalm 127:1–2

They got not the land in possession by their own sword, neither did their own arm save them: but thy right hand, and thine arm, and the light of thy countenance, because thou hadst a favour unto them. —— There be many that say, Who will shew us any good? Lord, lift thou up the light of thy countenance upon us.

—Psalm 44:3; 4:6

Saturday: *They sung as it were a new song.* —Revelations 14:3

A new and living way, which he hath consecrated for us. —— Not by works of righteousness which we have done, but according to his mercy he saved us, by the washing of regeneration, and renewing of the Holy Ghost; Which he shed on us abundantly through Jesus Christ our Saviour. —— By grace are ye saved through faith; and that not of yourselves: it is the gift of God: not of works, lest any man should boast.

—Hebrews 10:20; Titus 3:5–6; Ephesians 2:8–9

Not unto us, O Lord, not unto us, but unto thy name give glory. —— Unto him that loved us, and washed us from our sins in own blood, and hath made us kings and priests unto God and his Father; to him be glory and dominion for ever and ever. Amen. —— Thou wast slain, and hast redeemed us to God by thy blood out of every kindred, and tongue, and people, and nation. —— I beheld, and, lo, a great multitude, which no man could number...cried...saying, Salvation to our God which sitteth upon the throne, and unto the Lamb.

—Psalm 115:1; Revelations 1:5–6; 5:9; 7:9–10

WEEK 26 - TRUST GOD 1

S**unday**: *Trust in the Lord with all thine heart; and lean not unto thine own understanding.*

In all thy ways acknowledge him, and he shall direct thy paths.

—Proverbs 3:5–6

Trust in him at all times; ye people, pour out your heart before him:

God is a refuge for us.

—Psalm 62:8

I will instruct thee and teach thee in the way which thou shalt go: I will guide thee with mine eye. Be ye not as the horse, or as the mule, which have no understanding: whose mouth must be held in with bit and bridle, lest they come near unto thee. Many sorrows shall be to the wicked: but he that trusteth in the Lord, mercy shall compass him about. —— Thine ears shall hear a word behind thee, saying, This is the way, walk ye in it, when ye turn to the right hand, and when ye turn to the left.

—Psalm 32:8–10; Isaiah 30:21

If thy presence go not with me, carry us not up hence. For wherein shall it be known here that I and thy people have found grace in thy sight? is it not in that thou goest with us? so shall we be separated, I and thy people, from all the people that are upon the face of the earth.

—Exodus 33:15–16

. . .

Monday: *They that know thy name will put their trust in thee: for thou, Lord, hast not forsaken them that seek thee.*

—Psalm 9:10

The name of the Lord is a strong tower: the righteous runneth into it, and is safe. —— I will trust, and not be afraid: for the ***LORD*** *JEHOVAH is my strength and my song; he also is become my salvation.*

—Proverbs 18:10; Isaiah 12:2

I have been young, and now am old; yet have I not seen the righteous forsaken, nor his seed begging bread. ...For the Lord loveth judgment, and forsaketh not his saints; they are preserved for ever: but the seed of the wicked shall be cut off. —— The Lord will not forsake his people for his great name's sake: because it hath pleased the Lord to make you his people. —— Who delivered us from so great a death, and doth deliver: in whom we trust that he will yet deliver us.

—Psalm 37:25–28; 1 Samuel 12:22; 2 Corinthians 1:10

Be content with such things as ye have: for he hath said, I will never leave thee, nor forsake thee. So that we may boldly say, The Lord is my helper, and I will not fear what man shall do unto me.

—Hebrews 13:5–6

Tuesday: *He...bowed his shoulder to bear.*

—Genesis 49:15

Take, my brethren, the prophets, who have spoken in the name of the Lord, for an example of suffering affliction, and of patience. —— Now all these things happened unto them for ensamples: and they are written for our admonition, upon whom the ends of the world are come.

—James 5:10; 1 Corinthians 10:11

Shall we receive good at the hand of God, and shall we not receive evil? In all this did not Job sin with his lips. —— Aaron held his peace. —— It is the Lord: let him do what seemeth him good.

—Job 2:10; Leviticus 10:3; 1 Samuel 3:18

Cast thy burden upon the Lord, and he shall sustain thee. —— Surely he hath borne our griefs, and carried our sorrows.

—Psalm 55:22; Isaiah 53:4

Come unto me, all ye that labour and are heavy laden, and I will give you rest. Take my yoke upon you, and learn of me; for I am meek and lowly in heart: and ye shall find rest unto your souls. For my yoke is easy, and my burden is light.

—Matthew 11:28–30

. . .

Wednesday: *The Lord will provide.* —Genesis 22:14

God will provide himself a lamb for a burnt offering.

—Genesis 22:8

Behold, the Lord's hand is not shortened, that it cannot save; neither his ear heavy, that it cannot hear. —— There shall come out of Sion the Deliverer, and shall turn away ungodliness from Jacob.

—Isaiah 59:1; Romans 11:26

Happy is he that hath the God of Jacob for his help, whose hope is in the Lord his God. —— Behold, the eye of the Lord is upon them that fear him, upon them that hope in his mercy; To deliver their soul from death.

—Psalm 146:5; 33:18–19

My God shall supply all your need according to his riches in glory by Christ Jesus. —— He hath said, I will never leave thee, nor forsake thee. So that we may boldly say, The Lord is my helper, and I will not fear what man shall do unto me. —— The Lord is my strength and my shield; my heart trusteth in him, and I am helped: therefore my heart greatly rejoiceth: and with my song will I praise him.

—Philippians 4:19; Hebrews 13:5–6; Psalm 28:7

Thursday: *My times are in thy hand.*

—Psalm 31:15

All his saints are in thy hand. —— The word of the Lord came unto him [Elijah], saying, Get thee hence, and turn thee eastward, and hide thyself by the brook Cherith, that is before Jordan. And it shall be, that thou shalt drink of the brook; and I have commanded the ravens to feed thee there...And the word of the Lord came unto him, saying, Arise, get thee to Zarephath, which belongeth to Zidon, and dwell there: behold, I have commanded a widow woman there to sustain thee.

—Deuteronomy 33:3; 1 Kings 17:2–9

Take no thought for your life, what ye shall eat, or what ye shall drink; nor yet for your body, what ye shall put on. ...Your heavenly Father knoweth that ye have need of all these things.

—Matthew 6:25, 32

Trust in the Lord with all thine heart; and lean not unto thine own understanding. In all thy ways acknowledge him, and he shall direct thy paths. —— Casting all your care upon him; for he cares for you.

—Proverbs 3:5–6; 1 Peter 5:7

. . .

Friday: *Whoso trusteth in the Lord, happy is he.*
—Proverbs 16:20

[Abraham] staggered not at the promise of God through unbelief; but was strong in faith, giving glory to God; And being fully persuaded that, what he had promised, he was able also to perform. —— The children of Judah prevailed, because they relied upon the Lord God of their fathers.

—Romans 4:20–21; 2 Chronicles 13:18

God is our refuge and strength, a very present help in trouble. Therefore will not we fear, though the earth be removed, and though the mountains be carried into the midst of the sea. ——

It is better to trust in the Lord than to put confidence in man. It is better to trust in the Lord than to put confidence in princes. —— The steps of a good man are ordered by the Lord: and he delighteth in his way. Though he fall, he shall not be utterly cast down: for the Lord upholdeth him with his hand.

—Psalm 46:1–2; 118:8–9; 37:23–24

O taste and see that the Lord is good: blessed is the man that trusteth in him. O fear the Lord, ye his saints: for there is no want to them that fear him.

—Psalm 34:8–9

Saturday: *He is able...to save them to the uttermost that come unto God by him.* —Hebrews 7:25

I am the way, the truth, and the life: no man cometh unto the Father, but by me. —— Neither is there salvation in any other: for there is none other name under heaven given among men, whereby we must be saved.

—John 14:6; Acts 4:12

My sheep hear my voice, and I know them, and they follow me: And I give unto them eternal life; and they shall never perish, neither shall any man pluck them out of my hand. —— He which hath begun a good work in you will perform it until the day of Jesus Christ. —— Is any thing too hard for the Lord?

—John 10:27–28; Philippians 1:6; Genesis 18:14

Now unto him that is able to keep you from falling, and to present you faultless before the presence of his glory with exceeding joy, To the only wise God our Saviour, be glory and majesty, dominion and power, both now and ever. Amen.

—Jude 1:24–25

WEEK 27 - THE LOVE & COMPASSION OF GOD – 2

S**unday**: *Having loved his own which were in the world, he loved them unto the end.* —John 13:1

I pray for them: I pray not for the world, but for them which thou hast given me; for they are thine. And all mine are thine, and thine are mine; and I am glorified in them...and these things I speak in the world, that they might have my joy fulfilled in themselves. ....I pray not that thou shouldest take them out of the world, but that thou shouldest keep them from the evil. —— That they all may be one; as thou, Father, art in me, and I in thee, that they also may be one in us: that the world may believe that thou hast sent me. And the glory which thou gavest me I have given them; that they may be one, even as we are one: I in them, and thou in me, that they may be made perfect in one; and that the world may know that thou hast sent me, and hast loved them, as thou hast loved me. —— As the Father hath loved me, so have I loved you: continue ye in my love. ...Greater love hath no man than this, that a man lay down his life for his friends. Ye are my friends, if ye do whatsoever I command you.

—John 17:9–15; 17:21–23; 15:9–14

He which hath begun a good work in you will perform it until the day of Jesus Christ. —— Christ...loved the church, and gave himself for it; That he might sanctify and cleanse it with the washing of water by the word.

—Philippians 1:6; Ephesians 5:25–26

. . .

Monday: *His left hand is under my head, and his right hand doth embrace me.* —Songs 2:6

Underneath are the everlasting arms. —— When he [Peter] saw the wind boisterous, he was afraid; and beginning to sink, he cried, saying, Lord, save me. And immediately Jesus stretched forth his hand, and caught him, and said unto him, O thou of little faith, wherefore didst thou doubt? —— The steps of a good man are ordered by the Lord: and he delighteth in his way. Though he fall, he shall not be utterly cast down: for the Lord upholdeth him with his hand. —— An high Priest...touched with the feeling of our infirmities.

—Deuteronomy 33:27; Matthew 14:30–31; Psalm 37:23–24; Hebrews 4:15

The beloved of the Lord shall dwell in safety by him; and the Lord shall cover him all the day long, and he shall dwell between his shoulders. —— Casting all your care upon him, for he careth for you. —— Behold how he loved! —— He that toucheth you toucheth the apple of his eye.

—Deuteronomy 33:12; 1 Peter 5:7; John 11:36; Zechariah 2:8

They shall never perish, neither shall any man pluck them out of my hand. My Father, which gave them me, is greater than all. —John 10:28–29

Tuesday: *He calleth his own sheep by name, and leadeth them out.* —John 10:3

Behold, I have graven thee upon the palms of my hands; thy walls are continually before me. —— The foundation of God standeth sure, having this seal, The Lord knoweth them that are his. And, let every one that nameth the name of Christ depart from iniquity. —— And when he putteth forth his own sheep, he goeth before them, and the sheep follow him: for they know his voice. —— The Lord...knoweth them that trust in him. —— The Lord is my shepherd, I shall not want. —— He shall feed his flock like a shepherd: he shall gather the lambs with his arm, and carry them in his bosom, and shall gently lead those that are with young.

—Isaiah 49:16; 2 Timothy 2:19; John 10:4; Nahum 1:7; Psalm 23:1; Isaiah 40:11

In my Father's house are many mansions. ...I go to prepare a place for you, I will come again, and receive you unto myself; that where I am, there ye may be also. —— The Lamb which is in the midst of the throne shall feed them, and shall lead them unto living fountains of waters: and God shall wipe away all tears from their eyes.

—John 14:2–3; Revelations 7:17

. . .

W**ednesday**: *He will rest in his love.* —Zephaniah 3:17

The Lord did not set his love upon you, nor choose you, because ye were more in number than any people; for ye were the fewest of all people: But because the Lord loved you. —— We love him, because he first loved us. —— You...hath he reconciled In the body of his flesh through death, to present you holy and unblameable and unreproveable in his sight.

—Deuteronomy 7:7–8; 1 John 4:19; Colossians 1:21–22

Father, I will that they also...be with me where I am; that they may behold my glory, which thou hast given me: for thou lovedst me before the foundation of the world. —— His desire is toward me.

—John 17:24; Songs 7:10

Herein is love, not that we loved God, but that he loved us, and sent his Son to be the propitiation for our sins. —— His Son...Who being the brightness of his glory, and the express image of his person, and upholding all things by the word of his power, when he had by himself purged our sins, sat down on the right hand of the Majesty on high —— And hath raised us up together, and made us sit together in heavenly places in Christ Jesus. —— I will come again, and receive you unto myself; that where I am, there ye may be also.

—1 John 4:10; Hebrews 1:2–3; Ephesians 2:6; John 14:3

T**hursday**: *The deep things of God.* —1 Corinthians 2:10

Henceforth I call you not servants; for the servant knoweth not what his lord doeth; but I have called you friends; for all things that I have heard of my Father I have made known unto you. —— As the Father hath loved me, so have I loved you. ...These things have I spoken unto you, that my joy might remain in you, and that your joy might be full. —— It is given unto you to know the mysteries of the kingdom of heaven.

—John 15:15; 15:9–11; Matthew 13:11

We have received, not the spirit of the world, but the Spirit which is of God; that we might know the things that are freely given to us of God.

—1 Corinthians 2:12

For this cause I bow my knees unto the Father of our Lord Jesus Christ, Of whom the whole family in heaven and earth is named, That he would grant you, according to the riches of his glory, to be strengthened with might by his Spirit in the inner man; ...that ye, being rooted and grounded in love, May be able to comprehend with all saints what is the breadth, and length, and depth, and height; And to know the love of Christ, which passeth knowledge, that ye might be filled with all the fulness of God. —Ephesians 3:14–19

. . .

Friday: *We have known and believed the love that God hath to us.* —1 John 4:16

God, who is rich in mercy, for his great love wherewith he loved us, Even when we were dead in sins, hath quickened us together with Christ, (by grace ye are saved;) And hath raised us up together, and made us sit together in heavenly places in Christ Jesus: That in the ages to come he might shew the exceeding riches of his grace in his kindness toward us through Christ Jesus.

—Ephesians 2:4–7

God so loved the world, that he gave his only begotten Son, that whosoever believeth in him should not perish, but have everlasting life. —— He that spared not his own Son, but delivered him up for us all, how shall he not with him also freely give us all things? —— The Lord is good to all: and his tender mercies are over all his works. —— We love him, because he first loved us.

—John 3:16; Romans 8:32; Psalm 145:9; 1 John 4:19

Saturday: *Thou art a gracious God, and merciful, slow to anger, and of great kindness.*

—Jonah 4:2

And he arose, and came to his father. But when he was yet a great way off, his father saw him, and had compassion, and ran, and fell on his neck, and kissed him. —— His great love wherewith he loved us. —— God commendeth his love toward us, in that, while we were yet sinners, Christ died for us. —— The Lord hath laid on him the iniquity of us all. —— He died for all. —— Behold my servant, whom I uphold; mine elect, in whom my soul delighteth...He shall not cry, nor lift up, nor cause his voice to be heard in the street. A bruised reed shall he not break, and the smoking flax shall he not quench: he shall bring forth judnment unto truth.

—Luke 15:20; Ephesians 2:4; Romans 5:8; Isaiah 53:6; 2 Corinthians 5:15; Isaiah 42:1–3

Come unto me, all ye that labour and are heavy laden, and I will give you rest. Take my yoke upon you, and learn of me; for I am meek and lowly in heart: and ye shall find rest unto your souls. —— Mercy and truth are met together; righteousness and peace have kissed each other. —— Whom have I in heaven but thee? and there is none upon earth that I desire beside thee.

—Matthew 11:28–29; Psalm 85:10; 73:25

WEEK 28 - PEACE

S**unday**: *The Prince of Peace.*

—Isaiah 9:6

He shall judge thy people with righteousness, and thy poor with judgment. The mountains shall bring peace to the people, and the little hills, by righteousness. ...He shall come down like rain upon the mown grass; as showers that water the earth. In his days shall the righteous flourish; and abundance of peace so long as the moon endureth. —— Glory to God...on earth peace, good will toward men.

—Psalm 72:2–7; Luke .2:14

Let him take hold of my strength, that he may make peace with me; and he shall make peace with me. —— Acquaint now thyself with him, and be at peace. —— Being justified by faith, we have peace with God through our Lord Jesus Christ. —— A man is not justified by the works of the law, but by the faith of Jesus Christ. —— By the deeds of the law there shall no flesh be justified in his sight.

—Isaiah 27:5; Job .22:21; Romans 5:1; Galatians 2:16; Romans 3:20

Through the tender mercy of our God...the dayspring from on high hath visited us, To give light to them that sit in darkness and in the shadow of death, to guide our feet into the way of peace. —— Peace by Jesus Christ: (he is Lord of all). —— These things I have spoken unto you, that in me ye might have peace. In the world ye shall have tribulation: but be of good cheer; I have overcome the world.

—Luke .1:78–79; Acts 10:36; John 16:33

. . .

Monday: *The Lord of peace himself give you peace always by all means. The Lord be with you all.* —2 Thessalonians 3:16

Peace, from him which is, and which was, and which is to come. —— The peace of God, which passeth all understanding, shall keep your hearts and minds through Christ Jesus. —— Jesus himself stood in the midst of them, and saith unto them, Peace be unto you. —— Peace I leave with you, my peace I give unto you: not as the world giveth, give I unto you. Let not your heart be troubled, neither let it be afraid. —— The Comforter...even the Spirit of truth. —— The fruit of the Spirit is love, joy, peace. —— The Spirit itself beareth witness with our spirit, that we are the children of God.

—Revelations 1:4; Philippians 4:7; Luke 24:36; John 14:27; 15:26; Galatians 5:22; Romans 8:16

My presence shall go with thee, and I will give thee rest. And he said unto him, If thy presence go not with me, carry us not up hence. For wherein shall it be known here that I and thy people have found grace in thy sight? is it not in that thou goest with us? ——

The brightness of his glory, and the express image of his person. —— Blessed is the people that know the joyful sound: they shall walk, O Lord, in the light of thy countenance. —— The Lord will give strength unto his people; the Lord will bless his people with peace. —— "Be of good cheer; it is I; be not afraid."

—Exodus 33:14–16; 2 Corinthians 4:4; Hebrews 1:3; Psalm 89:15; 29:11; Matthew 14:27

Tuesday: *Thou wilt keep him in perfect peace, whose mind is stayed on thee: because he trusteth in thee.* —Isaiah 26:3

Cast thy burden upon the Lord, and he shall sustain thee: he shall never suffer the righteous to be moved. —— I will trust, and not be afraid: for the ***LORD JEHOVAH*** *is my strength and my song; he also is become my salvation.*

—Psalm 55:22; Isaiah 12:2

Be careful for nothing; but in every thing by prayer and supplication with thanksgiving let your requests be made known unto God. And the peace of God, which passeth all understanding, shall keep your hearts and minds through Christ Jesus. —— In quietness and in confidence shall be your strength. ——The effect of righteousness [shall be] quietness and assurance for ever. —— Peace I leave with you, my peace I give unto you: not as the world giveth, give I unto you. Let not your heart be troubled, neither let it be afraid. —— Peace, from him which is, and which was, and which is to come.

—Philippians 4:6–7; Isaiah 30:15; Isaiah 32:17; John 14:27; Revelations 1:4

. . .

Wednesday: *Acquaint now thyself with him, and be at peace.* —Job 22:21

It pleased the Father that in him should all fulness dwell; And, having made peace through the blood of his cross, by him to reconcile all things unto himself. —— Mercy and truth are met together; righteousness and peace have kissed each other.

—Colossians 1:19–20; Psalm 85:10

I know the thoughts that I think toward you, saith the Lord, thoughts of peace, and not of evil. —— Come now, and let us reason together, saith the Lord: though your sins be as scarlet, they shall be as white as snow; though they be red like crimson, they shall be as wool. —— Who is a God like unto thee, that pardoneth iniquity? —— Work out your own salvation with fear and trembling. For it is God which worketh in you both to will and to do of his good pleasure. —— Lord, thou wilt ordain peace for us: for thou also hast wrought all our works in us.

—Jeremiah 29:11; Isaiah 1:18; Micah 7:18; Philippians 2:12–13; Isaiah 26:12

Thursday: *He is our peace.* —Ephesians 2:14

God was in Christ, reconciling the world unto himself, not imputing their trespasses unto them; ...For he hath made him to be sin for us, who knew no sin; that we might be made the righteousness of God in him. —— Having made peace through the blood of his cross, by him to reconcile all things unto himself; ...And you, that were sometime alienated and enemies in your mind by wicked works, yet now hath he reconciled In the body of his flesh through death, to present you holy and unblameable and unreproveable in his sight.

—2 Corinthians 5:19,21; Colossians 1:20–22

Blotting out the handwriting of ordinances that was against us, which was contrary to us, and took it out of the way, nailing it to his cross. —— Having abolished in his flesh the enmity, even the law of commandments contained in ordinances; for to make in himself of twain one new man, so making peace. —— Grace be to you and peace from God the Father, and from our Lord Jesus Christ, Who gave himself for our sins, that he might deliver us from this present evil world, according to the will of God and our Father: To whom be glory for ever and ever. Amen.

—Colossians 2:14; Ephesians 2:15; Galatians 1:3–5

. . .

Friday: *The Lord will give strength unto his people; the Lord will bless his people with peace.* —Psalm 29:11

Depart from evil, and do good; seek peace, and pursue it. —— Mark the perfect man, and behold the upright: for the end of that man is peace.

—Psalm 34:14; 37:37

The world passeth away, and the lust thereof. —— Surely every man walketh in a vain shew: surely they are disquieted in vain: he heapeth up riches, and knoweth not who shall gather them. —— What fruit had ye then in those things whereof ye are now ashamed? for the end of those things is death. —— But the meek shall inherit the earth; and shall delight themselves in the abundance of peace. —1 John 2:17; Psalm 39:6; Romans 6:21; Psalm 37:11

Martha, Martha, thou are careful and troubled about many things: But one thing is needful: and Mary hath chosen that good part, which shall not be taken away from her. —— I would have you without carefulness.

—Luke 10:41–42; 1 Corinthians 7:32

Hear my prayer, O Lord, and give ear unto my cry; hold not thy peace at my tears: for I am a stranger with thee, and a sojourner, as all my fathers were. —— Hold not thy peace, O God of my praise. —— The Lord bless thee, and keep thee: The Lord make his face shine upon thee, and be gracious unto thee: The Lord lift up his countenance upon thee, and give thee peace.

—Psalm 39:12; 109:1; Numbers 6:24–26

Saturday: *The fruit of the Spirit is...peace.* —Galatians 5:22

To be spiritually minded is life and peace. —— God hath called us to peace. —— Peace I leave with you, my peace I give unto you: not as the world giveth, give I unto you. Let not your heart be troubled, neither let it be afraid. —— The God of hope fill you with all joy and peace in believing, that ye may abound in hope, through the power of the Holy Ghost. —— I know whom I have believed, and am persuaded that he is able to keep that which I have committed unto him against that day. —— Thou wilt keep him in perfect peace, whose mind is stayed on thee: because he trusteth in thee. —Romans 8:6; 1 Corinthians 7:15; John 14:27; Romans 15:13; 2 Timothy 1:12; Isaiah 26:3

The work of righteousness shall be peace; and the effect of righteousness quietness and assurance for ever. And my people shall dwell in a peaceable habitation, and in sure dwellings, and in quiet resting places. —— Whoso hearkeneth unto me shall dwell safely, and shall be quiet from fear of evil. —— Great peace have they which love thy law. —Isaiah 32:17–18; Proverbs 1:33; Psalm 119:165

WEEK 29 - JOY IN TRIALS

Sunday: *We glory in tribulations.* —Romans 5:3

Beloved, think it not strange concerning the fiery trial which is to try you, as though some strange thing happened unto you: But rejoice, inasmuch as ye are partakers of Christ's sufferings; that, when his glory shall be revealed, ye may be glad also with exceeding joy. —— Sorrowful, yet alway rejoicing.

—1 Peter 4:12–13; 2 Corinthians 6:10

Rejoice in the Lord alway: and again I say, Rejoice. —— They departed from the presence of the council, rejoicing that they were counted worthy to suffer shame for his name.

—Philippians 4:4; Acts 5:41

The God of hope fill you with all joy and peace in believing.

—Romans 15:13

Although the fig tree shall not blossom, neither shall fruit be in the vines; the labour of the olive shall fail, and the fields shall yield no meat; the flock shall be cut off from the fold, and there shall be no herd in the stalls: Yet I will rejoice in the Lord, I will joy in the God of my salvation.

—Habakkuk 3:17–18

How excellent is thy lovingkindness, O God! therefore the children of men put their trust under the shadow of thy wings. They shall be abundantly satisfied with the fatness of thy house; and thou shalt make them drink of the river of thy pleasures. For with thee is the fountain of life: in thy light shall we see light.

—Psalm 36:7–9

. . .

Monday: *We know that all things work together for good to them that love God.* —Romans 8:28

Surely the wrath of man shall praise thee: the remainder of wrath shalt thou restrain. —— Ye thought evil against me; but God meant it unto good.

—Psalm 76:10; Genesis 50:20

All things are yours; Whether...the world, or life, or death, or things present, or things to come; all are yours; And ye are Christ's; and Christ is God's. —— All things are for your sakes, that the abundant grace might through the thanksgiving of many redound to the glory of God. For which cause we faint not; but though our outward man perish, yet the inward man is renewed day by day. For our light affliction, which is but for a moment, worketh for us a far more exceeding and eternal weight of glory.

—1 Corinthians 3:21–23; 2 Corinthians 4:15–17

My brethren, count it all joy when ye fall into divers temptations; Knowing this, that the trying of your faith worketh patience. But let patience have her perfect work, that ye may be perfect and entire, wanting nothing. —— Make me to hear joy and gladness; that the bones which thou hast broken may rejoice. ... Restore unto me the joy of thy salvation; and uphold me with thy free spirit. —— My soul shall be satisfied as with marrow and fatness; and my mouth shall praise thee with joyful lips.

—James 1:2–4; Psalm 51:8–12; 63:5

Tuesday: *The fellowship of his sufferings.* —Philippians 3:10

He is despised and rejected of men; a man of sorrows, and acquainted with grief; and we hid as it were our faces from him; he was despised, and we esteemed him not. —— In the world ye shall have tribulation. —— Because ye are not of the world, but I have chosen you out of the world, therefore the world hateth you.

—Isaiah 53:3; John 16:33; 15:19

I looked for some to take pity, but there was none. —— At my first answer no man stood with me, but all men forsook me. —— The foxes have holes, and the birds of the air have nests; but the Son of man hath not where to lay his head. —— Here have we no continuing city, but we seek one to come.

—Psalm 69:20; 2 Timothy 4:16; Matthew 8:20; Hebrews 13:14

Let us run with patience the race that is set before us, Looking unto Jesus the author and finisher of our faith; who for the joy that was set before him endured the cross, despising the shame, and is set down at the right hand of the throne of God. —— In thy presence is fulness of joy. —Hebrews 12:1-2; Psalm 16:11

. . .

Wednesday: *Light is sown for the righteous,*
and gladness for the upright in heart. —Psalm 97:11

They that sow in tears shall reap in joy. He that goeth forth and weepeth, bearing precious seed, shall doubtless come again with rejoicing, bringing his sheaves with him. —— Be glad in the Lord, and rejoice, ye righteous: and shout for joy, all ye that are upright in heart. —— Blessed is the people that know the joyful sound: they shall walk, O Lord, in the light of thy countenance. —— And my soul shall be joyful in the Lord: it shall rejoice in his salvation.

—Psalm 126:5–6; 32:11; 89:15; 35:9

Blessed be the God and Father of our Lord Jesus Christ, which according to his abundant mercy hath begotten us again unto a lively hope by the resurrection of Jesus Christ from the dead. ...Wherein ye greatly rejoice, though now for a season, if need be, ye are in heaviness through manifold temptations: That the trial of your faith, being much more precious than of gold that perisheth, though it be tried with fire, might be found unto praise and honour and glory at the appearing of Jesus Christ.

—1 Peter 1:3, 6–7

Thursday: *Reproach hath broken my heart.*
—Psalm 69:20

Is not this the carpenter's son? —— Can there any good thing come out of Nazareth? —— Say we not well that thou are a Samaritan, and hast a devil? —— He casteth out devils through the prince of the devils. —— We know that this man is a sinner. —— He deceiveth the people. —— This man blasphemeth. —— Behold a man gluttonous, and a winebibber, a friend of publicans and sinners.

—Matthew 13:55; John 1:46; 8:48; Matthew 9:34; John 9:24; 7:12; Matthew 9:3; 11:19

It is enough for the disciple that he be as his master, and the servant as his lord. —— This is thankworthy, if a man for conscience toward God endure grief, suffering wrongfully. ...For even hereunto were ye called: because Christ also suffered for us, leaving us an example, that we should follow his steps: Who did no sin, neither was guile found in his mouth: Who when he was reviled, reviled not again; when he suffered, he threatened not; but committed himself to him that judgeth righteously. —— If ye be reproached for the name of Christ, happy are ye. —— In his favour is life: weeping may endure for a night, but joy cometh in the morning.

—Matthew 10:25; 1 Peter 2:19–23; 4:14; Psalm 30:5

. . .

Friday: *As the sufferings of Christ abound in us, so our consolation also aboundeth by Christ.* —2 Corinthians 1:5

The fellowship of his sufferings. —— Rejoice, inasmuch as ye are partakers of Christ's sufferings; that, when his glory shall be revealed, ye may be glad also with exceeding joy. —— For if we be dead with him, we shall also live with him. —— If children, then heirs; heirs of God, and joint-heirs with Christ; if so be that we suffer with him, that we may be also glorified together.

—Philippians 3:10; 1 Peter 4:13; 2 Timothy 2:11; Romans 8:17

God, willing more abundantly to shew unto the heirs of promise the immutability of his counsel, confirmed it by an oath: That by two immutable things, in which it was impossible for God to lie, we might have a strong consolation, who have fled for refuge to lay hold upon the hope set before us. —— For I know the thoughts that I think toward you, saith the Lord, thoughts of peace, and not of evil, to give you an expected end. —— Our Lord Jesus Christ himself, and God, even our Father, which hath loved us, and hath given us everlasting consolation and good hope through grace, Comfort your hearts, and stablish you in every good word and work.

—Hebrews 6:17–18; Jeremiah 29:11; 2 Thessalonians 2:16–17

Saturday: *Behold, we count them happy which endure.* —James 5:11

We glory in tribulations...knowing that tribulation worketh patience; And patience, experience; and experience, hope: And hope maketh not ashamed; because the love of God is shed abroad in our hearts by the Holy Ghost which is given unto us. —— No chastening for the present seemeth to be joyous, but grievous: nevertheless afterward it yieldeth the peaceable fruit of righteousness unto them which are exercised thereby.

—Romans 5:3–5; Hebrews 12:11

My brethren, count it all joy when ye fall into divers temptations; Knowing this, that the trying of your faith worketh patience. But let patience have her perfect work, that ye may be perfect and entire, wanting nothing. ...Blessed is the man that endureth temptation: for when he is tried, he shall receive the crown of life, which the Lord hath promised to them that love him. —— Most gladly therefore will I rather glory in my infirmities, that the power of Christ may rest upon me. ...For when I am weak, then am I strong. —— For the joy of the Lord is your strength.

—James 1:2–4, 12; 2 Corinthians 12:9–10; Nehemiah 8:10

WEEK 30 - REPLACE WORRY WITH FAITH

S**unday**: *I will both lay me down in peace, and sleep: for thou, Lord, only makest me dwell in safety.* —Psalm 4:8

Thou shalt not be afraid for the terror by night. ...He shall cover thee with his feathers, and under his wings shalt thou trust. —— Even as a hen gathereth her chickens under her wings. —— He will not suffer thy foot to be moved: he that keepeth thee will not slumber. Behold, he that keepeth Israel shall neither slumber nor sleep. The Lord is thy keeper: the Lord is thy shade upon thy right hand. —— As an eagle stirreth up her nest, fluttereth over her young, spreadeth abroad her wings, taketh them, beareth them on her wings: So the Lord alone did lead him, and there was no strange god with him. He made him ride on the high places of the earth, that he might eat the increase of the fields; and he made him to suck honey out of the rock.

—Psalm 91:5, 4; Matthew 23:37; Psalm 121:3–5; Deuteronomy 32:11–13

How excellent is thy lovingkindness, O God! therefore the children of men put their trust under the shadow of thy wings. They shall be abundantly satisfied with the fatness of thy house; and thou shalt make them drink of the river of thy pleasures. For with thee is the fountain of life: in thy light shall we see light. —— I will abide in thy tabernacle for ever: I will trust in the covert of thy wings. —— He that spared not his own Son, but delivered him up for us all, how shall he not with him also freely give us all things? —— I will trust, and not be afraid.

—Psalm 36:7–9; 61:4; Romans 8:32; Isaiah 12:2

. . .

Monday: *My God shall supply all your need according to his riches in glory by Christ Jesus.*

—Philippians 4:19

Seek ye first the kingdom of God, and his righteousness; and all...things shall be added unto you. —— He that spared not his Son, but delivered him up for us all, how shall he not with him freely give us all things? —— All things are yours; whether Paul, or Apollos, or Cephas, or the world, or life, or death, or things present, or things to come; all are yours; And ye are Christ's; and Christ is God's. —— As having nothing, and yet possessing all things.

—Matthew 6:33; Romans 8:32; 1 Corinthians 3:21–23; 2 Corinthians 6:10

The Lord is my shepherd; I shall not want. —— The Lord God is a sun and shield: the Lord will give grace and glory: no good thing will he withhold from them that walk uprightly. —— The living God...giveth us richly all things to enjoy. —— God is able to make all grace abound toward you; that ye, always having all sufficiency in all things, may abound to every good work.

—Psalm 23:1; 84:11; 1 Timothy 6:17; 2 Corinthians 9:8

Tuesday: *I will not fear what man shall do unto me.* —Hebrews 13:6

Who shall separate us from the love of Christ? shall tribulation, or distress, or persecution, or famine, or nakedness, or peril, or sword?...Nay, in all these things we are more than conquerors through him that loved us. —— Be not afraid of them that kill the body, and after that have no more that they can do. But I will forewarn you whom ye shall fear: Fear him, which after he hath killed hath power to cast into hell; yea, I say unto you, Fear him.

—Romans 8:35, 37; Luke 12:4–5

Blessed are they which are persecuted for righteousness' sake: for theirs is the kingdom of heaven. Blessed are ye, when men shall revile you, and persecute you, and shall say all manner of evil against you falsely, for my sake. Rejoice, and be exceeding glad: for great is your reward in heaven. —— None of these things move me, neither count I my life dear unto myself, so that I might finish my course with joy.

—Matthew 5:10–12; Acts 20:24

Have not I commanded thee? Be strong and of a good courage; be not afraid, neither be thou dismayed: for the Lord thy God is with thee whithersoever thou goest.

—Joshua 1:9

. . .

Wednesday: *Be not afraid nor dismayed by reason of this great multitude; for the battle is not yours, but God's.*

—2 Chronicles 20:15

Be of good courage, and let us behave ourselves valiantly for our people, and for the cities of our God: and let the Lord do that which is good in his sight. —— We made our prayer unto our God, and set a watch against them day and night. —— Watch and pray, that ye enter not into temptation. —— Watch ye, stand fast in the faith, ...be strong. —— Fervent in spirit; serving the Lord. —— Strengthen ye the weak hands, and confirm the feeble knees. Say to them that are of a fearful heart, Be strong, fear not....Then shall the lame man leap as an hart, and the tongue of the dumb sing: for in the wilderness shall waters break out, and streams in the desert.

—1 Chronicles 19:13; Nehemiah 4:9; Matthew 26:41; 1 Corinthians 16:13; Romans 12:11; Isaiah 35:3–6

Wherefore lift up the hands which hang down, and the feeble knees; And make straight paths for your feet, lest that which is lame be turned out of the way; but let it rather be healed. Follow peace with all men, and holiness, ...Looking diligently...lest any root of bitterness springing up trouble you, and thereby many be defiled.

—Hebrews 12:12–15

Thursday: *Sit still, my daughter.* —Ruth 3:18

Take heed, and be quiet; fear not, neither be fainthearted. —— Be still, and know that I am God. —— Said I not unto thee, that, if thou wouldest believe, thou shouldest see the glory of God? —— The loftiness of man shall be bowed down, and the haughtiness of men shall be made low: and the Lord alone shall be exalted in that day.

—Isaiah 7:4; Psalm 46:10; John 11:40; Isaiah 2:17

Mary...sat at Jesus' feet, and heard his word. —— Mary hath chosen that good part, which shall not be taken away from her. —— In returning and rest shall ye be saved; in quietness and in confidence shall be your strength. —— Commune with your own heart upon your bed, and be still. —— Rest in the Lord, and wait patiently for him: fret not thyself because of him who prospereth in his way, because of the man who bringeth wicked devices to pass. —— He shall not be afraid of evil tidings: his heart is fixed, trusting in the Lord. His heart is established. — He that believeth shall not make haste.

—Luke 10:39, 42; Isaiah 30:15; Psalm 4:4; 37:7; 112:7–8; Isaiah 28:16

. . .

Friday: *He shall call upon me, and I will answer him: I will be with him in trouble; I will deliver him.* —Psalm 91:15

Fear thou not; for I am with thee: be not dismayed; for I am thy God: I will strengthen thee; yea, I will help thee; yea, I will uphold thee with the right hand of my righteousness. Behold, all they that were incensed against thee shall be ashamed and confounded: they shall be as nothing; and they that strive with thee shall perish. Thou shalt seek them, and shalt not find them, even them that contended with thee: they that war against thee shall be as nothing, and as a thing of nought. For I the Lord thy God will hold thy right hand, saying unto thee, Fear not; I will help thee.

—Isaiah 41:10–13

Asa cried unto the Lord his God, and said, Lord, it is nothing with thee to help, whether with many, or with them that have no power. ...O Lord, thou art our God; let not man prevail against thee. So the Lord smote the Ethiopians before Asa. —— O thou that hearest prayer, unto thee shall all flesh come.

—2 Chronicles 14:11–12; Psalm 65:2

Saturday: *I know whom I have believed, and am persuaded that he is able.* —2 Timothy 1:12

Able to do exceeding abundantly above all that we ask or think. —— Able to make all grace abound toward you; that ye, always having all sufficiency in all things, may abound to every good work. —— Able to succour them that are tempted.

—Ephesians 3:20; 2 Corinthians 9:8; Hebrews 2:18

Able ... to save them to the uttermost that come unto God by him, seeing he ever liveth to make intercession for them.

—Hebrews 7:25

Able to keep you from falling, and to present you faultless before the presence of his glory with exceeding joy.

—Jude 1:24

Able to keep that which I have committed unto him against that day. —— Who shall change our vile body, that it may be fashioned like unto his glorious body, according to the working whereby he is able even to subdue all things unto himself.

—2 Timothy 1:12; Philippians 3:21

Believe ye that I am able to do this?...Yea, Lord. ...According to your faith be it unto you.

—Matthew 9:28–29

WEEK 31 - GOD OUR STRENGTH

S**unday**: *He giveth power to the faint;*
and to them that have no might he increaseth strength.

—Isaiah 40:29

When they shall lead you, and deliver you up, take no thought beforehand what ye shall speak, neither do ye premeditate: but whatsoever shall be given you in that hour, that speak ye: for it is not ye that speak, but the Holy Ghost. —— Take...no thought for the morrow: for the morrow shall take thought for the things of itself. Sufficient unto the day is the evil thereof.

—Mark 13:11; Matthew 6:34

The God of Israel is he that giveth strength and power unto his people. Blessed be God.

—Psalm 68:35

My grace is sufficient for thee: for my strength is made perfect in weakness. Most gladly therefore will I rather glory in my infirmities, that the power of Christ may rest upon me. Therefore I take pleasure in infirmities, in reproaches, in necessities, in persecutions, in distresses for Christ's sake: for when I am weak, then am I strong. —— I can do all things through Christ which strengtheneth me. —— O my soul, thou hast trodden down strength.

—2 Corinthians 12:9–10; Philippians 4:13; Judges 5:21

. . .

M**onday**: *Be strong in the grace that is in Christ Jesus.*
—2 Timothy 2:1

Strengthened with all might, according to his glorious power. —— As ye have therefore received Christ Jesus the Lord, so walk ye in him: Rooted and built up in him, and stablished in the faith, as ye have been taught, abounding therein with thanksgiving. —— Trees of righteousness, the planting of the Lord, that he might be glorified. —— Built upon the foundation of the apostles and prophets, Jesus Christ himself being the chief corner stone; In whom all the building fitly framed together groweth unto a holy temple in the Lord. —— That Christ may dwell in your hearts by faith; that ye, being rooted and grounded in love.

—Colossians 1:11; 2:6–17; Isaiah 61:3; Ephesians 2:20–21; 3:17

And he shall be like a tree planted by the rivers of water, that bringeth forth his fruit in his season; his leaf also shall not wither; and whatsoever he doeth shall prosper.

—Psalm 1:3

Being filled with the fruits of righteousness, which are by Jesus Christ, unto the glory and praise of God. —— Fight the good fight of faith. —— In nothing terrified by your adversaries. —— The joy of the Lord is your strength.

—Philippians 1:11; 1 Timothy 6:12; Philippians 1:28; Nehemiah 8:10

T**uesday**: *Be strong, and work; for I am with you, saith the Lord of hosts.* —Haggai 2:4

I am the vine, ye are the branches: He that abideth in me, and I in him, the same bringeth forth much fruit: for without me ye can do nothing. —— I can do all things through Christ which strengtheneth me. —— Strong in the Lord, and in the power of his might.

—John 15:5; Philippians 4:13; Ephesians 6:10

Thus said the Lord of hosts; Let your hands be strong, ye that hear in these days these words by the mouth of the prophets. —— Strengthen ye the weak hands, and confirm the feeble knees. Say to them that are of a fearful heart, Be strong, fear not. —— The Lord looked upon him, and said, Go in this thy might.

—Zechariah 8:9; Isaiah 35:3–4; Judges 6:14

If God be for us, who can be against us? —— Therefore seeing we have this ministry, as we have received mercy, we faint not. —— Let us not be weary in well doing: for in due season we shall reap, if we faint not. —— Thanks be to God, which giveth us the victory through our Lord Jesus Christ.

—Romans 8:31; 2 Corinthians 4:1; Galatians 6:9; 1 Corinthians 15:57

. . .

Wednesday: *My heart panteth, my strength faileth me.* —Psalm 38:10

Hear my cry, O God; attend unto my prayer. From the end of the earth will I cry unto thee, when my heart is overwhelmed: lead me to the rock that is higher than I. —— Blessed are the poor in spirit: for theirs is the kingdom of heaven. Blessed are they that mourn: for they shall be comforted. Blessed are the meek: for they shall inherit the earth.

—Psalm 61:1–2; Matthew 5:3–5

When [Peter] saw the wind boisterous, he was afraid; and beginning to sink, he cried, saying, Lord, save me. And immediately Jesus stretched forth his hand, and caught him, and said unto him, O thou of little faith, wherefore didst thou doubt? —— If thou faint in the day of adversity, thy strength is small. —— He giveth power to the faint; and to them that have no might he increaseth strength. —— The eternal God is thy refuge, and underneath are the everlasting arms. —— Strengthened with all might, according to his glorious power.

—Matthew 14:30–31; Proverbs 24:10; Isaiah 40:29; Deuteronomy 33:27; Colossians 1:11

Thursday: *Let him take hold of my strength, that he may make peace with me.* —Isaiah 27:5

I know the thoughts that I think toward you, saith the Lord, thoughts of peace, and not of evil. —— I will love thee, O Lord, my strength. The Lord is my rock, and my fortress, and my deliverer; my God, my strength, in whom I will trust; my buckler, and the horn of my salvation, and my high tower. I will call upon the Lord, who is worthy to be praised.

—Jeremiah 29:11; Psalm 18:1–3

For by thee I have run through a troop; and by my God have I leaped over a wall. As for God, his way is perfect: the word of the Lord is tried: he is a buckler to all those that trust in him. —Psalm 18:29–30

For who is God save the Lord? or who is a rock save our God? It is God that girdeth me with strength, and maketh my way perfect. He maketh my feet like hinds' feet, and setteth me upon my high places...Thou hast also given me the shield of thy salvation: and thy right hand hath holden me up, and thy gentleness hath made me great. Thou hast enlarged my steps under me, that my feet did not slip. ...The Lord liveth; and blessed be my rock; and let the God of my salvation be exalted. —— Trust ye in the Lord for ever, for in the ***LORD JEHOVAH*** *is everlasting strength.*

—Psalm 18: 31–36, 46; Isaiah 26:4

. . .

Friday: *God hath chosen the weak things of the world to confound the things which are mighty.* —1 Corinthians 1:27

When I am weak, then am I strong. —— God shall be my strength. —— He said unto me, My grace is sufficient for thee: for my strength is made perfect in weakness. Most gladly therefore will I rather glory in my infirmities, that the power of Christ may rest upon me. —— Let him take hold of my strength.

—2 Corinthians 12:10; Isaiah 49:5; 2 Corinthians 12:9; Isaiah 27:5

Cast thy burden upon the Lord, and he shall sustain thee. —— The arms of his hands were made strong by the hands of the mighty God of Jacob.

—Psalm 55:22; Genesis 49:24

I will not let thee go, except thou bless me. —Genesis 32:26

Thou comest to me with a sword, and with a spear, and with a shield: but I come to thee in the name of the Lord of hosts, the God of the armies of Israel, whom thou hast defied. ...And all this assembly shall know that the Lord saveth not with sword and spear: for the battle is the Lord's, and he will give you into our hands. —— Plead my cause, O Lord, with them that strive with me: fight against them that fight against me. Take hold of shield and buckler, and stand up for mine help.

—1 Samuel 17:45–47; Psalm 35:1–2

Saturday: *They that wait upon the Lord shall renew their strength.* —Isaiah 40:31

Woe to the rebellious children, saith the Lord, that take counsel, but not of me; and that cover with a covering, but not of my spirit, that they may add sin to sin: That walk to go down into Egypt, and have not asked at my mouth; to strengthen themselves in the strength of Pharaoh, and to trust in the shadow of Egypt! Therefore shall the strength of Pharaoh be your shame, and the trust in the shadow of Egypt your confusion. ...For thus saith the Lord God, the Holy One of Israel; In returning and rest shall ye be saved; in quietness and in confidence shall be your strength:

—Isaiah 30:1–3,15

It is better to trust in the Lord than to put confidence in man. It is better to trust in the Lord than to put confidence in princes...The Lord is my strength and song, and is become my salvation. —— Not by might, nor by power, but by my spirit, saith the Lord of hosts. —— My brethren, be strong in the Lord, and in the power of his might.

—Psalm 118:8–9,14; Zechariah 4:6; Ephesians 6:10

WEEK 32 - YOU ARE GOD'S TEMPLE

S**unday**: *Behold, I stand at the door, and knock: if any man hear my voice, and open the door, I will come in to him, and will sup with him, and he with me.* —Revelations 3:20

And I will pray the Father, and he shall give you another Comforter, that he may abide with you for ever; Even the Spirit of truth; whom the world cannot receive, because it seeth him not, neither knoweth him: but ye know him; for he dwelleth with you, and shall be in you.

...At that day ye shall know that I am in my Father, and ye in me, and I in you. He that hath my commandments, and keepeth them, he it is that loveth me: and he that loveth me shall be loved of my Father, and I will love him, and will manifest myself to him. ...Jesus answered and said unto him, If a man love me, he will keep my words: and my Father will love him, and we will come unto him, and make our abode with him. He that loveth me not keepeth not my sayings: and the word which ye hear is not mine, but the Father's which sent me.

...But the Comforter, which is the Holy Ghost, whom the Father will send in my name, he shall teach you all things, and bring all things to your remembrance, whatsoever I have said unto you.

—John 14:16–17,20–21,23–24, 26

But the anointing which ye have received of him abideth in you, and ye need not that any man teach you: but as the same anointing teacheth you of all things, and is truth, and is no lie, and even as it hath taught you, ye shall abide in him.

—1 John 2:27

. . .

Monday: *The house that is to be builded for the Lord must be exceeding magnifical.*

—1 Chronicles 22:5

They brought great stones, costly stones, and hewed stones, to lay the foundation of the house. —— The house, when it was in building, was built of stone made ready before it was brought thither: so that there was neither hammer nor axe nor any tool of iron heard in the house, while it was in building.

—I Kings 5:17, 6:7

Ye also, as lively stones, are built up a spiritual house. —— Built upon the foundation of the apostles and prophets, Jesus Christ himself being the chief corner stone; In whom all the building fitly framed together groweth unto an holy temple in the Lord: In whom ye also are builded together for an habitation of God through the Spirit. —— Which in time past were not a people, but are now the people of God.

—1 Peter 2:5; Ephesians 2:20–22; 1 Peter 2:10

Ye are God's building. —— Therefore if any man be in Christ, he is a new creature: old things are passed away; behold, all things are become new. —— Now he that hath wrought us for the selfsame thing is God, who also hath given unto us the earnest of the Spirit.

—1 Corinthians 3:9; 2 Corinthians 5:17; 2 Corinthians 5:5

Tuesday: *The temple of God is holy, which temple ye are.*

—1 Corinthians 3:17

What manner of persons ought ye to be in all holy conversation and godliness...without spot, and blameless? —— Give thanks at the remembrance of his holiness. —— Who is like unto thee, O Lord, among the gods? who is like thee, glorious in holiness? —— Holy, holy, holy, is the Lord of hosts.

—2 Peter 3:11, 14; Psalm 97:12; Exodus 15:11; Isaiah 6:3

As he which hath called you is holy, so be ye holy in all manner of conversation; Because it is written, Be ye holy; for I am holy. —— Partakers of his holiness. —— And that ye put on the new man, which after God is created in righteousness and true holiness.

—1 Peter 1:15–16; Hebrews 12:10; Ephesians 4:24

Let no corrupt communication proceed out of your mouth, but that which is good to the use of edifying. ...And grieve not the Holy Spirit of God, whereby ye are sealed unto the day of redemption.

—Ephesians 4:29–30

. . .

W**ednesday**: *Know ye not that ye are the temple of God, and that the Spirit of God dwelleth in you?* —1 Corinthians 3:16

And hereby we know that he abideth in us, by the Spirit which he hath given us. —— Where two or three are gathered together in my name, there am I in the midst of them. —— Lo, I am with you always, even unto the end of the world. —— My presence shall go with thee, and I will give thee rest.

—1 John 3:24; Matthew 18:20; 28:20; Exodus 33:14

Whither shall I go from thy spirit? or whither shall I flee from thy presence? If I ascend up into heaven, thou art there: if I make my bed in hell, behold, thou art there. —— Am I a God at hand, saith the Lord, and not a God afar off? Can any hide himself in secret places that I shall not see him? saith the Lord, Do not I fill heaven and earth? saith the Lord.

—Psalm 139:7–8; Jeremiah 23:23–24

Behold, the heaven and heaven of heavens cannot contain thee; how much less this house that I have builded? —— Thus saith the high and lofty One that inhabiteth eternity, whose name is Holy; I dwell in the high and holy place, with him also that is of a contrite and humble spirit, to revive the spirit of the humble, and to revive the heart of the contrite ones.

—1 Kings 8:27; Isaiah 57:15

T**hursday**: *The king of Israel...is in the midst of thee.*

—Zephaniah 3:15.

Fear thou not; for I am with thee: be not dismayed; for I am thy God: I will strengthen thee; yea, I will help thee; yea, I will uphold thee with the right hand of my righteousness.

—Isaiah 41:10

Strengthen ye the weak hands, and confirm the feeble knees. Say to them that are of a fearful heart, Be strong, fear not: behold, your God will come with vengeance, even God with a recompence; he will come and save you. —— The Lord thy God in the midst of thee is mighty; he will save, he will rejoice over thee with joy; he will rest in his love, he will joy over thee with singing. —— Wait on the Lord: be of good courage, and he shall strengthen thine heart.

—Isaiah 35:3–4; Zephaniah 3:17; Psalm 27:14

I heard a great voice out of heaven saying, Behold, the tabernacle of God is with men, and he will dwell with them, and they shall be his people, and God himself shall be with them, and be their God. And God shall wipe away all tears from their eyes; and there shall be no more death, neither sorrow, nor crying, neither shall there be any more pain. —Revelations 21:3–4

. . .

F**riday**: *What agreement hath the temple of God with idols? for ye are the temple of the living God; as God has said, I will dwell in them, and walk in them; and I will be their God, and they shall be my people.*

—2 Corinthians 6:16

Love not the world, neither the things that are in the world. If any man love the world, the love of the Father is not in him. —— But God hath chosen the foolish things of the world to confound the wise; and God hath chosen the weak things of the world to confound the things which are mighty. ...For the wisdom of this world is foolishness with God.

—1 John 2:15; 1 Corinthians 1:27, 3:19

Know ye not that your body is the temple of the Holy Ghost which is in you, which ye have of God, and ye are not your own? For ye are bought with a price: therefore glorify God in your body, and in your spirit, which are God's. —— I beseech you therefore, brethren, by the mercies of God, that ye present your bodies a living sacrifice, holy, acceptable unto God, which is your reasonable service. And be not conformed to this world: but be ye transformed by the renewing of your mind, that ye may prove what is that good, and acceptable, and perfect, will of God.

—1 Corinthians 6:19–20; Romans 12:1–2

S**aturday**: *Jehovah-shammah* (*The Lord is there.*) —Ezekiel 48:35

Behold, the tabernacle of God is with men, and he will dwell with them, and they shall be his people, and God himself shall be with them, and be their God. —— I saw no temple...for the Lord God Almighty and the Lamb are the temple. ...The city had no need of the sun, neither of the moon, to shine in it: for the glory of God did lighten it, and the Lamb is the light thereof.

—Revelations 21:3; 22–23

I shall be satisfied, when I awake, with thy likeness. —— Whom have I in heaven but thee? and there is none upon earth that I desire beside thee.

—Psalm 17:15; 73:25

Sing and rejoice, O daughter of Zion; for, lo, I come, and I will dwell in the midst of thee, saith the Lord. —— There shall be no more curse: but the throne of God and of the Lamb shall be in it; and his servants shall serve him.

—Zechariah 2:10; Revelations 22:3

Ye are the temple of living God. —2 Corinthians 6:16

WEEK 33 - PERFECTED BY TRIALS

S**unday**: *Every branch that beareth fruit, he purgeth it.* —John 15:2

He is like a refiner's fire, and like fullers' soap: And he shall sit as a refiner and purifier of silver: and he shall purify the sons of Levi, and purge them as gold and silver, that they may offer unto the Lord an offering in righteousness.

—Malachi 3:2–3

We glory in tribulations...knowing that tribulation worketh patience; And patience, experience; and experience, hope: And hope maketh not ashamed; because the love of God is shed abroad in our hearts by the Holy Ghost which is given unto us. —— If ye endure chastening, God dealeth with you as with sons, for what son is he whom the Father chasteneth not? But if ye be without chastisement, whereof all are partakers, then are ye bastards, and not sons. ...Now no chastening for the present seemeth to be joyous, but grievous: nevertheless afterward it yieldeth the peaceable fruit of righteousness unto them which are exercised thereby. Wherefore lift up the hands which hang down, and the feeble knees.

—Malachi 3:2–3. Romans 5:3–5; Hebrews 12:7–8,11–12

There is no man that hath left house, or brethren, or sisters, or father, or mother, or wife, or children, or lands, for my sake, and the gospel's, But he shall receive an hundredfold now in this time, houses, and brethren, and sisters, and mothers, and children, and lands, with persecutions; and in the world to come eternal life.

—Mark 10:29–30

. . .

M**onday**: *It is good for me that I have been afflicted; that I might learn thy statutes.*

—Psalm 119:71

Though he were a Son, yet learned he obedience by the things which he suffered. —— We suffer with him, that we may be also glorified together. For I reckon that the sufferings of this present time are not worthy to be compared with the glory which shall be revealed in us. —— He knoweth the way that I take: when he hath tried me, I shall come forth as gold. My foot hath held his steps, his way have I kept, and not declined.

—Hebrews 5:8; Romans 8:17–18; Job 23:10–11

Thou shalt remember all the way which the Lord thy God led thee these forty years in the wilderness, to humble thee, and to prove thee, to know what was in thine heart, whether thou wouldest keep his commandments, or no. ...Thou shalt also consider in thine heart, that, as a man chasteneth his son, so the Lord thy God chasteneth thee. Therefore thou shalt keep the commandments of the Lord thy God, to walk in his ways, and to fear him.

—Deuteronomy 8:2, 5–6

T**uesday**: *Whom the Lord loveth he correcteth.* —Proverbs 3:12

See now that I, even I, am he, and there is no god with me. —— I know the thoughts that I think toward you, saith the Lord, thoughts of peace, and not of evil, to give you an expected end. —— My thoughts are not your thoughts, neither are your ways my ways, saith the Lord.

—Deuteronomy 32:39; Jeremiah 29:11; Isaiah 55:8

I will allure her, and bring her into the wilderness, and speak comfortably unto her. —— As a man chasteneth his son, so the Lord thy God chasteneth thee. —— Now no chastening for the present seemeth to be joyous, but grievous: nevertheless afterward it yieldeth the peaceable fruit of righteousness unto them which are exercised thereby. —— Humble yourselves therefore under the mighty hand of God, that he may exalt you in due time.

—Hosea 2:14; Deuteronomy 8:5; Hebrews 12:11; 1 Peter 5:6

I know, O Lord, that thy judgments are right, and that thou in faithfulness hast afflicted me. —— This book of the law shall not depart out of thy mouth; but thou shalt meditate therein day and night, that thou mayest observe to do according to all that is written therein: for then thou shalt make thy way prosperous, and then thou shalt have good success.

—Psalm 119:75; Joshua 1:8

. . .

Wednesday: *Let patience have her perfect work, that ye may be perfect and entire, wanting nothing.* —James 1:4

Now for a season, if need be, ye are in heaviness through manifold temptations: That the trial of your faith, being much more precious than of gold that perisheth, though it be tried with fire, might be found unto praise and honour and glory at the appearing of Jesus Christ. —— We glory in tribulations...knowing that tribulation worketh patience; And patience, experience; and experience, hope.

—1 Peter 1:6–7; Romans 5:3–4

It is good that a man should both hope and quietly wait for the salvation of the Lord. —— Ye have in heaven a better and an enduring substance. Cast not away therefore your confidence, which hath great recompence of reward. For ye have need of patience, that, after ye have done the will of God, ye might receive the promise. —— Our Lord Jesus Christ himself, and God, even our Father, which hath loved us, and hath given us everlasting consolation and good hope through grace, Comfort your hearts.

—Lamentations 3:26; Hebrews 10:34–36; 2 Thessalonians 2:16–17

Thursday: *What I do thou knowest not now; but thou shalt know hereafter.* —John 13:7

Thou shalt remember all the way which the Lord thy God led thee these forty years in the wilderness, to humble thee, and to prove thee, to know what was in thine heart, whether thou wouldest keep his commandments, or no.

—Deuteronomy 8:2

When I passed by thee, and looked upon thee, behold, thy time was the time of love; ...yea, I sware unto thee, and entered into a covenant with thee, saith the Lord God, and thou becamest mine. —— Whom the Lord loveth he chasteneth.

—Ezekiel 16:8; Hebrews 12:6

Beloved, think it not strange concerning the fiery trial which is to try you, as though some strange thing happened unto you: But rejoice, inasmuch as ye are partakers of Christ's sufferings; that, when his glory shall be revealed, ye may be glad also with exceeding joy. —— Our light affliction, which is but for a moment, worketh for us a far more exceeding and eternal weight of glory; While we look not at the things which are seen, but at the things which are not seen.

—1 Peter 4:12–13; 2 Corinthians 4:17–18

. . .

Friday: *Endure hardness, as a good soldier of Jesus Christ.* —2 Timothy 2:3

I have given him for a witness to the people, a leader and commander to the people. —— It became him, for whom are all things, and by whom are all things, in bringing many sons unto glory, to make the captain of their salvation perfect through suffering. —— We must through much tribulation enter into the kingdom of God. —— We do not war after the flesh: (For the weapons of our warfare are not carnal, but mighty through God to the pulling down of strong holds.)

—Isaiah 55:4; Hebrews 2:10; Acts 14:22; 2 Corinthians 10:3–4

Add to your faith virtue; and to virtue knowledge; And to knowledge temperance; and to temperance patience; and to patience godliness; And to godliness brotherly kindness; and to brotherly kindness charity. For if these things be in you, and abound, they make you that ye shall neither be barren nor unfruitful in the knowledge of our Lord Jesus Christ. —— The God of all grace, who hath called us unto his eternal glory by Christ Jesus, after that ye have suffered a while, make you perfect, stablish, strengthen, settle you.

—2 Peter 1:5–8; 1 Peter 5:10.

Saturday: *Every thing that may abide the fire, ye shall make it go through the fire, and it shall be clean.* —Numbers 31:23

The Lord your God proveth you, to know whether ye love the Lord your God with all your heart, and with all your soul. —— He shall sit as a refiner and purifier of silver: and he shall purify the sons of Levi, and purge them as gold and silver, that they may offer unto the Lord an offering in righteousness. —— Every man's work shall be made manifest: for the day shall declare it, because it shall be revealed by fire; and the fire shall try every man's work of what sort it is.

—Deuteronomy 13:3; Malachi 3:3; 1 Corinthians 3:13

I will turn my hand upon thee, and purely purge away thy dross, and take away all thy tin. —— I will melt them, and try them. —— Thou, O God, hast proved us; thou hast tried us, as silver is tried. ...We went through fire and through water: but thou broughtest us out into a wealthy place. —— When thou walkest through the fire, thou shalt not be burned; neither shall the flame kindle upon thee.

—Isaiah 1:25; Jeremiah 9:7; Psalm 66:10–12; Isaiah 43:2

WEEK 34 - JESUS 2

Sunday: *I have laid help upon one that is mighty;*
I have exalted one chosen out of the people.

—Psalm 89:19

I, even I, am the Lord; and beside me there is no saviour. —— There is one God, and one mediator between God and men, the man Christ Jesus. —— There is none other name under heaven given among men, whereby we must be saved.

—Isaiah 43:11; 1 Timothy 2:5; Acts 4:12

The mighty God. —— Who, being in the form of God, thought it not robbery to be equal with God: But made himself of no reputation, and took upon him the form of a servant, and was made in the likeness of men: And being found in fashion as a man, he humbled himself, and became obedient unto death, even the death of the cross. Wherefore God also hath highly exalted him, and given him a name which is above every name: That at the name of Jesus every knee should bow, of things in heaven, and things in earth, and things under the earth. —— We see Jesus, who was made a little lower than the angels for the suffering of death, crowned with glory and honour; that he by the grace of God should taste death for every man...Forasmuch...as the children are partakers of flesh and blood, he also himself likewise took part of the same.

—Isaiah 9:6; Philippians 2:6–10; Hebrews 2:9, 14

. . .

M**onday**: *What think ye of Christ?* —Matthew 22:42

Who is this King of glory? The Lord of hosts, he is the King of glory. —— He hath on his vesture and on his thigh a name written, KING OF KINGS, AND LORD OF LORDS.

—Psalm 24:10; Revelations 19:16

Unto you...which believe he is precious: but unto them which be disobedient, the stone which the builders disallowed, the same is made the head of the corner. —— Christ crucified, unto the Jews a stumblingblock, and unto the Greeks foolishness; But unto them which are called, both Jews and Greeks, Christ the power of God, and the wisdom of God.

—1 Peter 2:7; 1 Corinthians 1:23–24

I count all things but loss for the excellency of the knowledge of Christ Jesus my Lord: for whom I have suffered the loss of all things, and do count them but dung, that I may win Christ. —— Lord, thou knowest all things; thou knowest that I love thee. —— Holy, holy, holy, Lord God Almighty, which was, and is, and is to come. ...Blessing, and honour, and glory, and power, be unto him that sitteth upon the throne, and unto the Lamb for ever and ever.

—Philippians 3:8; John 21:17; Revelations 4:8, 5:13

T**uesday**: *God gave Solomon...largeness of heart, even as the sand that is on the sea shore.* —1 Kings 4:29

Behold, a greater than Solomon is here. —— The Prince of Peace.

—Matthew 12:42; Isaiah 9:6

Scarcely for a righteous man will one die: yet peradventure for a good man some would even dare to die. But God commendeth his love toward us, in that, while we were yet sinners, Christ died for us. —— The love of Christ which passeth knowledge. —— To make all men see what is the fellowship of the mystery, which from the beginning of the world hath been hid in God, who created all things by Jesus Christ. —— For in him we live, and move, and have our being.

—Romans 5:7–8; Ephesians 3:19; 3:9; Acts 17:28

Christ the power of God, and the wisdom of God. —— Upholding all things by the word of his power. —— In whom are hid all the treasures of wisdom and knowledge. —— The unsearchable riches of Christ. —— Of him are ye in Christ Jesus, who of God is made unto us wisdom, and righteousness, and sanctification, and redemption.

—1 Corinthians 1:24; Hebrews 1:3; Colossians 2:3; Ephesians 3:8; 1 Corinthians 1:30

. . .

Wednesday: *And Jesus returned in the power of the Spirit into Galilee: and there went out a fame of him through all the region round about.* —Luke 4:14

And he taught in their synagogues, being glorified of all. And he came to Nazareth, where he had been brought up: and, as his custom was, he went into the synagogue on the sabbath day, and stood up for to read. And there was delivered unto him the book of the prophet Esaias. And when he had opened the book, he found the place where it was written, The Spirit of the Lord is upon me, because he hath anointed me to preach the gospel to the poor; he hath sent me to heal the brokenhearted, to preach deliverance to the captives, and recovering of sight to the blind, to set at liberty them that are bruised, To preach the acceptable year of the Lord. And he closed the book, and he gave it again to the minister, and sat down. And the eyes of all them that were in the synagogue were fastened on him.

—Luke 4:15–20

And he began to say unto them, ***This day is this scripture fulfilled in your ears****.*

—Luke 4:21

Thursday: *Jesus Christ our Lord.* —1 Corinthians 1:9

In him dwelleth all the fulness of the Godhead bodily. —— I have laid help upon one that is mighty; I have exalted one chosen out of the people.

—Colossians 2:9; Psalm 89:19

Great is the mystery of godliness: God was manifest in the flesh. —— Unto us a child is born, unto us a son is given: and the government shall be upon his shoulder: and his name shall be called Wonderful, Counsellor, The mighty God, The Everlasting Father, The Prince of Peace.

—1 Timothy 3:16; Isaiah 9:6

The brightness of his glory, and the express image of his person, and upholding all things by the word of his power, when he had by himself purged our sins, sat down on the right hand of the majesty on high. ...Unto the Son he saith, Thy throne, O God, is for ever and ever.

—Hebrews 1:3, 8

Let all the angels of God worship him. —— ***KINGS OF KINGS, AND LORD OF LORDS.***

—Hebrews 1:6; Revelations 19:16

. . .

Friday: *Thou shalt make a plate of pure gold, and grave upon it, like the engravings of a signet:* ***HOLINESS TO THE LORD.***

—Exodus 28:36

Holiness, without which no man shall see the Lord. —— God is a Spirit: and they that worship him must worship him in spirit and in truth. —— But we are all as an unclean thing, and all our righteousnesses are as filthy rags. —— Before all the people I will be glorified.

—Hebrews 12:14; John 4:24; Isaiah 64:6; Leviticus 10:3

This is the law of the house; Upon the top of the mountain the whole limit thereof round about shall be most holy. —— Holiness becometh thine house, O Lord, for ever.

—Ezekiel 43:12; Psalm 93:5

For their sakes I sanctify myself, that they also might be sanctified through the truth. —— Seeing...that we have a great high priest, that is passed into the heavens, Jesus the Son of God, let us...come boldly unto the throne of grace. that we may obtain mercy, and find grace to help in time of need.

—John 17:19; Hebrews 4:14, 16

Saturday: *He is before all things.* —Colossians 1:17

The Amen...the beginning of the creation of God. —— The beginning, the firstborn from the dead; that in all things he might have the preeminence.

—Revelations 3:14; Colossians 1:18

The Lord possessed me in the beginning of his way, before his works of old. I was set up from everlasting, from the beginning, or ever the earth was. ...When he prepared the heavens, I was there: when he set a compass upon the face of the depth: When he established the clouds above: when he strengthened the fountains of the deep; When he gave to the sea his decree, that the waters should not pass his commandment: when he appointed the foundations of the earth...I was daily his delight, rejoicing always before him. —— Yea, before the day was I am he.

—Proverbs 8:22–23, 27–30; Isaiah 43:13

The Lamb slain from the foundation of the world. —— The author and finisher of our faith; who for the joy that was set before him endured the cross, despising the shame, and is set down at the right hand of the throne of God.

—Revelations 13:8; Hebrews 12:2

WEEK 35 - OUR HEART'S TREASURE

S**unday**: *Jesus said unto him, Thou shalt love the Lord thy God with all thy heart, and with all thy soul, and with all thy mind.*

—Matthew 22:37

Love not the world, neither the things that are in the world. If any man love the world, the love of the Father is not in him. For all that is in the world, the lust of the flesh, and the lust of the eyes, and the pride of life, is not of the Father, but is of the world. And the world passeth away. —— No servant can serve two masters: for either he will hate the one, and love the other; or else he will hold to the one, and despise the other.

—1 John 2:15–17. Luke 16:13

That he would grant you, according to the riches of his glory, to be strengthened with might by his Spirit in the inner man; That Christ may dwell in your hearts by faith; that ye, being rooted and grounded in love, May be able to comprehend with all saints what is the breadth, and length, and depth, and height; And to know the love of Christ, which passeth knowledge, that ye might be filled with all the fulness of God.

—Ephesians 3:16–19

We walk by faith, not by sight...while we look not at the things which are seen, but at the things which are not seen: for the things which are seen are temporal; but the things which are not seen are eternal. —— An inheritance incorruptible, and undefiled, and that fadeth not away, reserved in heaven for you.

—2 Corinthians 5:7, 4:18; 1 Peter 1:4

. . .

M**onday**: *A man's life consisteth not in the abundance of the things which he possesseth.* —Luke 12:15

A little that a righteous man hath is better than the riches of many wicked. —— Better is little with the fear of the Lord than great treasure and trouble therewith. —— Godliness with contentment is great gain. ...Having food and raiment let us be therewith content. —— Give me neither poverty nor riches; feed me with food convenient for me: Lest I be full, and deny thee, and say, Who is the Lord? or lest I be poor, and steal, and take the name of my God in vain. —— Give us this day our daily bread.

—Psalm 37:16; Proverbs 15:16; 1 Timothy 6:6–8; Proverbs 30:8–9; Matthew 6:11

Take no thought for your life, what ye shall eat, or what ye shall drink; nor yet for your body, what ye shall put on. Is not the life more than meat, and the body than raiment? —— When I sent you without purse, and scrip, and shoes, lacked ye any thing? And they said, Nothing. —— Let your conversation be without covetousness; and be content with such things as ye have: for he hath said, I will never leave thee, nor forsake thee.

—Matthew 6:25; Luke 22:35; Hebrews 13:5

T**uesday**: *Whatsoever a man soweth, that shall he also reap.* —Galatians 6:7

They that plow iniquity, and sow wickedness, reap the same. —— They have sown the wind, and they shall reap the whirlwind. —— He that soweth to his flesh shall of the flesh reap corruption. —— And they that are Christ's have crucified the flesh with the affections and lusts.

—Job 4:8; Hosea 8:7; Galatians 6:8; 5:24

To him that soweth righteousness shall be a sure reward. —— He that soweth to the Spirit shall of the Spirit reap life everlasting. And let us not be weary in well doing: for in due season we shall reap, if we faint not. As we have therefore opportunity, let us do good unto all men, especially unto them who are of the household of faith.

—Proverbs 11:18; Galatians 6:8–10

There is that scattereth, and yet increaseth; and there is that withholdeth more than is meet, but it tendeth to poverty. ...The liberal soul shall be made fat: and he that watereth shall be watered also himself. —— Be kindly affectioned one to another with brotherly love; in honour preferring one another. —— He which soweth sparingly shall reap also sparingly; and he which soweth bountifully shall reap also bountifully. —Proverbs 11:24–25; Romans 12:10; 2 Corinthians 9:6

. . .

Wednesday: *One thing is needful.* —Luke 10:42

There be many that say, Who will shew us any good? Lord, lift thou up the light of thy countenance upon us. Thou hast put gladness in my heart, more than in the time that their corn and their wine increased.

—Psalm 4:6–7

As the hart panteth after the water brooks, so panteth my soul after thee, O God. My soul thirsteth for God, for the living God. —— O God, thou art my God; early will I seek thee: my soul thirsteth for thee, my flesh longeth for thee in a dry and thirsty land, where no water is.

—Psalm 42:1–2; 63:1

I am the bread of life: he that cometh to me shall never hunger; and he that believeth on me shall never thirst. ...Lord, evermore give us this bread. —— Mary... sat at Jesus' feet, and heard his word. —— One thing have I desired of the Lord, that will I seek after; that I may dwell in the house of the Lord all the days of my life, to behold the beauty of the Lord, and to enquire in his temple.

—John 6:35, 34; Luke 10:39; Psalm 27:4

Thursday: *My son, give me thine heart.* —Proverbs 23:26

Return unto the Lord with all your hearts, then put away the strange gods and Ashtaroth from among you, and prepare your hearts unto the Lord, and serve him only. —— Thy heart is not right in the sight of God. —— Because the carnal mind is enmity against God: for it is not subject to the law of God, neither indeed can be. So then they that are in the flesh cannot please God.

—1 Samuel 7:3; Acts 8:21; Romans 8:7–8

Little children, keep yourselves from idols. —— Come out from among them, and be ye separate. —— So the Lord alone did lead him, and there was no strange god with him. —— Ye shall walk after the Lord your God...and cleave unto him. —— Serve him with a perfect heart with a willing mind: for the Lord searcheth all hearts, and understandeth all the imaginations of the thoughts. ——

Man looketh on the outward appearance, but the Lord looketh on the heart. —— Keep thy heart with all diligence; for out of it are the issues of life. —— As the servants of Christ, doing the will of God from the heart; With good will doing service, as to the Lord, and not to men.

—1 John 5:21; 2 Corinthians 6:17; Deuteronomy 32:12; 13:4; 1 Chronicles 28:9; 1 Samuel 16:7; Proverbs 4:23; Ephesians 6:6–7

. . .

Friday: *Riches are not for ever; and doth the crown endure to every generation?* —Proverbs 27:24

Surely every man walketh in a vain shew: surely they are disquieted in vain: he heapeth up riches, and knoweth not who shall gather them. —— Set your affection on things above, not on things on the earth. —— Lay not up for yourselves treasures upon earth, where moth and rust doth corrupt, and where thieves break through and steal: But lay up for yourselves treasures in heaven. ... For where your treasure is, there will your heart be also. ...Ye cannot serve God and mammon. —Psalm 39:6; Colossians 3:2; Matthew 6:19–21, 24

They do it to obtain a corruptible crown; but we an incorruptible. —— We look not at the things which are seen, but at the things which are not seen. —— To him that soweth righteousness shall be a sure reward. —— There is laid up for me a crown of righteousness, which the Lord, the righteous judge, shall give me at that day: and not to me only, but unto all them also that love his appearing. —— A crown of glory that fadeth not away.

—1 Corinthians 9:25; 2 Corinthians 4:18; Proverbs 11:18; 2 Timothy 4:8; 1 Peter 5:4

Saturday: *The prize of the high calling of God in Christ Jesus.* —Philippians 3:14.

Thou shalt have treasure in heaven: ...come and follow me. —— I am...thy exceeding great reward. —— Well done, thou good and faithful servant: thou hast been faithful over a few things, I will make thee ruler over many things: enter thou into the joy of thy lord. —— They shall reign for ever and ever. —— Ye shall receive a crown of glory that fadeth not away. —— The crown of life. —— A crown of righteousness. —— An incorruptible [*crown*]. *—— For ye are dead, and your life is hid with Christ in God.*

—Matthew 19:21; Genesis 15:1; Matthew 25:21; Revelations 22:5; 1 Peter 5:4; James 1:12; 2 Timothy 4:8; 1 Corinthians 9:25; Colossians 3:3

Father, I will that they also, whom thou hast given me, be with me where I am; that they may behold my glory, which thou has given me. —— So shall we ever be with the Lord. —— For this cause we also, since the day we heard it, do not cease to pray for you...that ye might be filled with the knowledge of his will in all wisdom and spiritual understanding; That ye might walk worthy of the Lord...in the knowledge of God; Strengthened with all might, according to his glorious power, unto all patience...with joyfulness; Giving thanks unto the Father, which hath made us meet to be partakers of the inheritance of the saints in light.

—John 17:24; 1 Thessalonians 4:17; Colossians 1:9–12

WEEK 36 - TRUST GOD 2

S**unday**: *The floods lift up their waves.*

—Psalm 93:3

The Lord on high is mightier than the noise of many waters, yea, than the mighty waves of the sea. —— O Lord God of hosts, who is a strong Lord like unto thee? or to thy faithfulness round about thee? Thou rulest the raging of the sea: when the waves thereof arise, thou stillest them.

—Psalm 93:4; 89:8–9

Fear ye not me? saith the Lord: will ye not tremble at my presence, which have placed the sand for the bound of the sea by a perpetual decree, that it cannot pass it?

—Jeremiah 5:22

When thou passest through the waters, I will be with thee; and through the rivers, they shall not overflow thee.

—Isaiah 43:2

Peter...walked on the water, to go to Jesus. But when he saw the wind boisterous, he was afraid; and beginning to sink, he cried, saying, Lord, save me. And immediately Jesus stretched forth his hand, and caught him, and said unto him, O thou of little faith, wherefore didst thou doubt?

—Matthew 14:29–31

What time I am afraid, I will trust in thee.

—Psalm 56:3

. . .

Monday: *Call upon me in the day of trouble: I will deliver thee, and thou shalt glorify me.*

—Psalm 50:15

Why art thou cast down, O my soul? and why art thou disquieted within me? hope thou in God: for I shall yet praise him, who is the health of my countenance, and my God. —— Lord, thou hast heard the desire of the humble: thou wilt prepare their heart, thou wilt cause thine ear to hear. —— For thou, Lord, art good, and ready to forgive; and plenteous in mercy unto all them that call upon thee.

—Psalm 42:11; 10:17; 86:5

Jacob said unto his household...Let us arise, and go up to Bethel; and I will make there an altar unto God, who answered me in the day of my distress, and was with me in the way which I went. —— Bless the Lord, O my soul, and forget not all his benefits.

—Genesis 35:2–3; Psalm 103:2

I love the Lord, because he hath heard my voice and my supplications. Because he hath inclined his ear unto me, therefore will I call upon him as long as I live. The sorrows of death compassed me, and the pains of hell gat hold upon me: I found trouble and sorrow. Then called I on the name of the Lord.

—Psalm 116:1–4

Tuesday: *I will not fear what man shall do unto me.* —Hebrews 13:6.

Who shall separate us from the love of Christ? shall tribulation, or distress, or persecution, or famine, or nakedness, or peril, or sword?...Nay, in all these things we are more than conquerors through him that loved us.

—Romans 8:35–37

Be not afraid of them that kill the body, and after that have no more that they can do. But I will forewarn you whom ye shall fear: Fear him, which after he hath killed hath power to cast into hell; yea, I say unto you, Fear him.

—Luke 12:4–5

Blessed are they which are persecuted for righteousness' sake: for theirs is the kingdom of heaven. Blessed are ye, when men shall revile you, and persecute you, and shall say all manner of evil against you falsely, for my sake. Rejoice, and be exceeding glad: for great is your reward in heaven. —— None of these things move me, neither count I my life dear unto myself, so that I might finish my course with joy. —— I will speak of thy testimonies...before kings, and will not be ashamed.

—Matthew 5:10–12; Acts 20:24; Psalm 119:46

. . .

W**ednesday**: *Lead me to the rock that is higher than I.*
—Psalm 61:2

Be careful for nothing; but in every thing by prayer and supplication with thanksgiving let your requests be made known unto God. And the peace of God, which passeth all understanding, shall keep your hearts and minds through Christ Jesus.

—Philippians 4:6–7

When my spirit was overwhelmed within me, then thou knewest my path. —— He knoweth the way that I take: when he hath tried me, I shall come forth as gold. —— Lord, thou hast been our dwelling place in all generations. —— Thou hast been a strength to the poor, a strength to the needy in his distress, a refuge from the storm, a shadow from the heat.

—Psalm 142:3; Job 23:10; Psalm 90:1; Isaiah 25:4

Who is a rock save our God? —— They shall never perish, neither shall any man pluck them out of my hand. —— Uphold me according unto thy word, that I may live: and let me not be ashamed of my hope. —— Which hope we have as an anchor of the soul, both sure and stedfast, and which entereth into that within the veil.

—Psalm 18:31; John 10:28; Psalm 119:116; Hebrews 6:19

T**hursday**: *O God, my heart is fixed.* —Psalm 108:1

The Lord is my light and my salvation; whom shall I fear? the Lord is the strength of my life; of whom shall I be afraid?

—Psalm 27:1

Thou wilt keep him in perfect peace, whose mind is stayed on thee:

because he trusteth in thee. —— He shall not be afraid of evil tidings: his heart is fixed, trusting in the Lord. His heart is established, he shall not be afraid, until he see his desire upon his enemies.

—Isaiah 26:3; Psalm 112:7–8

What time I am afraid, I will trust in thee. —— In the time of trouble he shall hide me in his pavilion: in the secret of his tabernacle shall he hide me; he shall set me up upon a rock. And now shall mine head be lifted up above mine enemies round about me: therefore will I offer in his tabernacle sacrifices of joy; I will sing, yea, I will sing praises unto the Lord.

—Psalm 56:3; 27:5–6

The God of all grace, who hath called us unto his eternal glory by Christ Jesus, after that ye have suffered a while, make you perfect, stablish, strengthen, settle you. To him be glory and dominion for ever and ever. —1 Peter 5:10–11

. . .

Friday: *Whoso hearkeneth unto me shall dwell safely, and shall be quiet from fear of evil.*

—Proverbs 1:33.

Lord, thou hast been our dwelling place in all generations. —— He that dwelleth in the secret place of the most High shall abide under the shadow of the Almighty...His truth shall be thy shield and buckler.

—Psalm 90:1; 91:1, 4

Your life is hid with Christ in God. —— He that toucheth you toucheth the apple of his eye. —— Fear ye not, stand still, and see the salvation of the Lord. ... The Lord shall fight for you, and ye shall hold your peace. —— God is our refuge and strength, a very present help in trouble. Therefore will not we fear.

—Colossians 3:3; Zechariah 2:8; Exodus 14:13–14; Psalm 46:1–2

Jesus spake unto them, saying, Be of good cheer; it is I; be not afraid. —— Why are ye troubled? and why do thoughts arise in your hearts? Behold my hands and my feet, that it is I myself: handle me, and see; for a spirit hath not flesh and bones, as ye see me have. —— I know whom I have believed, and am persuaded that he is able to keep that which I have committed unto him against that day.

—Matthew 14:27; Luke 24:38–39; 2 Timothy 1:12

Saturday: *The Lord shall be thy confidence, and shall keep thy foot from being taken.*

—Proverbs 3:26

Surely the wrath of man shall praise thee: the remainder of wrath shalt thou restrain. —— The king's heart is in the hand of the Lord, as the rivers of water: he turneth it whithersoever he will. —— When a man's ways please the Lord, he maketh even his enemies to be at peace with him.

—Psalm 76:10; Proverbs 21:1; 16:7

I wait for the Lord, my soul doth wait, and in his word do I hope. My soul waiteth for the Lord more than they that watch for the morning: I say, more than they that watch for the morning. —— I sought the Lord, and he heard me, and delivered me from all my fears.

—Psalm 130:5–6; 34:4

The eternal God is thy refuge, and underneath are the everlasting arms: and he shall thrust out the enemy from before thee; and shall say, Destroy them. —— Blessed is the man that trusteth in the Lord, and whose hope the Lord is. —— What shall we then say to these things? If God be for us, who can be against us?

—Deuteronomy 33:27; Jeremiah 17:7; Romans 8:31

WEEK 37 - HUMILITY 2

S**unday**: *Let us not be desirous of vain glory.* —Galatians 5:26

Gideon said unto them, I would desire a request of you, that ye would give me every man the earrings of his prey. (For they had golden earrings, because they were Ishmaelites.) And they answered, We will willingly give them. And they spread a garment, and did cast therein every man the earrings of his prey. ...And Gideon made an ephod thereof, and put it in his city, even in Ophrah: and all Israel went thither a whoring after it: which thing became a snare unto Gideon, and to his house.

—Judges 8:24–25, 27

Seekest thou great things for thyself? seek them not. —— The sacrifices of God are a broken spirit: a broken and a contrite heart, O God, thou wilt not despise. —— Lest I should be exalted above measure through the abundance of the revelations, there was given to me a thorn in the flesh.

—Jeremiah 45:5; Psalm 51:17; 2 Corinthians 12:7

Let nothing be done through strife or vainglory; but in lowliness of mind let each esteem other better than themselves. —— Charity envieth not; charity vaunteth not itself, is not puffed up, Doth not behave itself unseemly, seeketh not her own.

—Philippians 2:3; 1 Corinthians 13:4–5

Take my yoke upon you, and learn of me.

—Matthew 11:29

. . .

Monday: *Mind not high things, but condescend to men of low estate.* —Romans 12:16

My brethren, have not the faith of our Lord Jesus Christ, the Lord of glory, with respect of persons. ...Hath not God chosen the poor of this world rich in faith, and heirs of the kingdom which he hath promised to them that love him?

—James 2:1,5; 1 Corinthians 10:24; 1 Timothy 6:8–9; 1 Corinthians 1:27–29; Psalm 131:1

Let no man seek his own, but every man another's wealth. —— Having food and raiment let us be therewith content. But they that will be rich fall into temptation and a snare, and into many foolish and hurtful lusts, which drown men in destruction and perdition.

—1 Corinthians 10:24; 1 Timothy 6:8–9

God hath chosen the foolish things of the world to confound the wise:

and God hath chosen the weak things of the world to confound the things which are mighty; And base things of the world, and things which are despised, hath God chosen, yea, and things which are not, to bring to nought things that are: That no flesh should glory in his presence.

—1 Corinthians 1:27–29

Lord, my heart is not haughty, nor mine eyes lofty.

—Psalm 131:1

Tuesday: *His mercy is on them that fear him.* —Luke 1:50

Oh how great is thy goodness, which thou hast laid up for them that fear thee; which thou hast wrought for them that trust in thee before the sons of men! Thou shalt hide them in the secret of thy presence from the pride of man: thou shalt keep them secretly in a pavilion from the strife of tongues.

—Psalm 31:19–20

If ye call on the Father, who without respect of persons judgeth according to every man's work, pass the time of your sojourning here in fear. —— The Lord is nigh unto all them that call upon him in truth. He will fulfill the desire of them that fear him: he also will hear their cry, and will save them.

—1 Peter 1:17; Psalm 145:18–19

Because thine heart was tender, and thou hast humbled thyself before the Lord...and hast rent thy clothes, and wept before me; I also have heard thee, saith the Lord. —— To this man will I look, even to him that is poor and of a contrite spirit, and trembleth at my word. —— The Lord is nigh unto them that are of a broken heart; and saveth such as be of a contrite spirit.

—2 Kings 22:19; Isaiah 66:2; Psalm 34:18

. . .

W**ednesday**: *Thy will be done.* —Matthew 26:42

O Lord, I know that the way of man is not in himself: it is not in man that walketh to direct his steps. —— Not as I will, but as thou wilt. —— Surely I have behaved and quieted myself, as a child that is weaned of his mother: my soul is even as a weaned child.

—Jeremiah 10:23; Matthew 26:39; Psalm 131:2

We know not what we should pray for as we ought: but the Spirit itself maketh intercession for us with groanings which cannot be uttered. And he that searcheth the hearts knoweth what is the mind of the Spirit, because he maketh intercession for the saints according to the will of God.

—Romans 8:26–27

Ye know not what ye ask. —— He gave them their request; but sent leanness into their soul. —— These things were our examples, to the intent we should not lust after evil things, as they also lusted.

—Matthew 20:22; Psalm 106:15; 1 Corinthians 10:6

I would have you without carefulness. —— Thou wilt keep him in perfect peace, whose mind is stayed on thee: because he trusteth in thee.

—1 Corinthians 7:32; Isaiah 26:3

T**hursday**: *The day shall declare it.* —1 Corinthians 3:13

Judge nothing before the time, until the Lord come, who both will bring to light the hidden things of darkness, and will make manifest the counsels of the hearts: and then shall every man have praise of God.

—1 Corinthians 4:5

Why dost thou judge thy brother? or why dost thou set at nought thy brother? for we shall all stand before the judgment seat of Christ. ...So then every one of us shall give account of himself to God. Let us not therefore judge one another any more.

—Romans 14:10, 12–13

God shall judge the secrets of men by Jesus Christ. —— The Father judgeth no man, but hath committed all judgment unto the Son...And hath given him authority to execute judgment also, because he is the Son of man.

—Romans 2:16; John 5:22, 27

The Great, the Mighty God, the Lord of hosts, is his name, Great in counsel, and mighty in work: for thine eyes are open upon all the ways of the sons of men: to give every one according to his ways, and according to the fruit of his doings.

—Jeremiah 32:18–19

. . .

Friday: *A bruised reed shall he not break.* —Matthew 12:20

The sacrifices of God are a broken spirit: a broken and a contrite heart, O God, thou wilt not despise. —— He healeth the broken in heart, and bindeth up their wounds. —— Thus saith the high and lofty One that inhabiteth eternity, whose name is Holy; I dwell in the high and holy place, with him also that is of a contrite and humble spirit, to revive the spirit of the humble, and to revive the heart of the contrite ones. For I will not contend for ever, neither will I be always wroth: for the spirit should fail before me, and the souls which I have made.

—Psalm 51:17, 147:3; Isaiah 57:15–16

I will seek that which was lost, and bring again that which was driven away, and will bind up that which was broken, and will strengthen that which was sick. —— Wherefore lift up the hands which hang down, and the feeble knees; And make straight paths for your feet, lest that which is lame be turned out of the way; but let it rather be healed. —— Behold, your God...will come and save you.

—Ezekiel 34:16; Hebrews 12:12–13; Isaiah 35:4

Saturday: *When ye shall have done all those things which are commanded you, say, We are unprofitable servants.* —Luke 17:10

Where is boasting then? It is excluded. By what law? of works? Nay: but by the law of faith. —— What hast thou that thou didst not receive? now if thou didst receive it, why dost thou glory, as if thou hadst not received it? —— By grace are ye saved through faith; and that not of yourselves: it is the gift of God: Not of works, lest any man should boast. For we are his workmanship, created in Christ Jesus unto good works, which God hath before ordained that we should walk in them.

—Romans 3:27; 1 Corinthians 4:7; Ephesians 2:8–10

By the grace of God I am what I am: and his grace which was bestowed upon me was not in vain; but I laboured more abundantly than they all: yet not I, but the grace of God which was with me. —— For of him, and through him, and to him, are all things. —— All things come of thee and of thine own have we given thee.

—1 Corinthians 15:10; Romans 11:36; 1 Chronicles 29:14

Enter not into judgment with thy servant: for in thy sight shall no man living be justified.

—Psalm 143:2

WEEK 38 - OUR FATHER

Sunday: *He said, Abba, Father.*

—Mark 14:36

Jesus...lifted up his eyes to heaven, and said, Father...Holy Father...O righteous Father. —— Because ye are sons, God hath sent forth the Spirit of his Son into your hearts, crying, Abba, Father. —— For through him we both have access by one Spirit unto the Father. Now therefore ye are no more strangers and foreigners, but fellowcitizens with the saints, and of the household of God.

—John 17:1, 11, 25; Galatians 4:6; Ephesians 2:18–19

Doubtless thou art our father...thou, O Lord, art our father, our redeemer; thy name is from everlasting. —— The Lord is very pitiful, and of tender mercy. —— The Lord is merciful and gracious, slow to anger, and plenteous in mercy. —— And when he came to himself, he said, How many hired servants of my father's have bread enough and to spare, and I perish with hunger!...And he arose, and came to his father. But when he was yet a great way off, his father saw him, and had compassion, and ran, and fell on his neck, and kissed him. ...But the father said to his servants, Bring forth the best robe, and put it on him; and put a ring on his hand, and shoes on his feet: And bring hither the fatted calf, and kill it; and let us eat, and be merry: For this my son was dead, and is alive again; he was lost, and is found. And they began to be merry.

—Isaiah 63:16; James 5:11; Psalm 103:8; Luke 15:17, 20, 22–24

But God, who is rich in mercy, for his great love wherewith he loved us.

—Ephesians 2:4

. . .

Monday: *My Father is greater than I.*
—John 14:28

When ye pray, say, Our Father which art in heaven. —— My Father, and your Father...my God and your God. —— As the Father gave me commandment, even so I do. —— The words that I speak unto you I speak not of myself: but the Father that dwelleth in me, he doeth the works.

—Luke 11:2; John 20:17; 14:31; 14:10

The Father loveth the Son, and hath given all things into his hand.

—John 3:35

Lord, show us the Father, and it sufficeth us. Jesus saith unto him, Have I been so long time with you, and yet hast thou not known me, Philip? he that hath seen me hath seen the Father; and how sayest thou then, Show us the Father? Believest thou not that I am in the Father, and the Father in me? —— I and my Father are one. —— As the Father hath loved me, so have I loved you: continue ye in my love. If ye keep my commandments, ye shall abide in my love; even as I have kept my Father's commandments, and abide in his love.

—John 14:8–10; 10:30; 15:9–10

Tuesday: *Thou shalt make them drink of the river of thy pleasures. For with thee is the fountain of life: in thy light shall we see light.*

—Psalm 36:8–9

If thou knewest the gift of God, and who it is that saith unto thee, Give me to drink; thou wouldest have asked of him, and he would have given thee living water. —— If any man thirst, let him come unto me and drink. ...(This spake he of the Spirit, which they that believe on him should receive.) —— Because ye are sons, God hath sent forth the Spirit of his Son into your hearts, crying, Abba, Father. —— Ye have not received the spirit of bondage again to fear; but ye have received the Spirit of adoption, whereby we cry, Abba, Father.

—John 4:10,7:37,39. Galatians 4:6; Romans 8:15

Prove me now herewith, saith the Lord of hosts, if I will not open you the windows of heaven, and pour you out a blessing, that there shall not be room enough to receive it. —— If ye...being evil, know how to give good gifts unto your children: how much more shall your heavenly Father give the Holy Spirit to them that ask him? —— Ask, and it shall be given you; seek, and ye shall find.

—Malachi 3:10; Luke 11:13; 9

. . .

Wednesday: *If children, then heirs; heirs of God, and joint-heirs with Christ.*

—Romans 8:17

If ye be Christ's, then are ye Abraham's seed, and heirs according to the promise.

—Galatians 3:29

Behold, what manner of love the Father hath bestowed upon us, that we should be called the sons of God. —— Thou art no more a servant, but a son; and if a son, then an heir of God through Christ. —— Having predestinated us unto the adoption of children by Jesus Christ to himself, according to the good pleasure of his will.

—1 John 3:1; Galatians 4:7; Ephesians 1:5

Jesus saith unto him, I am the way, the truth, and the life: no man cometh unto the Father, but by me. If ye had known me, ye should have known my Father also: and from henceforth ye know him, and have seen him. —— I and my Father are one. —— Be ye therefore followers of God, as dear children.

—John 14:6–7; 10:30; Ephesians 5:1

Thursday: *The whole family in heaven and earth.* —Ephesians 3:15

One God and Father of all, who is above all, and through all, and in you all. —— Ye are all the children of God by faith in Christ Jesus. —— That in the dispensation of the fulness of times he might gather together in one all things in Christ, both which are in heaven, and which are on earth; even in him.

—Ephesians 4:6; Galatians 3:26; Ephesians 1:10

He is not ashamed to call them brethren. —— Behold my mother and my brethren! ...Whosoever shall do the will of my Father which is in heaven, the same is my brother, and sister, and mother. —— Go to my brethren, and say unto them, I ascend unto my Father, and your Father.

— Hebrews 2:11; Matthew 12:49–50; John 20:17

I saw under the altar the souls of them that were slain for the word of God, and for the testimony which they held...And white robes were given unto every one of them; and it was said unto them, that they should rest yet for a little season, until their fellowservants also and their brethren, that should be killed as they were, should be fulfilled. —— That they without us should not be made perfect.

—Revelations 6:9–11; Hebrews 11:40

. . .

Friday: *The Lord delighteth in thee.* —Isaiah 62:4

Thus saith the Lord that created thee...Fear not: for I have redeemed thee, I have called thee by thy name; thou art mine. —— Can a woman forget her sucking child, that she should not have compassion on the son of her womb? yea, they may forget, yet will I not forget thee. Behold, I have graven thee upon the palms of mine hands; thy walls are continually before me.

—Isaiah 43:1; 49:15–16

The steps of a good man are ordered by the Lord: and he delighteth in his way. —— My delights were with the sons of men. —— The Lord taketh pleasure in them that fear him, in those that hope in his mercy. —— They shall be mine, saith the Lord of hosts, in that day when I make up my jewels; and I will spare them, as a man spareth his own son that serveth him.

—Psalm 37:23; Proverbs 8:31; Psalm 147:11; Malachi 3:17

Jesus answered and said unto him, If a man love me, he will keep my words: and my Father will love him, and we will come unto him, and make our abode with him. —— This is my commandment, That ye love one another, as I have loved you.

—John 14:23; 15:12

Be ye therefore merciful, as your Father also is merciful.

—Luke 6:36

Saturday: Jesus' Gethsemane Prayer To Our Father:

These words spake Jesus, and lifted up his eyes to heaven, and said, Father, the hour is come; glorify thy Son, that thy Son also may glorify thee: 2 As thou hast given him power over all flesh, that he should give eternal life to as many as thou hast given him. 3 And this is life eternal, that they might know thee the only true God, and Jesus Christ, whom thou hast sent.

4 I have glorified thee on the earth: I have finished the work which thou gavest me to do. 5 And now, O Father, glorify thou me with thine own self with the glory which I had with thee before the world was. 6 I have manifested thy name unto the men which thou gavest me out of the world: thine they were, and thou gavest them me; and they have kept thy word.

7 Now they have known that all things whatsoever thou hast given me are of thee. 8 For I have given unto them the words which thou gavest me; and they have received them, and have known surely that I came out from thee, and they have believed that thou didst send me. 9 I pray for them: I pray not for the world, but for them which thou hast given me; for they are thine. 10 And all mine are thine, and thine are mine; and I am glorified in them.

11 And now I am no more in the world, but these are in the world, and I come to thee. Holy Father, keep through thine own name those whom thou hast given me, that they may be one, as we are. 12 While I was with them in the world, I kept them in thy name: those that thou gavest me I have kept, and none of them is lost, but the son of perdition; that the scripture might be fulfilled. 13 And now come I to thee; and these things I speak in the world, that they might have my joy fulfilled in themselves.

14 I have given them thy word; and the world hath hated them, because they are not of the world, even as I am not of the world. 15 I pray not that thou shouldest take them out of the world, but that thou shouldest keep them from the evil. 16 They are not of the world, even as I am not of the world.

17 Sanctify them through thy truth: thy word is truth. 18 As thou hast sent me into the world, even so have I also sent them into the world. 19 And for their sakes I sanctify myself, that they also might be sanctified through the truth. 20 Neither pray I for these alone, but for them also which shall believe on me through their word; 21 That they all may be one; as thou, Father, art in me, and I in thee, that they also may be one in us: that the world may believe that thou hast sent me. 22 And the glory which thou gavest me I have given them; that they may be one, even as we are one: 23 I in them, and thou in me, that they may be made perfect in one; and that the world may know that thou hast sent me, and hast loved them, as thou hast loved me.

24 Father, I will that they also, whom thou hast given me, be with me where I am; that they may behold my glory, which thou hast given me: for thou lovedst me before the foundation of the world. 25 O righteous Father, the world hath not known thee: but I have known thee, and these have known that thou hast sent me.

26 And I have declared unto them thy name, and will declare it: that the love wherewith thou hast loved me may be in them, and I in them.

—John 17:1–26

WEEK 39 - FREE TO SERVE

Sunday: *Ye are dead, and your life is hid with Christ in God. ... Whatsoever ye do, do it heartily, as to the Lord.* —Colossians 3:3, 23

How shall we, that are dead to sin, live any longer therein?...In that he died, he died unto sin once: but in that he liveth, he liveth unto God. ...Being then made free from sin, ye became the servants of righteousness. —— He died for all, that they which live should not henceforth live unto themselves, but unto him which died for them, and rose again.

—Romans 6:2, 10, 18; 2 Corinthians 5:15

Ye cannot serve God and mammon. —— When ye were the servants of sin, ye were free from righteousness. What fruit had ye then in those things whereof ye are now ashamed? for the end of those things is death. But now being made free from sin, and become servants to God, ye have your fruit unto holiness, and the end everlasting life.

—Matthew 6:24; Romans 6:20–22

If any man serve me, let him follow me; and where I am, there shall also my servant be: if any man serve me, him will my Father honour. —— Take my yoke upon you, and learn of me: for I am meek and lowly in heart: and ye shall find rest unto your souls. For my yoke is easy, and my burden is light. —— If any man be in Christ, he is a new creature: old things are passed away; behold, all things are become new.

—John 12:26; Matthew 11:29–30; 2 Corinthians 5:17

. . .

M**onday**: *Fruitful in every good work, and increasing in the knowledge of God.* —Colossians 1:10

I beseech you...brethren, by the mercies of God, that ye present your bodies a living sacrifice, holy, acceptable unto God, which is your reasonable service. And be not conformed to this world: but be ye transformed by the renewing of your mind, that ye may prove what is that good, and acceptable, and perfect, will of God. —— As ye have yielded your members servants to uncleanness and to iniquity unto iniquity; even so now yield your members servants to righteousness unto holiness.

—Romans 12:1–2; 6:19

The night cometh, when no man can work. —— Whatsoever thy hand findeth to do, do it with thy might; for there is no work, nor device, nor knowledge, nor wisdom, in the grave, whither thou goest. —— The dead praise not the Lord, neither any that go down into silence.

—John 9:4; Ecclesiastes 9:10; Psalm 115:17

Herein is my Father glorified, that ye bear much fruit; so shall ye be my disciples. ...I have chosen you, and ordained you, that ye should go and bring forth fruit, and that your fruit should remain: that whatsoever ye shall ask of the Father in my name, he may give it you.

—John 15:8, 16

T**uesday**: *Son, go work today in my vineyard.* —Matthew 21:28

Thou are no more a servant, but a son; and if a son, then an heir of God through Christ.

—Galatians 4:7

Reckon ye...yourselves to be dead indeed unto sin, but alive unto God through Jesus Christ our Lord. Let not sin therefore reign in your mortal body, that ye should obey it in the lusts thereof. Neither yield ye your members as instruments of unrighteousness unto sin: but yield yourselves unto God, as those that are alive from the dead, and your members as instruments of righteousness unto God. —— As obedient children, not fashioning yourselves according to the former lusts in your ignorance: But as he which hath called you is holy, so be ye holy in all manner of conversation; Because it is written, Be ye holy; for I am holy. —— Sanctified, and meet for the master's use, and prepared unto every good work.

—Romans 6:11–13; 1 Peter 1:14–16; 2 Timothy 2:21

Therefore, my beloved brethren, be ye stedfast, unmoveable, always abounding in the work of the Lord, forasmuch as ye know that your labour is not in vain in the Lord. —1 Corinthians 15:58

. . .

W**ednesday**: *If any man will come after me, let him deny himself, and take up his cross daily, and follow me.* —Luke 9:23

Know ye not that the friendship of the world is enmity with God? whosoever therefore will be a friend of the world is the enemy of God. —— If one died for all, then were all dead: And that he died for all, that they which live should not henceforth live unto themselves, but unto him which died for them, and rose again.

—James 4:4; 2 Corinthians 5:14–15

God forbid that I should glory, save in the cross of our Lord Jesus Christ, by whom the world is crucified unto me, and I unto the world. —— I am crucified with Christ. —— They that are Christ's have crucified the flesh with the affections and lusts.

—Galatians 6:14; 2:20; 5:24

Forasmuch...as Christ hath suffered for us in the flesh, arm yourselves likewise with the same mind: for he that hath suffered in the flesh hath ceased from sin; That he no longer should live the rest of his time in the flesh to the lusts of men, but to the will of God.

—1 Peter 4:1–2

T**hursday**: *Seekest thou great things for thyself? seek them not.*
—Jeremiah 45:5

Take my yoke upon you, and learn of me; for I am meek and lowly in heart: and ye shall find rest unto your souls. —— Let this mind be in you, which was also in Christ Jesus: Who, being in the form of God, thought it not robbery to be equal with God: But made himself of no reputation, and took upon him the form of a servant, and was made in the likeness of men: And being found in fashion as a man, he humbled himself, and became obedient unto death, even the death of the cross.

—Matthew 11:29; Philippians 2:5–8

He that taketh not his cross, and followeth after me, is not worthy of me. —— Christ...suffered for us, leaving us an example, that ye should follow his steps.

—Matthew 10:38; 1 Peter 2:21

Godliness with contentment is great gain. For we brought nothing into this world, and it is certain we can carry nothing out. And having food and raiment let us be therewith content. —— I have learned, in whatsoever state I am, therewith to be content.

—1 Timothy 6:6–8; Philippians 4:11

. . .

F**riday**: *Thou renderest to every man according to his work.*
—Psalm 62:12

Other foundation can no man lay than that is laid, which is Jesus Christ. ...If any man's work abide which he hath built thereupon, he shall receive a reward. If any man's work shall be burned, he shall suffer loss: but he himself shall be saved; yet so as by fire. —— We must all appear before the judgment seat of Christ; that every one may receive the things done in his body, according to that he hath done, whether it be good or bad.

—1 Corinthians 3:11, 14–15; 2 Corinthians 5:10

They...first gave their own selves to the Lord. —— In every work that he [Hezekiah] began...to seek his God, he did it with all his heart, and prospered.

—2 Corinthians 8:5; 2 Chronicles 31:21

When thou doest alms, let not thy left hand know what thy right hand doeth: That thine alms may be in secret: and thy Father which seeth in secret himself shall reward thee openly. —— After a long time the lord of those servants cometh, and reckoneth with them. —— Not that we are sufficient of ourselves to think any thing as of ourselves; but our sufficiency is of God. —— Lord, thou wilt ordain peace for us: for thou also hast wrought all our works in us.

—Matthew 6:3–4; 25:19; 2 Corinthians 3:5; Isaiah 26:12

S**aturday**: *Christ...suffered for us, leaving us an example, that ye should follow his steps.* —1 Peter 2:21

Even the Son of man came not to be ministered unto, but to minister. —— Whosoever of you will be the chiefest, shall be servant of all.

—Mark 10:45; 10:44

Jesus of Nazareth...went about doing good. —— Bear ye one another's burdens, and so fulfill the law of Christ. —— The meekness and gentleness of Christ. —— In lowliness of mind let each esteem other better than themselves.

—Acts 10:38; Galatians 6:2; 2 Corinthians 10:1; Philippians 2:3

Father, forgive them; for they know not what they do. —— Be ye kind one to another, tenderhearted, forgiving one another, even as God for Christ's sake hath forgiven you. —— He that saith he abideth in him ought himself also so to walk, even as he walked. —— Looking unto Jesus the author and finisher of our faith; who for the joy that was set before him endured the cross, despising the shame, and is set down at the right hand of the throne of God.

—Luke 23:34; Ephesians 4:32—1 John 2:6; Hebrews 12:2

WEEK 40 - SPIRITUAL SITE

S**unday**: *Open thou mine eyes, that I may behold wondrous things out of thy law.*—Psalm 119:18

Then opened he their understanding, that they might understand the scriptures. —— It is given unto you to know the mysteries of the kingdom of heaven, but to them it is not given. —— I thank thee, O Father, Lord of heaven and earth, because thou hast hid these things from the wise and prudent, and hast revealed them unto babes. Even so, Father: for so it seemed good in thy sight. —— While we look not at the things which are seen, but at the things which are not seen: for the things which are seen are temporal; but the things which are not seen are eternal.

—Luke 24:45; Matthew 13:11; 11:25–26; 2 Corinthians 4:18

We have received, not the spirit of the world, but the spirit which is of God; that we might know the things that are freely given to us of God. —— O the depth of the riches both of the wisdom and knowledge of God! how unsearchable are his judgments, and his ways past finding out! For who hath known the mind of the Lord? or who hath been his counsellor?...For of him, and through him, and to him, are all things: to whom be glory for ever. Amen.

—1 Corinthians 2:12; Romans 11:33–36

Keep yourselves in the love of God, looking for the mercy of our Lord Jesus Christ unto eternal life.

—Jude 1:21

. . .

Monday: *The eyes of all wait upon thee.* —Psalm 145:15

He giveth to all life, and breath, and all things. —— The Lord is good to all: and his tender mercies are over all his works. —— Behold the fowls of the air: for they sow not, neither do they reap, nor gather into barns; yet your heavenly Father feedeth them. —— The same Lord over all is rich unto all that call upon him. —— I will lift up mine eyes unto the hills, from whence cometh my help. —— Behold, as the eyes of servants look unto the hand of their masters, and as the eyes of a maiden unto the hand of her mistress; so our eyes wait upon the Lord our God.

—Acts 17:25; Psalm 145:9; Matthew 6:26; Romans 10:12; Psalm 121:1; 123:2

The Lord is a God of judgment: blessed are all they that wait for him. —— And it shall be said in that day, Lo, this is our God; we have waited for him, and he will save us: this is the Lord; we have waited for him, we will be glad and rejoice in his salvation. —— If we hope for that we see not, then do we with patience wait for it.

—Isaiah 30:18; 25:9; Romans 8:25

Tuesday: *The light of the body is the eye: therefore when thine eye is single, thy whole body also is full of light.* —Luke 11:34

The natural man receiveth not the things of the Spirit of God: for they are foolishness unto him: neither can he know them, because they are spiritually discerned. —— O foolish people, and without understanding; which have eyes, and see not; which have ears, and hear not. —— Open thou mine eyes, that I may behold wondrous things out of thy law.

—1 Corinthians 2:14; Jeremiah 5:21; Psalm 119:18

I am the light of the world: he that followeth me shall not walk in darkness, but shall have the light of life. —— We all, with open face beholding as in a glass the glory of the Lord, are changed into the same image...even as by the Spirit of the Lord. —— God, who commanded the light to shine out of darkness, hath shined in our hearts, to give the light of the knowledge of the glory of God in the face of Jesus Christ.

—John 8:12; 2 Corinthians 3:18; 4:6

The God of our Lord Jesus Christ, the Father of glory, give unto you the spirit of wisdom and revelation in the knowledge of him...that ye may know what is the hope of his calling, and what the riches of the glory of his inheritance in the saints.

—Ephesians 1:17–18

. . .

W**ednesday**: *When he shall appear, we shall be like him; for we shall see him as he is.* —1 John 3:2

As many as received him, to them gave he power to become the sons of God, even to them that believe on his name. —— Whereby are given unto us exceeding great and precious promises: that by these ye might be partakers of the divine nature, having escaped the corruption that is in the world through lust. —— Since the beginning of the world men have not heard, nor perceived by the ear, neither hath the eye seen, O God, beside thee, what he hath prepared for him that waiteth for him.

—John 1:12; 2 Peter 1:4; Isaiah 64:4

Now we see through a glass, darkly; but then face to face: now I know in part; but then shall I know even as also I am known. —— Christ...shall change our vile body, that it may be fashioned like unto his glorious body, according to the working whereby he is able even to subdue all things unto himself. —— As for me, I will behold thy face in righteousness: I shall be satisfied, when I awake, with thy likeness.

—1 Corinthians 13:12; Philippians 3:20–21; Psalm 17:15

T**hursday**: *See...that ye walk circumspectly, not as fools, but as wise, Redeeming the time, because the days are evil.* —Ephesians 5:15–16

Take diligent heed to do the commandment and the law...to love the Lord your God, and to walk in all his ways, and to keep his commandments, and to cleave unto him, and to serve him with all your heart and with all your soul. —— Walk in wisdom toward them that are without, redeeming the time. Let your speech be always with grace, seasoned with salt, that ye may know how ye ought to answer every man. —— Abstain from all appearance of evil. —— Looking diligently lest any man fail of the grace of God; lest any root of bitterness springing up trouble you, and thereby many be defiled.

—Joshua 22:5; Colossians 4:5–6; 1 Thessalonians 5:22; Hebrews 12:15

While the bridegroom tarried, they all slumbered and slept. And at midnight there was a cry made, Behold, the bridegroom cometh; go ye out to meet him. ... Watch, therefore, for ye know neither the day nor the hour wherein the Son of man cometh.

—Matthew 25:5–6, 13

Brethren, give diligence to make your calling and election sure: for if ye do these things, ye shall never fall. —— Blessed are those servants, whom the lord when he cometh shall find watching.

—2 Peter 1:10; Luke 12:37

. . .

Friday: *We would see Jesus.* —John 12:21

O Lord, have we waited for thee; the desire of our soul is to thy name, and to the remembrance of thee. —— Looking unto Jesus the author and finisher of our faith. —— The Lord is nigh unto all them that call upon him, to all that call upon him in truth. —— Where two or three are gathered together in my name, there am I in the midst of them. —— I will not leave you comfortless: I will come to you. —— Lo, I am with you always, even unto the end of the world.

—Isaiah 26:8; Hebrews 12:2; Psalm 145:18; Matthew 18:20; John 14:18; Matthew 28:20

Now we see through a glass, darkly; but then face to face. —— Nevertheless we, according to his promise, look for new heavens and a new earth, wherein dwelleth righteousness. Wherefore, beloved, seeing that ye look for such things, be diligent that ye may be found of him in peace, without spot, and blameless. —— Let us run with patience the race that is set before us.

—1 Corinthians 13:12; 2 Peter 3:13–14; Hebrews 12:1

Beloved, now are we the sons of God, and it doth not yet appear what we shall be: but we know that, when he shall appear, we shall be like him; for we shall see him as he is. And every man that hath this hope in him purifieth himself, even as he is pure. —— Little children, abide in him.

—1 John 3:2–3; 2:28

Saturday: *What wilt thou that I shall do unto thee...*

Lord, that I may receive my sight.—Luke 18:41

Open thou mine eyes, that I may behold wondrous things out of thy law.

—Psalm 119:18

Then opened he their understanding, that they might understand the scriptures. —— The Comforter, which is the Holy Ghost, whom the Father will send in my name...shall teach you all things. —— Every good gift and every perfect gift is from above, and cometh down from the Father of lights.

—Luke 24:45; John 14:26; James 1:17

The God of our Lord Jesus Christ, the Father of glory...give unto you the spirit of wisdom and revelation in the knowledge of him: The eyes of your understanding being enlightened; that ye may know what is the hope of his calling, and what the riches of the glory of his inheritance in the saints, And what is the exceeding greatness of his power to us-ward who believe, according to the working of his mighty power.

—Ephesians 1:17–19

WEEK 41 - GOD'S GUIDANCE

S**unday**: *Teach me thy way, O Lord.*

—Psalm 27:11

I will instruct thee and teach thee in the way which thou shalt go: I will guide thee with mine eye. —— Good and upright is the Lord: therefore will he teach sinners in the way. The meek will he guide in judgment: and the meek will he teach his way.

—Psalm 32:8; 25:8–9

I am the door: by me if any man enter in, he shall be saved, and shall go in and out, and find pasture.

—John 10:9

Jesus saith unto him, I am the way, the truth, and the life: no man cometh unto the Father, but by me. —— Having...boldness to enter into the holiest by the blood of Jesus, By a new and living way, which he hath consecrated for us, through the veil, that is to say, his flesh; And having an high priest over the house of God; Let us draw near with a true heart in full assurance of faith.

—John 14:6; Hebrews 10:19–22

Then shall we know, if we follow on to know the Lord. —— All the paths of the Lord are mercy and truth unto such as keep his covenant and his testimonies.

—Hosea 6:3; Psalm 25:10

. . .

Monday: *This God is our God for ever and ever: he will be our guide even unto death.* —Psalm 48:14

O Lord, thou art my God; I will exalt thee, I will praise thy name; for thou hast done wonderful things; thy counsels of old are faithfulness and truth. —— The Lord is the portion of mine inheritance, and of my cup. ...Thou wilt shew me the path of life: in thy presence is fulness of joy; at thy right hand there are pleasures for evermore.

—Isaiah 25:1; Psalm 16:5, 11

Thou hast holden me by my right hand. Thou shalt guide me with thy counsel, and afterward receive me to glory. Whom have I in heaven but thee? and there is none upon earth that I desire beside thee. My flesh and my heart faileth: but God is the strength of my heart, and my portion for ever. —— I am the vine, ye are the branches: He that abideth in me, and I in him, the same bringeth forth much fruit: for without me ye can do nothing. —— Our heart shall rejoice in him, because we have trusted in his holy name. —— The Lord will perfect that which concerneth me: thy mercy. —— For in him we live, and move, and have our being...For we are also his offspring.

—Psalm 73:23–26; John 15:5; Psalm 33:21; 138:8; Acts 17:28

Tuesday: *The meek will he teach his way.* —Psalm 25:9

Blessed are the meek. —— For thus saith the high and lofty One that inhabiteth eternity, whose name is Holy; I dwell in the high and holy place, with him also that is of a contrite and humble spirit.

—Matthew 5:5; Isaiah 57:15

A man's heart deviseth his way: but the Lord directeth his steps. —— This I say then, Walk in the Spirit, and ye shall not fulfill the lust of the flesh. For the flesh lusteth against the Spirit, and the Spirit against the flesh: and these are contrary the one to the other. —— When he, the Spirit of truth, is come, he will guide you into all truth.

—Proverbs 16:9; Galatians 5:16–17; John 16:13

Unto thee lift I up mine eyes, O thou that dwellest in the heavens. Behold, as the eyes of servants look unto the hand of their masters, and as the eyes of a maiden unto the hand of her mistress; so our eyes wait upon the Lord our God. —— Cause me to know the way wherein I should walk; for I lift up my soul unto thee. —— If any of you lack wisdom, let him ask of God, that giveth to all men liberally, and upbraideth not; and it shall be given him.

—Psalm 123:1–2; 143:8; James 1:5

. . .

W**ednesday**: *He led them forth by the right way.* —Psalm 107:7

He found [Jacob] in a desert land, and in the waste howling wilderness; he led him about, he instructed him, he kept him as the apple of his eye. As an eagle stirreth up her nest, fluttereth over her young, spreadeth abroad her wings, taketh them, beareth them on her wings: So the Lord alone did lead him. —— Even to your old age I am he; and even to hoar hairs will I carry you: I have made, and I will bear; even I will carry, and will deliver you. —— He restoreth my soul: he leadeth me in the paths of righteousness for his name's sake. Yea, though I walk through the valley of the shadow of death, I will fear no evil: for thou art with me; thy rod and thy staff they comfort me.

—Deuteronomy 32:10–12; Isaiah 46:4; Psalm 23:3–4

The Lord shall guide thee continually, and satisfy thy soul in drought, and make fat thy bones: and thou shalt be like a watered garden, and like a spring of water, whose waters fail not. —— For this God is our God for ever and ever: he will be our guide even unto death. —— Who teacheth like him?

—Isaiah 58:11; Psalm 48:14; Job 36:22

T**hursday**: *What man is he that feareth the Lord?*

Him shall he teach in the way that he shall choose. —Psalm 25:12

The light of the body is the eye: if therefore thine eye be single, thy whole body shall be full of light. —— Thy word is a lamp unto my feet, and a light unto my path. —— Thine ears shall hear a word behind thee, saying, This is the way, walk ye in it, when ye turn to the right hand, and when ye turn to the left. —— I will instruct thee and teach thee in the way which thou shalt go: I will guide thee with mine eye. Be ye not as the horse, or as the mule, which have no understanding: whose mouth must be held in with bit and bridle, lest they come near unto thee. ... He that trusteth in the Lord, mercy shall compass him about. Be glad in the Lord, and rejoice, ye righteous: and shout for joy, all ye that are upright in heart.

—Matthew 6:22; Psalm 119:105; Isaiah 30:21; Psalm 32:8–11

O Lord, I know that the way of man is not in himself: it is not in man that walketh to direct his steps. —— Make me to go in the path of thy commandments; for therein do I delight. Incline my heart unto thy testimonies, and not to covetousness. Turn away mine eyes from beholding vanity; and quicken thou me in thy way. ...Through thy precepts I get understanding: therefore I hate every false way.

—Jeremiah 10:23; Psalm 119:35–37, 104

. . .

Friday: *Lead me in thy truth, and teach me.*
—Psalm 25:5

When he, the Spirit of truth, is come, he will guide you into all truth. —— Ye have an unction from the Holy One, and ye know all things.

—John 16:13; 1 John 2:20

To the law and to the testimony: if they speak not according to this word, it is because there is no light in them. —— All scripture is given by inspiration of God, and is profitable for doctrine, for reproof, for correction, for instruction in righteousness: That the man of God may be perfect, thoroughly furnished unto all good works. —— The holy Scriptures...are able to make thee wise unto salvation through faith which is in Christ Jesus.

—Isaiah 8:20; 2 Timothy 3:16–17; 3:15

I will instruct thee and teach thee in the way which thou shalt go: I will guide thee with mine eye. —— If any man will do his will, he shall know of the doctrine, whether it be of God. —— As ye have therefore received Christ Jesus the Lord, so walk ye in him: Rooted and built up in him, and stablished in the faith, as ye have been taught, abounding therein with thanksgiving.

—Psalm 32:8; John 7:17; Col 2:6–7

Saturday: *He led them on safely.*
—Psalm 78:53

I lead in the way of righteousness, in the midst of the paths of judgment.

—Proverbs 8:20

Behold, I send an Angel before thee, to keep thee in the way, and to bring thee into the place which I have prepared. —— In all their affliction he was afflicted, and the angel of his presence saved them: in his love and in his pity he redeemed them; and he bare them, and carried them all the days of old.

—Exodus 23:20; Isaiah 63:9

They got not the land in possession by their own sword, neither did their own arm save them: but thy right hand, and thine arm, and the light of thy countenance, because thou hadst a favour unto them. —— So didst thou lead thy people, to make thyself a glorious name. ——

Lead me, O Lord, in thy righteousness because of mine enemies; make thy way straight before my face. —— O send out thy light and thy truth: let them lead me; let them bring me unto thy holy hill, and to thy tabernacles. Then will I go unto the altar of God, unto God my exceeding joy: yea, upon the harp will I praise thee, O God my God.

—Psalm 44:3; Isaiah 63:14; Psalm 5:8; 43:3–4

WEEK 42 - JESUS' 2ND COMING

S**unday**: *He hath prepared for them a city.* —Hebrews 11:16

If I go and prepare a place for you, I will come again, and receive you unto myself; that where I am, there ye may be also. —— An inheritance incorruptible, and undefiled, and that fadeth not away, reserved in heaven for you. —— Here have we no continuing city, but we seek one to come. —— As it is written, Eye hath not seen, nor ear heard, neither have entered into the heart of man, the things which God hath prepared for them that love him. But God hath revealed them unto us by his Spirit.

—John 14:3; 1 Peter 1:4; Hebrews 13:14; 1 Corinthians 2:9–10

This same Jesus, which is taken up from you into heaven, shall so come in like manner as ye have seen him go into heaven. —— Behold, he cometh with clouds; and every eye shall see him, and they also which pierced him: and all kindreds of the earth shall wail because of him. Even so, Amen.

—Acts 1:11; Revelations 1:7

Be patient therefore, brethren, unto the coming of the Lord. Behold, the husbandman waiteth for the precious fruit of the earth, and hath long patience for it, until he receive the early and latter rain. Be ye also patient; stablish your hearts: for the coming of the Lord draweth nigh. —— Yet a little while, and he that shall come will come, and will not tarry. —— We which are alive and remain shall be caught up together with them in the clouds, to meet the Lord in the air: and so shall we ever be with the Lord. Wherefore comfort one another with these words.

—James 5:7–8; Hebrews 10:37; 1 Thessalonians 4:17–18

. . .

Monday: *When the Son of man cometh, shall he find faith on the earth?*

—Luke 18:8

He came unto his own, and his own received him not. —— The Spirit speaketh expressly, that in the latter times some shall depart from the faith.

—John 1:11; 1 Timothy 4:1

Preach the word; be instant in season, out of season; reprove, rebuke, exhort with all long suffering and doctrine. For the time will come when they will not endure sound doctrine; but after their own lusts shall they heap to themselves teachers, having itching ears; And they shall turn away their ears from the truth and shall be turned unto fables.

—2 Timothy 4:2–4

Of that day and that hour knoweth no man, no, not the angels which are in heaven, neither the Son, but the Father. Take ye heed, watch and pray: for ye know not when the time is. —— Blessed are those servants, whom the lord when he cometh shall find watching. —— Looking for that blessed hope...the glorious appearing of the great God and our Saviour Jesus Christ,

—Mark 13:32–33; Luke 12:37; Titus 2:13

Tuesday: *Sell that ye have, and give alms; provide yourselves bags which wax not old, a treasure in the heavens that faileth not, where no thief approacheth, neither moth corrupteth. For where your treasure is, there will your heart be also.*

Let your loins be girded about, and your lights burning; And ye yourselves like unto men that wait for their lord, when he will return from the wedding; that when he cometh and knocketh, they may open unto him immediately. Blessed are those servants, whom the lord when he cometh shall find watching: verily I say unto you, that he shall gird himself, and make them to sit down to meat, and will come forth and serve them.

And if he shall come in the second watch, or come in the third watch, and find them so, blessed are those servants. And this know, that if the goodman of the house had known what hour the thief would come, he would have watched, and not have suffered his house to be broken through.

Be ye therefore ready also: for the Son of man cometh at an hour when ye think not.

—Luke 12:33–40

. . .

Wednesday: *Who is she that looketh forth as the morning, fair as the moon, clear as the sun, and terrible as an army with banners?*

—Songs 6:10

The church of God, which he hath purchased with his own blood.

—Acts 20:28

Christ...loved the church, and gave himself for it; That he might sanctify and cleanse it with the washing of water by the word, That he might present it to himself a glorious church, not having spot, or wrinkle, or any such thing; but that it should be holy and without blemish.

—Ephesians 5:25–27

There appeared a great wonder in heaven; a woman clothed with the sun. —— The marriage of the Lamb is come, and his wife hath made herself ready. And to her was granted that she should be arrayed in fine linen, clean and white: for the fine linen is the righteousness of saints. —— The righteousness of God which is by faith of Jesus Christ unto all and upon all them that believe.

—Revelations 12:1; 19:7–8; Romans 3:22

The glory which thou gavest me I have given them.

—John 17:22

Thursday: *Behold, I create new heavens and a new earth.*

—Isaiah 65:17

The new heavens and the new earth, which I will make, shall remain before me...so shall your seed and your name remain.

—Isaiah 66:22

We, according to his promise, look for new heavens and a new earth, wherein dwelleth righteousness.

—2 Peter 3:13

I saw a new heaven and a new earth: for the first heaven and the first earth were passed away; and there was no more sea. And I John saw the holy city, new Jerusalem, coming down from God out of heaven, prepared as a bride adorned for her husband. And I heard a great voice out of heaven saying, Behold, the tabernacle of God is with men, and he will dwell with them, and they shall be his people, and God himself shall be with them, and be their God. And God shall wipe away all tears from their eyes; and there shall be no more death, neither sorrow, nor crying, neither shall there be any more pain: for the former things are passed away. And he that sat upon the throne said, Behold, I make all things new.

—Revelations 21:1–5

. . .

Friday: *Oh that thou wouldest rend the heavens, that thou wouldest come down.*

—Isaiah 64:1

Make haste, my beloved, and be thou like to a roe or to a young hart upon the mountains of spices. —— We ourselves groan within ourselves, waiting for the adoption, to wit, the redemption of our body. —— Bow thy heavens, O Lord, and come down: touch the mountains, and they shall smoke.

—Song 8:14; Romans 8:23; Psalm 144:5

This same Jesus, which is taken up from you into heaven, shall so come in like manner as ye have seen him go into heaven. —— Unto them that look for him shall he appear the second time without sin unto salvation. —— It shall be said in that day, Lo, this is our God; we have waited for him, and he will save us: this is the Lord; we have waited for him, we will be glad and rejoice in his salvation.

—Acts 1:11; Hebrews 9:28; Isaiah 25:9

He which testifieth these things saith, Surely I come quickly. Amen. Even so, come, Lord Jesus. —— That blessed hope, ...the glorious appearing of the great God and our Saviour Jesus Christ.

—Revelations 22:20; Titus 2:13

Saturday: *Watch, ...for ye know neither the day nor the hour wherein the Son of man cometh.*

—Matthew 25:13

Take heed to yourselves, lest at any time your hearts be overcharged with surfeiting, and drunkenness, and cares of this life, and so that day come upon you unawares. For as a snare shall it come on all them that dwell on the face of the whole earth. Watch ye therefore, and pray always, that ye may be accounted worthy to escape all these things that shall come to pass, and to stand before the Son of man.

—Luke 21:34–36

The day of the Lord so cometh as a thief in the night. For when they shall say, Peace and safety; then sudden destruction cometh upon them, as travail upon a woman with child; and they shall not escape. But ye, brethren, are not in darkness, that that day should overtake you as a thief. Ye are all the children of light, and the children of the day: we are not of the night, nor of darkness. Therefore let us not sleep, as do others; but let us watch and be sober.

—1 Thessalonians 5:2–6

. . .

Special Readings on Jesus' 2nd Coming:

Then shall the kingdom of heaven be likened unto ten virgins,
which took their lamps, and went forth to meet the bridegroom. 2 And five of
them were wise, and five were foolish. 3 They that were foolish took their lamps,
and took no oil with them: 4 But the wise took oil in their vessels with their lamps.
5 While the bridegroom tarried, they all slumbered and slept. 6 And at midnight
there was a cry made, Behold, the bridegroom cometh; go ye out to meet him.
7 Then all those virgins arose, and trimmed their lamps. 8 And the foolish said
unto the wise, Give us of your oil, for our lamps are gone out. 9 But the wise
answered, saying, 'Not so; lest there be not enough for us and you: but go ye rather
to them that sell, and buy for yourselves. 10 And while they went to buy, the
bridegroom came; and they that were ready went in with him to the marriage: and
the door was shut. 11 Afterward came also the other virgins, saying, Lord, Lord,
open to us. 12 But he answered and said, Verily I say unto you, I know you not.
13 Watch therefore, for ye know neither the day nor the hour wherein the Son of
man cometh.

—Matthew 25:1–13

"When the Son of Man shall come in his glory, and all the holy
angels with him, then shall he sit on the throne of his glory:
32 And before him shall be gathered all nations: and he shall separate them one
from another, as a shepherd divideth his sheep from the goats: 33 And he shall set
the sheep on his right hand, but the goats on the left. 34 Then shall the King say
unto them on his right hand, Come, ye blessed of my Father, inherit the kingdom
prepared for you from the foundation of the world: 35 For I was an hungred and
you gave me meat: I was thirsty, and ye gave me drink: I was a stranger and ye
took me in: 36 Naked, and ye clothed me: I was sick, and ye visited me: I was in
prison, and ye came unto me.

37 Then shall the righteous answer him, saying, Lord, when saw we see thee
an hungred, and fed thee? or thirsty, and give thee drink? 38 When saw we see
thee a stranger, and took thee in? or naked, and clothed thee? 39 Or when saw we
thee sick, or in prison, and came unto thee? 40 And the King shall answer and say
unto them, Verily I say unto you, Inasmuch as you have done it unto one of the
least of these my brethren, ye have done it unto me.

41 Then shall he say also unto them on the left hand, Depart from me, ye
cursed, into everlasting fire, prepared for the devil and his angels: 42 For I was an
hungred, and ye gave me no meat: I was thirsty, and ye gave me no drink: 43 I

was a stranger, and ye took me not in: naked, and ye clothed me not: sick, and in prison, and ye visited me not.

44 *Then shall they also answer him, saying, Lord, when saw we thee an hungred, or athirst, or a stranger, or naked, or sick, or in prison, and did not minister unto thee?* 45 *Then shall he answer them, saying, 'Verily I say unto you, Inasmuch as ye did it not to one of the least of these, you did it not to me.* 46 *And these shall go away into everlasting punishment: but the righteous into eternal life.*

—Matthew 25:31–46

Ye shall know them by their fruits. Do men gather grapes of thorns, or figs of thistles? 17 *Even so every good tree bringeth forth good fruit; but a corrupt tree bringeth forth evil fruit.* 18 *A good tree cannot bring forth evil fruit, neither can a corrupt tree bring forth good fruit.* 19 *Every tree that bringeth not forth good fruit is hewn down, and cast into the fire.* 20 *Wherefore by their fruits ye shall know them.*

21 *Not every one that saith unto me, Lord, Lord, shall enter into the kingdom of heaven; but he that doeth the will of my Father which is in heaven.* 22 *Many will say to me in that day, Lord, Lord, have we not prophesied in thy name? and in thy name have cast out devils? and in thy name done many wonderful works?* 23 *And then will I profess unto them, I never knew you: depart from me, ye that work iniquity.*

—Matthew 7:16–23

WEEK 43 - BLESSINGS OF GOD

S**unday**: *Oh that thou wouldest bless me indeed,*
...and that thou wouldest keep me from evil!
And God granted him that which he requested.

—I Chronicles 4:10

The blessing of the Lord, it maketh rich, and he addeth no sorrow with it. —— When he giveth quietness, who then can make trouble? and when he hideth his face, who then can behold him?

—Proverbs 10:22; Job 34:29

Salvation belongeth unto the Lord: thy blessing is upon thy people. —— How great is thy goodness, which thou hast laid up for them that fear thee; which thou hast wrought for them that trust in thee before the sons of men! —— I pray not that thou shouldest take them out of the world, but that thou shouldest keep them from the evil.

—Psalm 3:8; 31:19; John 17:15

Ask, and it shall be given you; seek, and ye shall find; knock, and it shall be opened unto you: For every one that asketh receiveth; and he that seeketh findeth; and to him that knocketh it shall be opened. —— The Lord redeemeth the soul of his servants: and none of them that trust in him shall be desolate.

—Matthew 7:7–8; Psalm 34:22

Thou, Lord, wilt bless the righteous; with favour wilt thou compass him as with a shield.

—Psalm 5:12

. . .

M**onday**: *Thou hast given me the heritage of those that fear thy name.* —Psalm 61:5

No weapon that is formed against thee shall prosper; and every tongue that shall rise against thee in judgment thou shalt condemn. This is the heritage of the servants of the Lord, and their righteousness is of me, saith the Lord. —— The angel of the Lord encampeth round about them that fear him, and delivereth them. O taste and see that the Lord is good: blessed is the man that trusteth in him. O fear the Lord, ye his saints: for there is no want to them that fear him. The young lions do lack, and suffer hunger: but they that seek the Lord shall not want any good thing. —— The lines are fallen unto me in pleasant places; yea, I have a goodly heritage.

—Isaiah 54:17; Psalm 34:7–10; 16:6

Unto you that fear my name shall the Sun of righteousness arise with healing in his wings; and ye shall go forth, and grow up as calves of the stall. —— He that spared not his own Son, but delivered him up for us all, how shall he not with him also freely give us all things?

—Malachi 4:2; Romans 8:32

T**uesday**: *When thou has eaten and are full... thou shalt bless the Lord thy God for the good land which he hath given thee.*

—Deuteronomy 8:10

Beware that thou forget not the Lord thy God. —— One of them, when he saw that he was healed, turned back, and with a loud voice glorified God, And fell down on his face at his feet, giving him thanks: and he was a Samaritan. And Jesus answering said, Were there not ten cleansed? but where are the nine? There are not found that returned to give glory to God, save this stranger.

—Deuteronomy 8:11; Luke 17:15–18

Every creature of God is good, and nothing to be refused, if it be received with thanksgiving: For it is sanctified by the word of God and prayer. —— He that eateth, eateth to the Lord, for he giveth God thanks. —— The blessing of the Lord, it maketh rich, and he addeth no sorrow with it.

—1 Timothy 4:4–5; Romans 14:6; Proverbs 10:22

Bless the Lord, O my soul: and all that is within me, bless his holy name. Bless the Lord, O my soul...Who forgiveth all thine iniquities...who crowneth thee with lovingkindness and tender mercies.

—Psalm 103:1–4

. . .

Wednesday: *The trees of the Lord are full of sap.*
—Psalm 104:16

I will be as the dew unto Israel: he shall grow as the lily, and cast forth his roots as Lebanon. His branches shall spread, and his beauty shalt be as the olive tree, and his smell as Lebanon. —— Blessed is the man that trusteth in the Lord, and whose hope the Lord is. For he shall be as a tree planted by the waters, and that spreadeth out her roots by the river, and shall not see when heat cometh, but her leaf shall be green; and shall not be careful in the year of drought, neither shall cease from yielding fruit.

—Hosea 14:5–6; Jeremiah 17:7–8

I the Lord have brought down the high tree, have exalted the low tree, have dried up the green tree, and have made the dry tree to flourish.

Ezekiel 17:24

The righteous shall flourish like the palm tree: he shall grow like a cedar in Lebanon. Those that be planted in the house of the Lord shall flourish in the courts of our God. They shall still bring forth fruit in old age; they shall be fat and flourishing.

—Psalm 92:12–14

Thursday: *Thou hast cast all my sins behind thy back.*
—Isaiah 38:17

Who is a God like unto thee, that pardoneth iniquity, and passeth by the transgression of the remnant of his heritage? he retaineth not his anger for ever, because he delighteth in mercy. He will turn again, he will have compassion upon us; he will subdue our iniquities; and thou wilt cast all their sins into the depths of the sea. —— I will forgive their iniquity, and I will remember their sin no more.

—Micah 7:18–19; Jeremiah 31:34

Blessed is he whose transgression is forgiven, whose sin is covered. Blessed is the man unto whom the Lord imputeth not iniquity, and in whose spirit there is no guile. —— The blood of Jesus Christ his Son cleanseth us from all sin.

—Psalm 32:1–2; 1 John 1:7

God giveth not the Spirit by measure unto him. —— And of his fulness have all we received, and grace for grace. —— It is like the precious ointment upon the head...even Aaron's...that went down to the skirts of his garments.

—John 3:34; 1:16; Psalm 133:2

. . .

Friday: *How great is thy goodness, which thou hast laid up for them that fear thee!* —Psalm 31:19

Since the beginning of the world men have not heard, nor perceived by the ear, neither hath the eye seen, O God, beside thee, what he hath prepared for him that waiteth for him. —— Eye hath not seen, nor ear heard, neither have entered into the heart of man, the things which God hath prepared for them that love him. But God hath revealed them unto us by his Spirit. —— Thou wilt shew me the path of life: in thy presence is fulness of joy; at thy right hand there are pleasures for evermore.

—Isaiah 64:4; 1 Corinthians 2:9–10; Psalm 16:11

How excellent is thy lovingkindness, O God! therefore the children of men put their trust under the shadow of thy wings. They shall be abundantly satisfied with the fatness of thy house; and thou shalt make them drink of the river of thy pleasures. For with thee is the fountain of life: in thy light shall we see light.

—Psalm 36:7–9

Godliness is profitable unto all things, having promise of the life that now is, and of that which is to come.

—1 Timothy 4:8

Saturday: *My cup runneth over.* —Psalm 23:5

O taste and see that the Lord is good: blessed is the man that trusteth in him. O fear the Lord, ye his saints: for there is no want to them that fear him. The young lions do lack, and suffer hunger: but they that seek the Lord shall not want any good thing. —— His compassions fail not. They are new every morning: great is thy faithfulness.

—Psalm 34:8–10; Lamentations 3:22–23

The Lord is the portion of mine inheritance and of my cup: thou maintainest my lot. The lines are fallen unto me in pleasant places; yea, I have a goodly heritage. —— Whether...the world, or life, or death, or things present, or things to come; all are your's [sic]. *—— Blessed be the God and Father of our Lord Jesus Christ, who hath blessed us with all spiritual blessings in heavenly places in Christ.*

—Psalm 16:5–6; 1 Corinthians 3:22; Ephesians 1:3

I have learned, in whatsoever state I am, therewith to be content. —— Godliness with contentment is great gain. —— My God shall supply all your need according to his riches in glory by Christ Jesus.

—Philippians 4:11; 1 Timothy 6:6; Philippians 4:19

WEEK 44 - GOD OUR PROTECTOR 1

Sunday: *God is my defense.* —Psalm 59:9

The Lord is my rock, and my fortress, and my deliverer; The God of my rock; in him will I trust: he is my shield, and the horn of my salvation, my high tower, and my refuge, my saviour. —— The Lord is my strength and my shield; my heart trusted in him, and I am helped: therefore my heart greatly rejoiceth; and with my song will I praise him.

—2 Samuel 22:2–3; Psalm 28:7

When the enemy shall come in like a flood, the Spirit of the Lord shall lift up a standard against him. —— We may boldly say, The Lord is my helper, and I will not fear what man shall do unto me.

—Isaiah 59:19; Hebrews 13:6

The Lord is my light and my salvation; whom shall I fear? the Lord is the strength of my life; of whom shall I be afraid? —— As the mountains are round about Jerusalem, so the Lord is round about his people from henceforth even for ever. —— Because thou hast been my help, therefore in the shadow of thy wings will I rejoice. —— For thy name's sake lead me, and guide me.

—Psalm 27:1; 125:2; 63:7; 31:3

O give thanks unto the Lord; for he is good: because his mercy endureth for ever. ...The Lord is on my side; I will not fear: what can man do unto me?...It is better to trust in the Lord than to put confidence in man. ...I will praise thee: for thou hast heard me, and art become my salvation.

—Psalm 118:1, 6, 8 ,21

. . .

Monday: *Whoso putteth his trust in the Lord shall be safe. [Or, set on high]* —Proverbs 29:25

The Lord is exalted; for he dwelleth on high. —— The Lord is high above all nations, and his glory above the heavens. ...He raiseth up the poor out of the dust, and lifteth the needy out of the dunghill; That he may set him with princes. —— God, who is rich in mercy, for his great love wherewith he loved us, Even when we were dead in sins, hath quickened us together with Christ, (by grace ye are saved;) And hath raised us up together, and made us sit together in heavenly places in Christ Jesus.

—Isaiah 33:5; Psalm 113:4, 7–8; Ephesians 2:4–6

He that spared not his own Son, but delivered him up for us all, how shall he not with him also freely give us all things? ...For I am persuaded, that neither death, nor life, nor angels, nor principalities, nor powers, nor things present, nor things to come, Nor height, nor depth, nor any other creature, shall be able to separate us from the love of God, which is in Christ Jesus our Lord. —— It is better to trust in the Lord than to put confidence in princes.

—Romans 8:32, 38–39; Psalm 118:9

Tuesday: *Thou hast given a banner to them that fear thee, that it may be displayed because of the truth.* —Psalm 60:4

Jehovahnissi. [The Lord my banner.] —— When the enemy shall come in like a flood, the Spirit of the Lord shall lift up a standard against him.

—Exodus 17:15; Isaiah 59:19

We will rejoice in thy salvation, and in the name of our God we will set up our banners. —— The Lord hath brought forth our righteousness: come, and let us declare in Zion the work of the Lord our God. —— We are more than conquerors through him that loved us. —— Thanks be to God, which giveth us the victory through our Lord Jesus Christ, —— the captain of their salvation.

—Psalm 20:5; Jeremiah 51:10; Romans 8:37; 1 Corinthians 15:57; Hebrews 2:10

My brethren, be strong in the Lord, and in the power of his might. —— Valiant for the truth. —— Fight the Lord's battles. —— Be strong, all ye people of the land, saith the Lord, and work. —— Lift up your eyes, and look on the fields; for they are white already to harvest. —— Yet a little while, and he that shall come will come, and will not tarry. —— His banner over me was love.

—Ephesians 6:10; Jeremiah 9:3; 1 Samuel 18:17; Haggai 2:4,5; John 4:35; Hebrews 10:37; Songs 2:4

. . .

Wednesday: *Oh...that thou wouldest keep me from evil.* —1 Chronicles 4:10

Fear thou not; for I am with thee: be not dismayed; for I am thy God: I will strengthen thee; yea, I will help thee; yea, I will uphold thee with the right hand of my righteousness. —— Why sleep ye? rise and pray, lest ye enter into temptation. —— Offer the sacrifices of righteousness, and put your trust in the Lord. —— The Lord shall preserve thee from all evil: he shall preserve thy soul. —— I will deliver thee out of the hand of the wicked, and I will redeem thee out of the hand of the terrible. —— He that is begotten of God keepeth himself, and that wicked one toucheth him not.

—Isaiah 41:10; Luke 22:46; Psalm 4:5; 121:7; Jeremiah 15:21; 1 John 5:18

Because thou hast kept the word of my patience, I also will keep thee from the hour of temptation, which shall come upon all the world, to try them that dwell upon the earth. —— The Lord is my strength and song, and is become my salvation. The voice of rejoicing and salvation is in the tabernacles of the righteous: the right hand of the Lord doeth valiantly. ...I shall not die, but live, and declare the works of the Lord. ...This is the day which the Lord hath made; we will rejoice and be glad in it. ...O give thanks unto the Lord; for he is good: for his mercy endureth for ever.

—Revelations 3:10; Psalm 118:14–15, 17, 24, 29

Thursday: *Thou art my help and my deliverer; make no tarrying, O my God.* —Psalm 40:17

The steps of a good man are ordered by the Lord: and he delighteth in his way. Though he fall, he shall not be utterly cast down: for the Lord upholdeth him with his hand. —— In the fear of the Lord is strong confidence: and his children shall have a place of refuge. —— Who art thou, that thou shouldest be afraid of a man that shall die, and of the son of man which shall be made as grass; And forgettest the Lord thy maker?

—Psalm 37:23–24; Proverbs 14:26; Isaiah 51:12–13

I am with thee to deliver thee. —— Be strong and of a good courage, fear not, nor be afraid of them: for the Lord thy God, he it is that doth go with thee; he will not fail thee, nor forsake thee. —— I will sing of thy power; yea, I will sing aloud of thy mercy in the morning: for thou hast been my defence and refuge in the day of my trouble. —— Thou art my hiding place; thou shalt preserve me from trouble; thou shalt compass me about with songs of deliverance.

—Jeremiah 1:8; Deuteronomy 31:6; Psalm 59:16; Psalm 32:7

. . .

Friday: *The Lord was my stay.* —Psalm 18:18

Truly in vain is salvation hoped for from the hills, and from the multitude of mountains: truly in the Lord our God is the salvation of Israel. —— The Lord is my rock, and my fortress, and my deliverer; my God, my strength, in whom I will trust; my buckler, and the horn of my salvation, and my high tower. —— Cry out and shout, thou inhabitant of Zion: for great is the Holy One of Israel in the midst of thee.

—Jeremiah 3:23; Psalm 18:2; Isaiah 12:6

The angel of the Lord encampeth round about them that fear him, and delivereth them. ...The righteous cry, and the Lord heareth, and delivereth them out of all their troubles. —— The eternal God is thy refuge, and underneath are the everlasting arms. —— So that we may boldly say, The Lord is my helper, and I will not fear what man shall do unto me. —— For who is God save the Lord? or who is a rock save our God? It is God that girdeth me with strength, and maketh my way perfect. —— By the grace of God I am what I am.

—Psalm 34:7, 17; Deuteronomy 33:27; Hebrews 13:6; Psalm 18:31–32; 1 Corinthians 15:10

Saturday: *He spread a cloud for a covering; and fire to give light in the night.* —Psalm 105:39

Like as a father pitieth his children, so the Lord pitieth them that fear him. For he knoweth our frame; he remembereth that we are dust. —— The sun shall not smite thee by day, nor the moon by night. —— There shall be a tabernacle for a shadow in the day time from the heat, and for a place of refuge, and for a covert from storm and from rain.

—Psalm 103:13–14;121:6; Isaiah 4:6

The Lord is thy keeper: the Lord is thy shade upon thy right hand. ...The Lord shall preserve thy going out and thy coming in from this time forth, and even for evermore.

—Psalm 121:5–8

I will say of the Lord, He is my refuge and my fortress: my God; in him will I trust. ...He shall cover thee with his feathers, and under his wings shalt thou trust: his truth shall be thy shield and buckler. ...Because thou hast made the Lord, which is my refuge, even the most High, thy habitation; There shall no evil befall thee, neither shall any plague come nigh thy dwelling. For he shall give his angels charge over thee, to keep thee in all thy ways. —— Jesus Christ the same yesterday, and to day, and for ever.

—Psalm 91:2, 4, 9–11; Hebrews 13:8

WEEK 45 - GOD OUR PROTECTOR 2

Sunday: *The children of Israel pitched before them like two little flocks of kids; but the Syrians filled the country.*

—1 Kings 20:27

Thus saith the Lord, Because the Syrians have said, the Lord is God of the hills, but he is not God of the valleys, therefore will I deliver all this great multitude into thine hand, and ye shall know that I am the Lord. And they pitched one over against the other seven days. And so it was, that in the seventh day the battle was joined: and the children of Israel slew of the Syrians an hundred thousand footmen in one day. —— Ye are of God, little children, and have overcome them: because greater is he that is in you, than he that is in the world.

—1 Kings 20:28–29; 1 John 4:4

Fear thou not; for I am with thee: be not dismayed; for I am thy God: I will strengthen thee; yea, I will help thee; yea, I will uphold thee with the right hand of my righteousness.

—Isaiah 41:10

They shall fight against thee; but they shall not prevail against thee; for I am with thee, saith the Lord, to deliver thee.

—Jeremiah 1:19

. . .

Monday: *The Lord is my rock and my fortress, and my deliverer.* —2 Samuel 22:2

God...my rock; in him will I trust: he is my shield, and the horn of my salvation, my high tower, and my refuge, my savior; thou savest me from violence. I will call on the Lord, who is worthy to be praised: so shall I be saved from mine enemies. ...Through the brightness before him were coals of fire kindled. The Lord thundered from heaven, And the most High uttered his voice. And he sent out arrows, and scattered them; lightning, and discomfited them.

—2 Samuel 22:3–4; 13–15

And the channels of the sea appeared, the foundations of the world were discovered, at the rebuking of the Lord, at the blast of the breath of his nostrils. He sent from above, he took me; he drew me out of many waters; He delivered me from my strong enemy, and from them that hated me: for they were too strong for me. They prevented me in the day of my calamity: but the Lord was my stay. He brought me forth also into a large place: he delivered me, because he delighted in me.

—2 Samuel 22:16–20

Tuesday: *For thou art my lamp, O Lord: and the Lord will lighten my darkness. For by thee I have run through a troop: By my God I have leaped over a wall.* —2 Samuel 22:29–30

As for God, his way is perfect; the word of the Lord is tried: he is a buckler to all them that trust in him. For who is God, save the Lord? And who is a rock, save our God?

—2 Samuel 22:31–32

God is my strength and power: and he maketh my way perfect. He maketh my feet like hinds' feet,: and setteth me upon my high places. He teacheth my hands to war; so that a bow of steel is broken by mine arms. Thou hast also given me the shield of thy salvation: And thy gentleess hath made me great. Thou hast enlarged my steps under me; so that my feet did not slip.

—2 Samuel 22:33-37

The Lord liveth; and blessed be my rock; and exalted be the God of the rock of my salvation. It is God that avengeth me, and that bringeth down the people under me. And that bringeth me forth from my enemies: thou also hast lifted me up on high above them that rose up against me: thou hast delivered me from the violent man. Therefore I will give thanks unto thee, O Lord, among the heathen, and I will sing praises unto thy name.

—2 Samuel 22:31–37, 47–50

. . .

Wednesday: *Strengthen thou me according unto thy word.*
—Psalm 119:28

Remember the word unto thy servant, upon which thou has caused me to hope. —— He shall call upon me, and I will answer him: I will be with him in trouble; I will deliver him, and honour him. With long life will I satisfy him, and shew him my salvation. —— Heaven and earth shall pass away: but my words shall not pass away. —— Ye know in all your hearts and in all your souls, that not one thing hath failed of all the good things which the Lord your God spake concerning you; all are come to pass unto you, and not one thing hath failed thereof.

—Psalm 119:49; 91:15–16; Luke 21:33; Joshua 23:14

Fear not: peace be unto thee, be strong, yea, be strong. And when he had spoken unto me, I was strengthened, and said, Let my lord speak; for thou hast strengthened me. —— Be strong...and work: for I am with you, saith the Lord of hosts. —— Not by might, nor by power, but by my spirit, saith the Lord of hosts. —— Be strong in the Lord, and in the power of his might.

—Daniel 10:19; Haggai 2:4; Zechariah 4:6; Ephesians 6:10

Thursday: *The darkness hideth not from thee.* —Psalm 139:12

His eyes are upon the ways of man, and he seeth all his goings. There is no darkness, nor shadow of death, where the workers of iniquity may hide themselves. —— Can any hide himself in secret places that I shall not see him?... Do not I fill heaven and earth? saith the Lord.

—Job 34:21–22; Jeremiah 23:24

He that dwelleth in the secret place of the most High shall abide under the shadow of the Almighty. I will say of the Lord, He is my refuge and my fortress: my God; in him will I trust. ...Thou shalt not be afraid for the terror by night; nor for the arrow that flieth by day; Nor for the pestilence that walketh in darkness; nor for the destruction that wasteth at noonday. ...Because he hath set his love upon me, therefore will I deliver him: I will set him on high, because he hath known my name. —— He that keepeth thee will not slumber. ...The Lord is thy keeper: the Lord is thy shade upon thy right hand. The sun shall not smite thee by day, nor the moon by night. The Lord shall preserve thee from all evil.

—Psalm 91:1–2, 5–6; 14; 121:3,5–7

Yea, though I walk through the valley of the shadow of death, I will fear no evil: for thou art with me.

—Psalm 23:4

. . .

Friday: *How wilt thou do in the swelling of Jordan?* —Jeremiah 12:5

For Jordan overfloweth all his banks all the time of harvest. ...The priests that bare the ark of the covenant of the Lord stood firm on dry ground in the midst of Jordan, and all the Israelites passed over on dry ground, until all the people were passed clean over Jordan.

—Joshua 3:15,17

We see Jesus, who was made a little lower than the angels for the suffering of death, crowned with glory and honour; that he by the grace of God should taste death for every man.

—Hebrews 2:9

Though I walk through the valley of the shadow of death, I will fear no evil: for thou art with me; thy rod and thy staff they comfort me. —— When thou passest through the waters, I will be with thee; and through the rivers, they shall not overflow thee.

—Psalm 23:4; Isaiah 43:2

Fear not; I am the first and the last: I am he that liveth, and was dead; and, behold, I am alive for evermore, Amen; and have the keys of hell and of death.

—Revelations 1:17–18

Saturday: *The Lord taketh my part.* —Psalm 118:7

The Lord hear thee in the day of trouble; the name of the God of Jacob defend thee; Send thee help from the sanctuary, and strengthen thee out of Zion. ...We will rejoice in thy salvation, and in the name of our God we will set up our banners. ...Some trust in chariots, and some in horses: but we will remember the name of the Lord our God. They are brought down and fallen: but we are risen, and stand upright.

—Psalm 20:1–2, 5, 7–8

When the enemy shall come in like a flood, the Spirit of the Lord shall lift up a standard against him. —— There hath no temptation taken you but such as is common to man: but God is faithful, who will not suffer you to be tempted above that ye are able: but will with the temptation also make a way to escape, that ye may be able to bear it.

—Isaiah 59:19; 1 Corinthians 10:13

If God be for us, who can be against us? —— The Lord is on my side; I will not fear. ——

Our God whom we serve is able to deliver us...and he will deliver us.

—Romans 8:31; Psalm 118:6; Daniel 3:17

WEEK 46 - OUR LOVE FOR GOD

S**unday**: *And thou shalt love the Lord thy God with all thine heart, and with all thy soul, and with all thy might.*

—Deuteronomy 6:5

Master, which is the great commandment in the law? Jesus said unto him, Thou shalt love the Lord thy God with all thy heart, and with all thy soul, and with all thy mind. This is the first and great commandment. —— I will love thee, O Lord, my strength.

—Matthew 22:36–38; Psalm 18:1

And ye shall seek me, and find me, when ye shall search for me with all your heart. —— Ask, and it shall be given you; seek, and ye shall find; knock, and it shall be opened unto you: For every one that asketh receiveth; and he that seeketh findeth; and to him that knocketh it shall be opened.

—Jeremiah 29:13; Matthew 7:7–8

But take diligent heed to do the commandment and the law, which Moses the servant of the Lord charged you, to love the Lord your God, and to walk in all his ways, and to keep his commandments, and to cleave unto him, and to serve him with all your heart and with all your soul. —— Take good heed therefore unto yourselves, that ye love the Lord your God.

—Joshua 22:5; 23:11

. . .

Monday: *He is altogether lovely.* —Song 5:16

My meditation of him shall be sweet. —— My beloved is...the chiefest among ten thousand. —— A chief corner stone, elect, precious: and he that believeth on him shall not be confounded. —— Thou art fairer than the children of men: grace is poured into thy lips. —— God...hath highly exalted him, and given him a name which is above every name.

—Psalm 104:34; Song 5:10; 1 Peter 2:6; Psalm 45:2; Philippians 2:9

Whom having not seen, ye love; in whom, though now ye see him not, yet believing, ye rejoice with joy unspeakable and full of glory.

—1 Peter 1:8

O love the Lord, all ye his saints: for the Lord preserveth the faithful. —— Let all those that seek thee rejoice and be glad in thee: let such as love thy salvation say continually, The Lord be magnified. —— But ye, beloved, building up yourselves on your most holy faith, praying in the Holy Ghost, Keep yourselves in the love of God, looking for the mercy of our Lord Jesus Christ unto eternal life.

—Psalm 31:23; 40:16; Jude 1:20–21

Tuesday: *My meditation of him shall be sweet: I will be glad in the Lord.* —Psalm 104:34

As the apple tree among the trees of the wood, so is my beloved among the sons. I sat down under his shadow with great delight, and his fruit was sweet to my taste. —— For who in the heaven can be compared unto the Lord? who among the sons of the mighty can be likened unto the Lord?

—Song 2:3; Psalm 89:6

My beloved is white and ruddy, —— one pearl of great price. —— The prince of the kings of the earth.

—Song 5:10; Matthew 13:46; Revelations 1:5

His head is as the most fine gold, his locks are bushy, and black as a raven. —— The head over all things. —— He is the head of the body, the church.

—Song 5:11; Ephesians 1:22; Colossians 1:18

His cheeks are as a bed of spices, as sweet flowers: his lips like lilies, dropping sweet smelling myrrh. —— Never man spake like this man.

—Song 5:13; John 7:46

His countenance is as Lebanon, excellent as the cedars. —— Make thy face to shine upon thy servant. —— Lord, lift thou up the light thy countenance upon us.

—Song 5:15; Psalm 31:16; 4:6

. . .

W**ednesday**: *Jesus said unto him, Thou shalt love the Lord thy God with all thy heart, and with all thy soul, and with all thy mind.*

—Matthew 22:37

Love not the world, neither the things that are in the world. If any man love the world, the love of the Father is not in him. For all that is in the world, the lust of the flesh, and the lust of the eyes, and the pride of life, is not of the Father, but is of the world. And the world passeth away. —— No servant can serve two masters: for either he will hate the one, and love the other; or else he will hold to the one, and despise the other. Ye cannot serve God and mammon.

—1 John 2:15–17; Luke 16:13

And the Lord thy God will circumcise thine heart, and the heart of thy seed, to love the Lord thy God with all thine heart, and with all thy soul, that thou mayest live. —— That he would grant you, according to the riches of his glory, to be strengthened with might by his Spirit in the inner man; That Christ may dwell in your hearts by faith; that ye, being rooted and grounded in love, May be able to comprehend with all saints what is the breadth, and length, and depth, and height; And to know the love of Christ, which passeth knowledge, that ye might be filled with all the fulness of God.

—Deuteronomy 30:6; Ephesians 3:16–19

T**hursday**: *Unto you...which believe he is precious.* —1 Peter 2:7

Thy name is as ointment poured forth. —— And His name shall be called Wonderful —— and His name is called The Word of God...And he hath on his vesture and on his thigh a name written, King Of Kings, And Lord Of Lords.

—Song 1:3; Isaiah 9:6; Revelations 19:13, 16

Again, the kingdom of heaven is like unto treasure hid in a field; the which when a man hath found, he hideth, and for joy thereof goeth and selleth all that he hath, and buyeth that field.

—Matthew 13:44

Lay not up for yourselves treasures upon earth, where moth and rust doth corrupt, and where thieves break through and steal: But lay up for yourselves treasures in heaven, where neither moth nor rust doth corrupt, and where thieves do not break through nor steal: For where your treasure is, there will your heart be also. —— My beloved is mine, and I am his.

—Matthew 6:19–21; Song 2:16

. . .

Friday: *If ye love me, keep my commandments.* —John 14:15

He that hath my commandments, and keepeth them, he it is that loveth me: and he that loveth me shall be loved of my Father, and I will love him, and will manifest myself to him.

—John 14:21

Jesus answered and said unto him, If a man love me, he will keep my words: and my Father will love him, and we will come unto him, and make our abode with him. He that loveth me not keepeth not my sayings: and the word which ye hear is not mine, but the Father's which sent me.

—John 14:23–24

This is my commandment, That ye love one another, as I have loved you. Greater love hath no man than this, that a man lay down his life for his friends.

—John 15:12–13

We love him, because he first loved us. If a man say, I love God, and hateth his brother, he is a liar: for he that loveth not his brother whom he hath seen, how can he love God whom he hath not seen? And this commandment have we from him, That he who loveth God love his brother also.

—1 John 4:19–21

Saturday: *Jesus saith to Simon Peter, Simon, son of Jonas, lovest thou me more than these? He saith unto him, Yea, Lord; thou knowest that I love thee. He saith unto him,*

Feed my lambs.

He saith to him again the second time, Simon, son of Jonas, lovest thou me? He saith unto him, Yea, Lord; thou knowest that I love thee. He saith unto him,

Feed my sheep.

He saith unto him the third time, Simon, son of Jonas, lovest thou me? ... And he said unto him, Lord, thou knowest all things; thou knowest that I love thee. Jesus saith unto him,

Feed my sheep.

—John 21:15–17

And Jesus came and spake unto them, saying, All power is given unto me in heaven and in earth. Go ye therefore, and teach all nations, baptizing them in the name of the Father, and of the Son, and of the Holy Ghost: Teaching them to observe all things whatsoever I have commanded you: and, lo, I am with you always, even unto the end of the world. Amen.

—Matthew 28:18–20

WEEK 47 - HIS WORD

S**unday**: *The words that I speak unto you,*
they are spirit, and they are life. —John 6:63

Of his own will begat he us with the word of truth. —— *For the word of God is quick, and powerful, and sharper than any twoedged sword, piercing even to the dividing asunder of soul and spirit, and of the joints and marrow, and is a discerner of the thoughts and intents of the heart.*

—James 1:18; Hebrews 4:12

Christ...loved the church, and gave himself for it; That he might sanctify and cleanse it with the washing of water by the word, That he might present it to himself a glorious church, not having spot, or wrinkle, or any such thing.

—Ephesians 5:25–27

Wherewithal shall a young man cleanse his way? by taking heed thereto according to thy word. ...Thy word hath quickened me. ...Thy word have I hid in mine heart, that I might not sin against thee. ...I will delight myself in thy statutes: I will not forget thy word. ...I trust in thy word. ...The law of thy mouth is better unto me than thousands of gold and silver. ...I will never forget thy precepts: for with them thou hast quickened me. ...How sweet are thy words unto my taste! yea, sweeter than honey to my mouth! Through thy precepts I get understanding: therefore I hate every false way.

—Psalm 119:9, 50, 11, 16, 42, 72, 93, 103–104

. . .

Monday: *Thy word is a lamp unto my feet, and a light unto my path.*

—Psalm 119:105

By the word of thy lips I have kept me from the paths of the destroyer. Hold up my goings in thy paths, that my footsteps slip not. —— When thou goest, it shall lead thee; when thou sleepest, it shall keep thee; and when thou awakest, it shall talk with thee. For the commandment is a lamp; and the law is light. —— Thine ears shall hear a word behind thee, saying, This is the way, walk ye in it, when ye turn to the right hand, and when ye turn to the left.

—Psalm 17:4–5; Proverbs 6:22–23; Isaiah 30:21

I am the light of the world: he that followeth me shall not walk in darkness, but shall have the light of life. —— We have also a...sure word of prophecy; whereunto ye do well that ye take heed, as unto a light that shineth in a dark place.

—John 8:12; 2 Peter 1:19

Order my steps in thy word, and let not any iniquity have dominion over me.

—Psalm 119:133

Tuesday: *Seek ye out of the book of the Lord.* —Isaiah 34:16

Shall ye lay up these my words in your heart and in your soul, and bind them for a sign upon your hand, that they may be as frontlets between your eyes. —— This book of the law shall not depart out of thy mouth; but thou shalt meditate therein day and night, that thou mayest observe to do according to all that is written therein: for then thou shalt make thy way prosperous, and then thou shalt have good success.

—Deuteronomy 11:18; Joshua 1:8

The law of his God is in his heart; none of his steps shall slide. —— By the word of thy lips I have kept me from the paths of the destroyer. —— Thy word have I hid in mine heart, that I might not sin against thee.

—Psalm 37:31; 17:4; 119:11

We have...a more sure word of prophecy; whereunto ye do well that ye take heed, as unto a light that shineth in a dark place, until the day dawn, and the day star arise in your hearts. —— That we through patience and comfort of the scriptures might have hope.

—2 Peter 1:19; Romans 15:4

. . .

Wednesday: *Write the things which thou hast seen, and the things which are, and the things which shall be hereafter.*

—Revelations 1:19

For the prophecy came not in old time by the will of man: but holy men of God spake as they were moved by the Holy Ghost. —— That which we have seen and heard declare we unto you, that ye also may have fellowship with us: and truly our fellowship is with the Father, and with his Son Jesus Christ.

—2 Peter 1:21; 1 John 1:3

Behold my hands and my feet, that it is I myself: handle me, and see; for a spirit hath not flesh and bones, as ye see me have. And when he had thus spoken, he shewed them his hands and his feet. —— He that saw it bare record, and his record is true: and he knoweth that he saith true, that ye might believe. —— We have not followed cunningly devised fables, when we made known unto you the power and coming of our Lord Jesus Christ, but were eyewitnesses of his majesty. —— That your faith should not stand in the wisdom of men, but in the power of God.

—Luke 24:39–40; John 19:35; 2 Peter 1:16; 1 Corinthians 2:5

Thursday: *Yea, hath God said?* —Genesis 3:1

Then was Jesus led up of the Spirit into the wilderness to be tempted of the devil. ...When the tempter came to him [Jesus], he said, If thou be the Son of God. ...Jesus said unto him, It is written...it is written. ...Then the devil leaveth him. —— And thou shalt remember all the way which the Lord thy God led thee these forty years in the wilderness, to humble thee, and to prove thee, to know what was in thine heart, whether thou wouldest keep his commandments, or no.

—Matthew 4:1, 3–4, 7, 10–11; Deuteronomy 8:2

Order my steps in thy word: and let not any iniquity have dominion over me. ...The sum of Your word is truth, And every one of Your righteous ordinances is everlasting. Thy word is true from the beginning: and every one of thy righteous judgments endureth for ever.

—Psalm 119:133, 160

Then Simon Peter answered him, Lord, to whom shall we go? thou hast the words of eternal life. —— Though we, or an angel from heaven, preach any other gospel unto you than that which we have preached unto you, let him be accursed. —— Thy word have I hid in mine heart, that I might not sin against thee. ...I will meditate in thy precepts, and have respect unto thy ways.

—John 6:68; Galatians 1:8; Psalm 119:11,15

. . .

Friday: *What is the thing that the Lord hath said unto thee?* —1 Samuel 3:17

He hath shewed thee, O man, what is good; and what doth the Lord require of thee, but to do justly, and to love mercy, and to walk humbly with thy God? —— To keep the commandments of the Lord, and his statutes, which I command thee this day for thy good.

—Micah 6:8; Deuteronomy 10:13

As many as are of the works of the law are under the curse: for it is written, Cursed is every one that continueth not in all things which are written in the book of the law to do them. But that no man is justified by the law in the sight of God, it is evident: for, The just shall live by faith. ...Wherefore then serveth the law? It was added because of transgressions, till the seed should come to whom the promise was made. —— But be ye doers of the word, and not hearers only, deceiving your own selves.

—Galatians 3:10–11, 19; James 1:22

God, who at sundry times and in divers manners spake in time past unto the fathers by the prophets, Hath in these last days spoken unto us by his Son. —— Speak, Lord; for thy servant heareth.

—Hebrews 1:1–2; 1 Samuel 3:9

Saturday: *The words of the Lord are pure words.* —Psalm 12:6

Thy word is very pure: therefore thy servant loveth it. —— The statutes of the Lord are right, rejoicing the heart: the commandment of the Lord is pure, enlightening the eyes. —— Every word of God is pure: he is a shield unto them that put their trust in him. Add thou not unto his words, lest he reprove thee, and thou be found a liar. —— We are not as many, which corrupt the word of God: but as of sincerity, but as of God, in the sight of God speak we in Christ. —— Nor handling the word of God deceitfully.

—Psalm 119:140; 19:8; Proverbs 30:5–6; 2 Corinthians 2:17; 4:2

Brethren, whatsoever things are true, whatsoever things are honest, whatsoever things are just, whatsoever things are pure, whatsoever things are lovely, whatsoever things are of good report; if there be any virtue, and if there be any praise, think on these things. —— As newborn babes, desire the sincere milk of the word, that ye may grow thereby. —— But he answered and said, It is written, Man shall not live by bread alone, but by every word that proceedeth out of the mouth of God.

—Philippians 4:8; 1 Peter 2:2; Matthew 4:4

. . .

Special C. Spurgeon Devotional

I will meditate in thy precepts.

—Psalm 119:15

There are times when solitude is better than society, and silence is wiser than speech. We should be better Christians if we were more alone, waiting upon God, and gathering through meditation on His Word spiritual strength for labor in His service.

We ought to muse upon the things of God, because we get the real nutrition out of them. Truth is something like the cluster of the vine: if we would have wine from it, we must bruise it; we must press and squeeze it many times. The bruiser's feet must come down joyfully upon the bunches, or else the juice will not flow; and they must well tread the grapes, or else much of the precious liquid will be wasted. So we must, by meditation, tread the clusters of truth, if we would get the wine of consolation from it.

Likewise, our bodies are not supported by merely taking food into the mouth, but the process which really supplies the muscle, and the nerve, and the sinew, and the bone, is the process of digestion. It is by digestion that the outward food becomes assimilated with the inner life.

Our souls are not nourished merely by listening awhile to this, and then to that, and then to the other part of divine truth. Hearing, reading, marking, and learning, all require inwardly digesting to complete their usefulness, and the inward digesting of the truth lies for the most part in meditating upon it.

Why is it that some Christians, although they hear many sermons, make but slow advances in the divine life? Because they neglect their closets, and do not thoughtfully meditate on God's Word. They love the wheat, but they do not grind it; they would have the corn, but they will not go forth into the fields to gather it; the fruit hangs upon the tree, but they will not pluck it; the water flows at their feet, but they will not stoop to drink it.

From such folly deliver us, O Lord, and be this our resolve this morning, "*I will meditate in thy precepts.*"

WEEK 48 - RESURRECTION

S**unday**: *Christ the firstfruits.*
—1 Corinthians 15:23

Except a corn of wheat fall into the ground and die, it abideth alone: but if it die, it bringeth forth much fruit. —— If the firstfruit be holy, the lump is also holy: and if the root be holy, so are the branches. —— Now is Christ risen from the dead, and become the firstfruits of them that slept. —— If we have been planted together in the likeness of his death, we shall be also in the likeness of his resurrection. —— The Lord Jesus Christ...shall change our vile body, that it may be fashioned like unto his glorious body, according to the working whereby he is able even to subdue all things unto himself.

—John 12:24; Romans 11:16; 1 Corinthians 15:20; Romans 6:5; Philippians 3:20–21

The firstborn from the dead. —— Him God raised up the third day, and shewed him openly...unto witnesses...even to us, who did eat and drink with him after he arose from the dead. —— If the Spirit of him that raised up Jesus from the dead dwell in you, he that raised up Christ from the dead shall also quicken your mortal bodies by his Spirit that dwelleth in you.

—Colossians 1:18; Acts 10:40; Romans 8:11

I am the resurrection, and the life: he that believeth in me, though he were dead, yet shall he live.

—John 11:25

. . .

Monday: *Then shall the dust return to the earth as it was...*
—Ecclesiastes 12:7

So also is the resurrection of the dead. It is sown in corruption; it is raised in incorruption: It is sown in dishonour; it is raised in glory: it is sown in weakness; it is raised in power: It is sown a natural body; it is raised a spiritual body. There is a natural body, and there is a spiritual body. ...The first man is of the earth, earthy.

—1 Corinthians 15:42–44, 47

Dust thou art, and unto dust shalt thou return. —— One dieth in his full strength, being wholly at ease and quiet. ...And another dieth in the bitterness of his soul, and never eateth with pleasure. They shall lie down alike in the dust, and the worms shall cover them.

—Genesis 3:19; Job 21:23, 25–26

My flesh...shall rest in hope. —— Though after my skin worms destroy this body, yet in my flesh shall I see God. —— Lord, make me to know mine end, and the measure of my days, what it is: that I may know how frail I am. —— So teach us to number our days, that we may apply our hearts unto wisdom.

—Psalm 16:9; Job 19:26; Psalm 39:4; 90:12

Tuesday: *...The spirit shall return unto God who gave it.*
—Ecclesiastes 12:7

The Lord God formed man of the dust of the ground, and breathed into his nostrils the breath of life; and man became a living soul. —— There is a spirit in man: and the inspiration of the Almighty giveth them understanding. —— The first man Adam was made a living soul. —— The spirit of man that goeth upward.

—Genesis 2:7; Job 32:8; 1 Corinthians 15:45; Ecclesiastes 3:21

Whilst we are at home in the body, we are absent from the Lord. ...We are confident...and willing rather to be absent from the body, and to be present with the Lord. —— With Christ; which is far better. —— I would not have you to be ignorant, brethren, concerning them which are asleep, that ye sorrow not, even as others which have no hope. For if we believe that Jesus died and rose again, even so them also which sleep in Jesus will God bring with him.

—2 Corinthians 5:6,8; Philippians 1:23; 1 Thessalonians 4:13–14

I go to prepare a place for you. And if I go and prepare a place for you, I will come again, and receive you unto myself; that where I am, there ye may be also.

—John 14:2–3

. . .

Wednesday: *They shall see his face.*
—Revelations 22:4

I beseech thee, shew me thy glory. —— No man hath seen God at any time, the only begotten Son, which is in the bosom of the Father, he hath declared him.
—Exodus 33:18; John 1:18

He hath prepared for them a city. —— An inheritance incorruptible, and undefiled, and that fadeth not away, reserved in heaven for you. —— Here have we no continuing city, but we seek one to come.
—Hebrews 11:16; 1 Peter 1:4; Hebrews 13:14

Every eye shall see him, and they also which pierced him: and all kindreds of the earth shall wail because of him. —— I shall see him, but not now: I shall behold him, but not nigh. —— For now we see through a glass, darkly; but then face to face: now I know in part; but then shall I know even as also I am known. —— I will behold thy face in righteousness: I shall be satisfied, when I awake, with thy likeness. —— We shall be like him; for we shall see him as he is.
—Revelations 1:7; Numbers 24:17; 1 Corinthians 13:12; Psalm 17:15; 1 John 3:2

Thursday: *The days of thy mourning shall be ended.*
—Isaiah 60:20

In the world ye shall have tribulation. —— The whole creation groaneth and travaileth in pain together until now. And not only they, but ourselves also, which have the firstfruits of the Spirit, even we ourselves groan within ourselves, waiting for the adoption, to wit, the redemption of our body. —— We that are in this tabernacle do groan, being burdened: not for that we would be unclothed, but clothed upon, that mortality might be swallowed up of life.
—John 16:33; Romans 8:22–23; 2 Corinthians 5:4

These are they which came out of great tribulation, and have washed their robes, and made them white in the blood of the Lamb. Therefore are they before the throne of God, and serve him day and night in his temple: and he that sitteth on the throne shall dwell among them. They shall hunger no more, neither thirst any more; neither shall the sun light on them, nor any heat. For the Lamb which is in the midst of the throne shall feed them, and shall lead them unto living fountains of waters: and God shall wipe away all tears from their eyes.
—Revelations 7:14–17

. . .

Friday: *How are the dead raised up?*
And with what body do they come?
—1 Corinthians 15:35

Beloved, now are we the sons of God, ...it doth not yet appear what we shall be: but we know that, when he shall appear, we shall be like him. —— As we have borne the image of the earthy, we shall also bear the image of the heavenly. —— Now for a season, if need be, ye are in heaviness through manifold temptations. —— For this corruptible must put on incorruption, and this mortal must put on immortality. So when this corruptible shall have put on incorruption, and this mortal shall have put on immortality, then shall be brought to pass the saying that is written, Death is swallowed up in victory.

—1 John 3:2; 1 Corinthians 15:49; 1 Peter 1:6; 1 Corinthians 15:53–54

Jesus himself stood in the midst of them, and saith unto them, Peace be unto you. But they were terrified and affrighted, and supposed that they had seen a spirit. —— He was seen of Cephas, then of the twelve: After that, he was seen of above five hundred brethren at once. —— If the Spirit of him that raised up Jesus from the dead dwell in you, he that raised up Christ from the dead shall also quicken your mortal bodies by his Spirit that dwelleth in you.

—Luke 24:36–37; 1 Corinthians 15:5–6; Romans 8:11

Saturday: *And when they heard of the resurrection of the dead,*
some mocked: and others said,
We will hear thee again of this matter. —Acts 17:32

The same day came to him the Sadducees, which say that there is no resurrection, and asked him, Saying, Master, Moses said, If a man die, having no children, his brother shall marry his wife, and raise up seed unto his brother. Now there were with us seven brethren: and the first, when he had married a wife, deceased, and, having no issue, left his wife unto his brother: Likewise the second also, and the third, unto the seventh. And last of all the woman died also. Therefore in the resurrection whose wife shall she be of the seven? for they all had her.

Jesus answered and said unto them, Ye do err, not knowing the scriptures, nor the power of God. For in the resurrection they neither marry, nor are given in marriage, but are as the angels of God in heaven. But as touching the resurrection of the dead, have ye not read that which was spoken unto you by God, saying, I am the God of Abraham, and the God of Isaac, and the God of Jacob? God is not the God of the dead, but of the living.

—Matthew 22:23–32

WEEK 49 - GOD IS SUPREME, OMNIPOTENT, SOVEREIGN

Sunday: *Holy, holy, holy, Lord God Almighty.*
—Revelations 4:8

Thine, O Lord is the greatness, and the power, and the glory, and the victory, and the majesty: for all that is in the heaven and in the earth is thine; thine is the kingdom, O Lord, and thou art exalted as head above all. Both riches and honour come of thee, and thou reignest over all; and in thine hand is power and might; and in thine hand it is to make great, and to give strength unto all. —— Draw not nigh hither: put off thy shoes from off thy feet, for the place whereon thou standest is holy ground...I am the God of thy father, the God of Abraham, the God of Isaac, and the God of Jacob. And Moses hid his face; for he was afraid to look upon God. —— To whom then will ye liken me, or shall I be equal? saith the Holy One. —— I am the Lord thy God, the Holy One of Israel, thy Saviour. ...I, even I, am the Lord; and beside me there is no saviour.

—1 Chronicles 29:11–12; Exodus 3:5–6; Isaiah 40:25; 43:3,11

As he which hath called you is holy, so be ye holy in all manner of conversation; Because it is written, Be ye holy; for I am holy. —— Know ye not that your body is the temple of the Holy Ghost which is in you, which ye have of God, and ye are not your own? —— Ye are the temple of the living God; as God hath said, I will dwell in them, and walk in them; and I will be their God, and they shall be my people.

—1 Peter 1:15–16; 1 Corinthians 6:19; 2 Corinthians 6:16

. . .

Monday: *The Lord God omnipotent reigneth.* —Revelations 19:6

I know that thou canst do every thing. —— The things which are impossible with men are possible with God. —— He doeth according to his will in the army of heaven, and among the inhabitants of the earth: and none can stay his hand, or say unto him, What doest thou? ——There is none that can deliver out of my hand: I will work, and who shall let it? —— Abba, Father, all things are possible unto thee.

—Job 42:2; Luke 18:27; Daniel 4:35; Isaiah 43:13; Mark 14:36

Believe ye that I am able to do this? They said unto him, Yea, Lord. Then touched he their eyes, saying, According to your faith be it unto you. —— Lord, if thou wilt, thou canst make me clean. And Jesus put forth his hand, and touched him, saying, I will; be thou clean. —— The mighty God. —— All power is given unto me in heaven and in earth.

—Matthew 9:28–29; 8:2–3; Isaiah 9:6; Matthew 28:18

Some trust in chariots, and some in horses: but we will remember the name of the Lord our God. —— Be strong and courageous, be not afraid nor dismayed... there be more with us than with him.

—Psalm 20:7; 2 Chronicles 32:7

Tuesday: *The Lord reigneth.* —Psalm 99:1

Fear ye not me? saith the Lord: will ye not tremble at my presence, which have placed the sand for the bound of the sea by a perpetual decree, that it cannot pass it: and though the waves thereof toss themselves, yet can they not prevail; though they roar, yet can they not pass over it? —— He changeth the times and the seasons: he removeth kings, and setteth up kings: he giveth wisdom unto the wise, and knowledge to them that know understanding. —— Promotion cometh neither from the east, nor from the west, nor from the south. But God is the judge: he putteth down one, and setteth up another. —— Ye shall hear of wars and rumours of wars: see that ye be not troubled.

—Jeremiah 5:22; Daniel 2:21; Psalm 75:6–7; Matthew 24:6

For by him were all things created, that are in heaven, and that are in earth, visible and invisible, whether they be thrones, or dominions, or principalities, or powers: all things were created by him, and for him: And he is before all things, and by him all things consist. And he is the head of the body, the church: who is the beginning, the firstborn from the dead; that in all things he might have the preeminence. For it pleased the Father that in him should all fulness dwell.

—Colossians 1:16–19

. . .

Wednesday: *The mighty God.*

—Isaiah 9:6

Thou art fairer than the children of men: grace is poured into thy lips: therefore God hath blessed thee for ever. Gird thy sword upon thy thigh, O most mighty, with thy glory and thy majesty. And in thy majesty ride prosperously. ... Thy throne, O God, is for ever and ever: the sceptre of thy kingdom is a right sceptre. —— Thou spakest in vision to thy holy one, and saidst, I have laid help upon one that is mighty. —— The man that is my fellow, saith the Lord of hosts.

—Psalm 45:2–6; 89:19; Zechariah 13:7

Behold, God, is my salvation; I will trust, and not be afraid: for the ***LORD JEHOVAH*** *is my strength and my song; he also is become my salvation. —— Thanks be unto God, which always causes us to triumph in Christ.*

—Isaiah 12:2; 2 Corinthians 2:14

Now unto him that is able to keep you from falling, and to present you faultless before the presence of his glory with exceeding joy, To the only wise God our Saviour, be glory and majesty, dominion and power, both now and ever.

—Jude 1:24–25

Thursday: *Upon the likeness of the throne was the likeness as the appearance of a man above upon it.*

—Ezekiel 1:26

The man Christ Jesus. —— Made in the likeness of men...found in fashion as a man. —— Forasmuch...as the children are partakers of flesh and blood, he also himself likewise took part of the same; that through death he might destroy him that had the power of death.

—1 Timothy 2:5; Philippians 2:7–8; Hebrews 2:14

I am he that liveth, and was dead; and, behold, I am alive for evermore. —— Christ being raised from the dead dieth no more; death hath no more dominion over him. For in that he died, he died unto sin once: but in that he liveth, he liveth unto God. —— What and if ye shall see the Son of man ascend up where he was before?—— He raised him from the dead, and set him at his own right hand in the heavenly places. —— In him dwelleth all the fulness of the Godhead bodily.

—Revelations 1:18; Romans 6:9–10; John 6:62; Ephesians 1:20; Colossians 2:9

Though he was crucified through weakness, yet he liveth by the power of God. For we also are weak in him, but we shall live with him by the power of God.

—2 Corinthians 13:4

. . .

F**riday**: *Thou art the same, and thy years shall have no end.*
—Psalm 102:27

Before the mountains were brought forth, or ever thou hadst formed the earth and the world, even from everlasting to everlasting, thou art God. —— I am the Lord, I change not; therefore ye sons of Jacob are not consumed. —— The same yesterday, and to day, and for ever.

—Psalm 90:2; Malachi 3:6; Hebrews 13:8

Every good gift and every perfect gift is from above, and cometh down from the Father of lights, with whom is no variableness, neither shadow of turning. —— God is not a man, that he should lie; neither the son of man, that he should repent. —— It is of the Lord's mercies that we are not consumed, because his compassions fail not. —— This man, because he continueth ever, hath an unchangeable priesthood. Wherefore he is able also to save them to the uttermost that come unto God by him, seeing he ever liveth to make intercession for them. —— Fear not; I am the first and the last.

—James 1:17; Numbers 23:19; Lamentations 3:22; Hebrews 7:24–25; Revelations 1:17

S**aturday**: *What God is there in heaven or in earth, that can do according to thy works, and according to thy might?*

—Deuteronomy 3:24

Who in the heaven can be compared unto the Lord? who among the sons of the mighty can be likened unto the Lord?...O Lord God of hosts, who is a strong Lord like unto thee? or to thy faithfulness round about thee? —— Among the gods there is none like unto thee, O Lord; neither are there any works like unto thy works. —— For thy word's sake, and according to thine own heart, hast thou done all these great things, to make thy servant know them. Wherefore thou art great, O Lord God: for there is none like thee, neither is there any God beside thee, according to all that we have heard with our ears.

—Psalm 89:6–8; 86:8; 2 Samuel 7:21–22

And Jesus came and spake unto them, saying, All power is given unto me in heaven and in earth. Go ye therefore, and teach all nations, baptizing them in the name of the Father, and of the Son, and of the Holy Ghost: Teaching them to observe all things whatsoever I have commanded you: and, lo, I am with you always, even unto the end of the world. Amen.

—Matthew 28:18–20

WEEK 50 - LIFE IN THE SPIRIT 2

Sunday: *The communion of the Holy Ghost, be with you all.*

—2 Corinthians 13:14

I will pray the Father, and he shall give you another Comforter, that he may abide with you for ever; Even the Spirit of truth; whom the world cannot receive, because it seeth him not, neither knoweth him: but ye know him; for he dwelleth with you, and shall be in you. —— He shall not speak of himself. ...He shall glorify me: for he shall receive of mine, and shall shew it unto you.

—John 14:16–17; 16:13–14

The love of God is shed abroad in our hearts by the Holy Ghost which is given unto us. ——

He that is joined unto the Lord is one spirit. ...Know ye not that your body is the temple of the Holy Ghost which is in you, which ye have of God, and ye are not your own?

—Romans 5:5; 1 Corinthians 6:17; 6:19

Grieve not the holy Spirit of God, whereby ye are sealed unto the day of redemption.

—Ephesians 4:30

Monday: *Take thou also unto thee principal spices...and thou shalt make it an oil of holy ointment.* —Exodus 30:23–25

Upon man's flesh shall it not be poured, neither shall ye make any other like it, after the composition of it: it is holy, and it shall be holy unto you. —— One Spirit. —— Diversities of gifts, but the same Spirit.

—Exodus 30:32; Ephesians 4:4; 1 Corinthians 12:4

God, thy God, hath anointed thee with the oil of gladness above thy fellows. —— God anointed Jesus of Nazareth with the Holy Ghost and with power. —— God giveth not the Spirit by measure unto him.

—Psalm 45:7; Acts 10:38; John 3:34

Of his fulness have all we received. —— As the same anointing teacheth you of all things, and is truth, and is no lie, and even as it hath taught you, ye shall abide in him. —— He which...hath anointed us, is God; Who hath also sealed us, and given the earnest of the Spirit in our hearts.

—John 1:16; 1 John 2:27; 2 Corinthians 1:21–22

The fruit of the Spirit is love, joy, peace, longsuffering, gentleness, goodness, faith, Meekness, temperance: against such there is no law.

—Galatians 5:22–23

Tuesday: *Things which are despised, hath God chosen.*

—1 Corinthians 1:28

Behold, are not all these which speak Galilaeans?

—Acts 2:7

Jesus...saw two brethren...casting a net into the sea: for they were fishers. And he saith unto them, Follow me. —— Now when they saw the boldness of Peter and John , and perceived that they were unlearned and ignorant men, they marvelled; and they took knowledge of them, that they had been with Jesus.

—Matthew 4:18–19; Acts 4:13

My speech and my preaching was not with enticing words of man's wisdom, but in demonstration of the Spirit and of power: That your faith should not stand in the wisdom of men, but in the power of God.

—1 Corinthians 2:4–5

Ye have not chosen me, but I have chosen you, and ordained you, that ye should go and bring forth fruit. ...He that abideth in me, and I in him, the same bringeth forth much fruit: for without me ye can do nothing. —— We have this treasure in earthen vessels, that the excellency of the power may be of God.

—John 15:16, 5; 2 Corinthians 4:7

. . .

Wednesday: *Not by might, nor by power, but by my spirit, saith the Lord of hosts.*

—Zechariah 4:6

Who hath directed the Spirit of the Lord, or being his counsellor hath taught him?

—Isaiah 40:13

God hath chosen the foolish things of the world to confound the wise; and God hath chosen the weak things of the world to confound the things which are mighty; And base things of the world, and things which are despised, hath God chosen, yea, and things which are not, to bring to nought things that are: That no flesh should glory in his presence.

—1 Corinthians 1:27–29

The wind bloweth where it listeth, and thou hearest the sound thereof, but canst not tell whence it cometh, and whither it goeth: so is every one that is born of the Spirit. —— Born, not of blood, nor of the will of the flesh, nor of the will of man, but of God.

—John 3:8; 1:13

My spirit remaineth among you: fear ye not. —— The battle is not yours, but God's.

—Haggai 2:5; 2 Chronicles 20:15

The Lord saveth not with sword and spear: for the battle is the Lord's.

—1 Samuel 17:47

Thursday: *Grieve not the holy Spirit of God, whereby ye are sealed unto the day of redemption.* —Ephesians 4:30

The love of the Spirit. —— The Comforter, which is the Holy Ghost. —— In all their affliction he was afflicted, and the angel of his presence saved them: in his love and in his pity he redeemed them; and he bare them, and carried them all the days of old. But they rebelled, and vexed his holy Spirit: therefore he was turned to be their enemy, and he fought against them.

—Romans 15:30; John 14:26; Isaiah 63:9–10

After that ye believed, ye were sealed with that holy Spirit of promise, Which is the earnest of our inheritance until the redemption of the purchased possession. —— This I say then, Walk in the Spirit, and ye shall not fulfil the lust of the flesh. For the flesh lusteth against the Spirit, and the Spirit against the flesh: and these are contrary the one to the other: so that ye cannot do the things that ye would.

—Ephesians 1:13–14; Galatians 5:16–17

. . .

F**riday**: *Quicken us, and we will call upon thy name.*
—Psalm 80:18

It is the Spirit that quickeneth. —— The Spirit also helpeth our infirmities: for we know not what we should pray for as we ought: but the Spirit itself maketh intercession for us with groanings which cannot be uttered. And he that searcheth the hearts knoweth what is the mind of the Spirit, because he maketh intercession for the saints according to the will of God. —— Praying always with all prayer and supplication in the Spirit, and watching thereunto with all perseverance.

—John 6:63; Romans 8:26–27; Ephesians 6:18

I will never forget thy precepts: for with them thou hast quickened me. —— The words that I speak unto you, they are spirit, and they are life. —— The letter killeth, but the spirit giveth life. —— If ye abide in me, and my words abide in you, ye shall ask what ye will, and it shall be done unto you. —— This is the confidence that we have in him, that, if we ask any thing according to his will, he heareth us.

—Psalm 119:93; John 6:63; 2 Corinthians 3:6; John 15:7; 1 John 5:14

No man can say that Jesus is the Lord, but by the Holy Ghost.

—1 Corinthians 12:3

S**aturday**: *It is expedient for you that I go away: for if I go not away, the Comforter will not come unto you;*

but if I depart, I will send him unto you.

—John 16:7

The Spirit itself beareth witness with our spirit, that we are the children of God. —— Ye have not received the spirit of bondage again to fear; but ye have received the Spirit of adoption, whereby we cry, Abba, Father.

—Romans 8:16, 15

The God of hope fill you with all joy and peace in believing, that ye may abound in hope, through the power of the Holy Ghost. —— Hope maketh not ashamed; because the love of God is shed abroad in our hearts by the Holy Ghost which is given unto us.

—Romans 15:13; 5:5

Hereby know we that we dwell in him, and he in us, because he hath given us of his Spirit.

—1 John 4:13

WEEK 51 - JESUS, LAMB OF GOD

Sunday: *The blood of sprinkling, that speaketh better things than that of Abel.*

—Hebrews 12:24

Behold the Lamb of God, which taketh away the sin of the world. —— The Lamb slain from the foundation of the world. —— It is not possible that the blood of bulls and of goats should take away sins. Wherefore when he cometh into the world, he saith, Sacrifice and offering thou wouldest not, but a body hast thou prepared me. ...By the which will we are sanctified through the offering of the body of Jesus Christ once for all.

—John 1:29; Revelations 13:8; Hebrews 10:4–5,10

Abel...brought of the firstlings of his flock and of the fat thereof. ...The Lord had respect unto Abel and to his offering. —— Christ...hath loved us, and hath given himself for us an offering and a sacrifice to God for a sweetsmelling savour.

—Genesis 4:4; Ephesians 5:2

Ye know that ye were not redeemed with corruptible things, as silver and gold...but with the precious blood of Christ, as of a lamb without blemish and without spot...manifest in these last times for you.

—1 Peter 1:18–20

Monday: *The Son of man came to give his life a ransom for many.* —Matthew 20:28

If the blood of bulls and of goats, and the ashes of an heifer sprinkling the unclean, sanctifieth to the purifying of the flesh: How much more shall the blood of Christ, who through the eternal Spirit offered himself without spot to God, purge your conscience from dead works to serve the living God?

—Hebrews 9:13–14

He is brought as a lamb to the slaughter. —— I lay down my life for the sheep. —— Not my will, but thine, be done. —— For God so loved the world, that he gave his only begotten Son, that whosoever believeth in him should not perish, but have everlasting life. For God sent not his Son into the world to condemn the world; but that the world through him might be saved.

—Isaiah 53:7; John 10:15; Luke 22:42; John 3:16–17

He [Jesus] said unto them, This is my blood of the new testament, which is shed for many. —— While we were yet sinners, Christ died for us. Much more then, being now justified by his blood, we shall be saved from wrath through him.

—Mark 14:24; Romans 5:8–9

Tuesday: *The life of the flesh is in the blood: and I have given it to you upon the altar to make an atonement for your souls: for it is the blood that maketh an atonement for the soul.*

—Leviticus 17:11

The blood of the Lamb. —— The precious blood of Christ, as of a lamb without blemish and without spot. —— Behold the blood of the covenant, which the Lord hath made with you. —— Without shedding of blood is no remission. —— The blood of Jesus Christ his Son cleanseth us from all sin. —— By his own blood he entered in once into the holy place, having obtained eternal redemption for us.

—Revelations 7:14; 1 Peter 1:19; Exodus 24:8; Hebrews 9:22; 1 John 1:7; Hebrews 9:12

Having therefore, brethren, boldness to enter into the holiest by the blood of Jesus, By a new and living way, which he hath consecrated for us, through the veil, that is to say, his flesh; ...Let us draw near with a true heart in full assurance of faith.

—Hebrews 10:19–22

Ye are bought with a price: therefore glorify God in your body, and in your spirit, which are God's.

—1 Corinthians 6:20

. . .

Wednesday: *The Lamb slain from the foundation of the world.* —Revelations 13:8

Your lamb shall be without blemish...and the whole assembly of the congregation of Israel shall kill it in the evening. And they shall take of the blood, and strike it on the two side posts and on the upper door post of the houses, wherein they shall eat it...and when I see the blood, I will pass over you. —— The blood of sprinkling. —— Christ our passover is sacrificed for us. —— Being delivered by the determinate counsel and foreknowledge of God. —— According to his own purpose and grace, which was given us in Christ Jesus before the world began.

—Exodus 12:5–13; Hebrews 12:24; 1 Corinthians 5:7; Acts 2:23; 2 Timothy 1:9

We have redemption through his blood, the forgiveness of sins.

—Ephesians 1:7

Forasmuch then as Christ hath suffered for us in the flesh, arm yourselves likewise with the same mind: for he that hath suffered in the flesh hath ceased from sin; That he no longer should live the rest of his time in the flesh to the lusts of men, but to the will of God.

—1 Peter 4:1–2

Thursday: *It is a night to be much observed unto the Lord for bringing them out from the land of Egypt.* —Exodus 12:42

The Lord Jesus the same night in which he was betrayed took bread: And when he had given thanks, he brake it, and said, Take, eat: this is my body, which is broken for you: this do in remembrance of me. After the same manner also he took the cup, when he had supped, saying, this cup is the new testament in my blood: this do ye, as oft as ye drink it, in remembrance of me.

—1 Corinthians 11:23–25

He...kneeled down, and prayed. ...And being in an agony he prayed more earnestly: and his sweat was as it were great drops of blood falling down to the ground.

—Luke 22:41 ,44

It was the preparation of the passover, and about the sixth hour...they took Jesus, and led him away...into a place called...Golgotha: where they crucified him.

—John 19:14–18

Christ our passover is sacrificed for us: Therefore let us keep the feast.

—1 Corinthians 5:7–8

. . .

Friday: *Ye know that he was manifested to take away our sins; and in him is no sin.*

—1 John 3:5

God...Hath in these last days spoken unto us by his Son, ...Who being the brightness of his glory, and the express image of his person, and upholding all things by the word of his power, when he had by himself purged our sins, sat down on the right hand of the Majesty on high. —— He hath made him to be sin for us, who knew no sin; that we might be made the righteousness of God in him.

—Hebrews 1:1–3; 2 Corinthians 5:21

Pass the time of your sojourning here in fear: Forasmuch as ye know that ye were not redeemed with corruptible things, as silver and gold...But with the precious blood of Christ, as of a lamb without blemish and without spot: Who verily was foreordained before the foundation of the world, but was manifest in these last times for you. —— The love of Christ constraineth us; because we thus judge, that if one died for all, then were all dead: And that he died for all, that they which live should not henceforth live unto themselves, but unto him which died for them, and rose again.

—1 Peter 1:17–20; 2 Corinthians 5:14–15

Saturday: *If his offering be a burnt sacrifice of the herd, let him offer a male without blemish: he shall offer it of his own voluntary will. ...And he shall put his hand upon the head of the burnt offering; and it shall be accepted for him to make atonement for him.*

—Leviticus 1:3–4

God will provide himself a lamb for a burnt offering. —— Behold the Lamb of God, which taketh away the sin of the world. —— We are sanctified through the offering of the body of Jesus Christ once for all. —— A ransom for many.

—Genesis 22:8; John 1:29; Hebrews 10:10; Matthew 20:28

No man taketh it from me, but I lay it down of myself. I have power to lay it down, and I have power to take it again. —— I will love them freely. —— The Son of God...loved me, and gave himself for me.

—John 10:18; Hosea 14:4; Galatians 2:20

He hath made him to be sin for us, who knew no sin; that we might be made the righteousness of God in him. —— He hath made us accepted in the beloved.

—2 Corinthians 5:21; Ephesians 1:6

WEEK 52 - CHRISTMAS WEEK

S**unday**: Jesus' birth in Prophecy

Therefore the Lord himself shall give you a sign; Behold, a virgin shall conceive, and bear a son, and shall call his name Immanuel.

—Isaiah 7:14

For unto us a child is born, unto us a son is given: and the government shall be upon his shoulder: and his name shall be called Wonderful, Counsellor, The mighty God, The everlasting Father, The Prince of Peace.

—Isaiah 9:6–8

Of the increase of his government and peace there shall be no end, upon the throne of David, and upon his kingdom, to order it, and to establish it with judgment and with justice from henceforth even for ever. The zeal of the Lord of hosts will perform this.

—Isaiah 9:7

The Lord sent a word into Jacob, and it hath lighted upon Israel. —— There shall come a Star out of Jacob, and a Sceptre shall rise out of Israel.

—Isaiah 9:8; Numbers 24:17

But thou, Bethlehem Ephratah, though thou be little among the thousands of Judah, yet out of thee shall he come forth unto me that is to be ruler in Israel; whose goings forth have been from of old, from everlasting.

—Micah 5:2

. . .

Monday: Jesus' Lineage Foretold

And the angel of the Lord called unto Abraham out of heaven...And said...in thy seed shall all the nations of the earth be blessed; because thou hast obeyed my voice.

—Genesis 22:15–18

And it came to pass that night, that the word of the Lord came unto Nathan, saying, Go and tell my servant David, Thus saith the Lord. ...I will set up thy seed after thee, which shall proceed out of thy bowels, and I will establish his kingdom. He shall build an house for my name, and I will stablish the throne of his kingdom for ever.

—2 Samuel 7:4–13

Behold, the days come, saith the Lord, that I will raise unto David a righteous Branch, and a King shall reign and prosper, and shall execute judgment and justice in the earth. In his days Judah shall be saved, and Israel shall dwell safely: and this is his name whereby he shall be called, The Lord Our Righteousness.

—Jeremiah 23:5–6

So all the generations from Abraham to David are fourteen generations; and from David until the carrying away into Babylon are fourteen generations; and from the carrying away into Babylon unto Christ are fourteen generations.

—Matthew 1:17

Tuesday: The Birth of Jesus Foretold

And in the sixth month the angel Gabriel was sent from God unto a city of Galilee, named Nazareth, To a virgin espoused to a man whose name was Joseph, of the house of David; and the virgin's name was Mary.

And the angel came in unto her, and said, Hail, thou that art highly favoured, the Lord is with thee: blessed art thou among women. And when she saw him, she was troubled at his saying, and cast in her mind what manner of salutation this should be. And the angel said unto her, Fear not, Mary: for thou hast found favour with God. And, behold, thou shalt conceive in thy womb, and bring forth a son, and shalt call his name Jesus. He shall be great, and shall be called the Son of the Highest: and the Lord God shall give unto him the throne of his father David: And he shall reign over the house of Jacob for ever; and of his kingdom there shall be no end.

Then said Mary unto the angel, How shall this be, seeing I know not a man?

And the angel answered and said unto her, The Holy Ghost shall come upon thee, and the power of the Highest shall overshadow thee: therefore also that holy thing which shall be born of thee shall be called the Son of God. And, behold, thy cousin Elisabeth, she hath also conceived a son in her old age: and this is the sixth month with her, who was called barren. For with God nothing shall be impossible.

And Mary said, Behold the handmaid of the Lord; be it unto me according to thy word. And the angel departed from her...

And Mary said,

My soul doth magnify the Lord,
And my spirit hath rejoiced in God my Saviour.
For he hath regarded the low estate of his handmaiden:
for, behold, from henceforth all generations shall call me blessed.
For he that is mighty hath done to me great things;
and holy is his name.
And his mercy is on them that fear him
from generation to generation.
He hath shewed strength with his arm;
he hath scattered the proud in the imagination of their hearts.
He hath put down the mighty from their seats,
and exalted them of low degree.
He hath filled the hungry with good things;
and the rich he hath sent empty away.
He hath helped his servant Israel,
in remembrance of his mercy;
As he spake to our fathers,
to Abraham, and to his seed for ever.
—Luke 1:26–38,46–55

Wednesday: Before Jesus' Birth

Now the birth of Jesus Christ was on this wise: When as his mother Mary was espoused to Joseph, before they came together, she was found with child of the Holy Ghost. Then Joseph her husband, being a just man, and not willing to make her a public example, was minded to put her away privily.

But while he thought on these things, behold, the angel of the Lord appeared unto him in a dream, saying, Joseph, thou son of David, fear not to take unto thee Mary thy wife: for that which is conceived in her is of the Holy Ghost. And she shall bring forth a son, and thou shalt call his name Jesus: for he shall save his people from their sins.

Now all this was done, that it might be fulfilled which was spoken of the Lord by the prophet, saying, Behold, a virgin shall be with child, and shall bring forth a son, and they shall call his name Emmanuel, which being interpreted is, God with us. Then Joseph being raised from sleep did as the angel of the Lord had bidden him, and took unto him his wife: And knew her not till she had brought forth her firstborn son: and he called his name Jesus.

—Matthew 1:18–25

Thursday: Jesus' Birth

And it came to pass in those days, that there went out a decree from Caesar Augustus that all the world should be taxed.

(And this taxing was first made when Cyrenius was governor of Syria.)

And all went to be taxed, every one into his own city.

And Joseph also went up from Galilee, out of the city of Nazareth, into Judaea, unto the city of David, which is called Bethlehem; (because he was of the house and lineage of David:) To be taxed with Mary his espoused wife, being great with child.

And so it was, that, while they were there, the days were accomplished that she should be delivered.

And she brought forth her firstborn son, and wrapped him in swaddling clothes, and laid him in a manger; because there was no room for them in the inn.

—Luke 2:1–7

Friday: The Shepherds Told by Angels

And there were in the same country shepherds abiding in the field, keeping watch over their flock by night. And, lo, the angel of the Lord came upon them, and the glory of the Lord shone round about them: and they were sore afraid. And the angel said unto them,

Fear not: for, behold,
I bring you good tidings of great joy, which shall be to all people.
For unto you is born this day in the city of David a Saviour,
which is Christ the Lord.
And this shall be a sign unto you;
Ye shall find the babe wrapped in swaddling clothes,
lying in a manger.

And suddenly there was with the angel a multitude of the heavenly host praising God, and saying,

Glory to God in the highest,
and on earth peace,
good will toward men.

And it came to pass, as the angels were gone away from them into heaven, the shepherds said one to another, Let us now go even unto Bethlehem, and see this thing which is come to pass, which the Lord hath made known unto us.

And they came with haste, and found Mary, and Joseph, and the babe lying in a manger. And when they had seen it, they made known abroad the saying which was told them concerning this child.

And all they that heard it wondered at those things which were told them by the shepherds.

But Mary kept all these things, and pondered them in her heart.

And the shepherds returned, glorifying and praising God for all the things that they had heard and seen, as it was told unto them.

—Luke 2:8–20

Saturday: The Magi

Now when Jesus was born in Bethlehem of Judaea in the days of Herod the king, behold, there came wise men from the east to Jerusalem, Saying,

Where is he that is born King of the Jews?
for we have seen his star in the east,
and are come to worship him.

When Herod the king had heard these things, he was troubled, and all Jerusalem with him. And when he had gathered all the chief priests and scribes of the people together, he demanded of them where Christ should be born.

And they said unto him, In Bethlehem of Judaea: for thus it is written by the prophet,

And thou Bethlehem, in the land of Juda, art not the least among the princes of Juda: for out of thee shall come a Governor, that shall rule my people Israel.

Then Herod, when he had privily called the wise men, enquired of them diligently what time the star appeared. And he sent them to Bethlehem, and said, Go and search diligently for the young child; and when ye have found him, bring me word again, that I may come and worship him also. When they had heard the king, they departed; and, lo, the star, which they saw in the east, went before them, till it came and stood over where the young child was.

When they saw the star, they rejoiced with exceeding great joy. And when they were come into the house, they saw the young child with Mary his mother, and fell down, and worshipped him: and when they had opened their treasures, they presented unto him gifts; gold, and frankincense and myrrh.

And being warned of God in a dream that they should not return to Herod, they departed into their own country another way. And when they were departed, behold, the angel of the Lord appeareth to Joseph in a dream, saying, Arise, and take the young child and his mother, and flee into Egypt, and be thou there until I bring thee word: for Herod will seek the young child to destroy him.

When he arose, he took the young child and his mother by night, and departed into Egypt: And was there until the death of Herod: that it might be fulfilled which was spoken of the Lord by the prophet, saying, Out of Egypt have I called my son.

—Matthew 2:1–15

And the child grew, and waxed strong in spirit, filled with wisdom: and the grace of God was upon him.

—Luke 2:40

Hark The Herald Angels Sing

Hark! the herald angels sing,
"Glory to the newborn King:
peace on earth, and mercy mild,
God and sinners reconciled!"
Joyful, all ye nations, rise,
join the triumph of the skies;
with th'angelic hosts proclaim,
"Christ is born in Bethlehem!"
...
Refrain:
Hark! the herald angels sing,
"Glory to the newborn King"
...
Christ, by highest heaven adored,
Christ, the everlasting Lord,
late in time behold him come,
offspring of the Virgin's womb:
veiled in flesh the Godhead see;
hail th'incarnate Deity,
pleased with us in flesh to dwell,
Jesus, our Immanuel. [Refrain]
...
Hail the heaven-born Prince of Peace!
Hail the Sun of Righteousness!
Light and life to all he brings,
risen with healing in his wings.

Mild he lays his glory by,
born that we no more may die,
born to raise us from the earth,
born to give us second birth. [Refrain]
—Charles Wesley, 1739

O Little Town Of Bethlehem

O little town of Bethlehem,
how still we see thee lie;
above thy deep and dreamless sleep
the silent stars go by:
yet in thy dark streets shineth
the everlasting Light;
the hopes and fears of all the years
are met in thee tonight.
...
For Christ is born of Mary,
and gathered all above,
while mortals sleep, the angels keep
their watch of wond'ring love.
O morning stars, together
proclaim the holy birth!
And praises sing to God the King,
and peace to men on earth.
...
How silently, how silently,
the wondrous gift is giv'n!
So God imparts to human hearts
the blessings of his heav'n.
No ear may hear his coming,
but in this world of sin,
where meek souls will receive him still,
the dear Christ enters in.
...
O holy child of Bethlehem,
descend to us, we pray;
cast out our sin and enter in;
be born in us today.
We hear the Christmas angels

the great glad tidings tell;
O come to us, abide with us,
our Lord Emmanuel!
—Phillips Brooks, 1868

Silent Night! Holy Night

Silent night! Holy night!
All is calm, all is bright
'round yon virgin mother and child.
Holy infant, so tender and mild,
sleep in heavenly peace,
sleep in heavenly peace.
...
Silent night! Holy night!
Shepherds quake at the sight!
Glories stream from heaven afar,
heav'nly hosts sing alleluia;
Christ, the Savior, is born!
Christ, the Savior, is born!
...
Silent night! Holy night!
Son of God, love's pure light
radiant beams from thy holy face,
with the dawn of redeeming grace,
Jesus, Lord, at thy birth,
Jesus, Lord, at thy birth.
...
Silent night! Holy night!
wondrous star, lend thy light;
with the angels let us sing
alleluias to our King;
Christ, the Savior, is born!
Christ, the Savior, is born!
—Joseph Mohr, date unknown

Made in the USA
Columbia, SC
24 October 2024

45018489R00143